Language and Literacy Development in Children Who Are Deaf

Language and Literacy Development in Children Who Are Deaf

Barbara R. Schirmer

Lewis & Clark College

Merrill, an imprint of
Macmillan Publishing Company
New York

Maxwell Macmillan Canada
Toronto

Maxwell Macmillan International
New York Oxford Singapore Sydney

Editor: Ann Castel
Production Editor: Mary M. Irvin
Art Coordinator: Peter A. Robison
Photo Editor: Anne Vega
Cover Designer: Cathleen Norz
Production Buyer: Jeff Smith
Artist: Jane Lopez
Electronic Text Management: Ben Ko, Marilyn Wilson Phelps

This book was set in New Baskerville by Macmillan Publishing Company and was printed and bound by Book Press, Inc., a Quebecor America Book Group Company. The cover was printed by Phoenix Color Corp.

Macmillan Publishing Company
866 Third Avenue
New York, NY 10022

Macmillan Publishing Company is part of the
Maxwell Communication Group of Companies.

Maxwell Macmillan Canada, Inc.
1200 Eglinton Avenue East, Suite 200
Don Mills, Ontario M3C 3N1

Library of Congress Cataloging-in-Publication Data
Schirmer, Barbara R.
     Language and literacy development in children who are deaf /
Barbara R. Schirmer.
          p. cm.
     Includes bibliographical references and index.
     ISBN 0-675-21295-2
     1. Deaf—Means of communication—Study and teaching (Elementary)
2. Children, Deaf—Language. 3. Deaf—Education. I. Title.
HV2443.S33 1994
305.9'08162—dc20   92–39428
                                                                           CIP

Printing: 1 2 3 4 5 6 7 8 9   Year: 4 5 6 7

Preface

The purpose of this text is to provide teachers with comprehensive information regarding how children who are deaf learn to use language in face-to-face communication, reading, and writing. The audience is preservice and inservice teachers who want to know how to create classroom environments that foster the development of language and literacy in children who are deaf.

Throughout the text, I have tried to maintain a balance between theory and practice because I believe that outstanding teachers of deaf children understand the theoretical foundations on which their teaching strategies are built. Trends in education come and go. The best teachers are those who are able to examine a trend in light of what they know about the processes involved in learning language for deaf children, and so are able to use what is valuable and ignore what is unproductive.

The theories, models, and strategies discussed in this text are those that are currently relevant to teachers of children who are deaf. To this end, I have drawn on the literature in deafness, special education, early childhood, linguistics, bilingual education, psychology, child language, reading, cognition, research in education, educational technology, communication disorders, child development, children's literature, curriculum, and language arts.

Chapter 1 focuses on the acquisition of linguistic knowledge in the child who is deaf, how this information can be applied to language goals for classroom instruction, the role of language assessment, methods and techniques for using informal approaches and formal tests to assess the language of children who are deaf, and how the classroom teacher can use assessment information to develop individualized language goals for each child.

Chapter 2 presents language as a curricular base on which the full school day is organized. It explains for the reader how to embed each deaf child's language goals into an array of daily learning experiences. Teaching models and strategies, the use of conversation, and interdisciplinary curriculum are all described and used to illustrate how the teacher can encourage language growth in children who are deaf. A final important feature of this chapter is an in-depth discussion of the issues surrounding bilingual/bicultural education for children who are deaf.

In Chapter 3 whole language is defined and the rationale for using whole language principles in teaching children who are deaf is discussed. This chapter also includes a thorough description of current views of reading and writing development, the kinds of reading materials that can enhance the development of literacy in youngsters who are deaf, and the instructional implications of the relationship between language, literacy, and cognitive development.

Chapter 4 builds on the theoretical framework of literacy development that was presented in Chapter 3. In this chapter, theory is linked with practice through descriptions of teaching activities that form the core of a literacy program for children who are deaf. Included are activities that foster emergent literacy, that promote growth in reading and writing, and that enable children who are deaf to become autonomous readers and writers.

Chapter 5 presents strategies for helping deaf children to read and write in the content areas. This chapter includes descriptions of reading strategies and study strategies with subject area text material, the teaching of expository text structure, the use of organizers and overviews, and the role of writing across the curriculum.

Chapter 6 focuses on assessment in reading and writing. It begins with a description of the principles that should guide teachers in monitoring the literacy development of children who are deaf. Portfolio assessment is described in detail, and both informal approaches and standardized test information are explained.

In Chapter 7, the role of parents in the language and literacy development of their children is highlighted and the importance of family-school partnerships is discussed.

This book should be used primarily by students in undergraduate and graduate programs preparing teachers of individuals who are deaf. It fits particularly well in the Language Development and Literacy Development/Methods of Teaching Reading courses that students take as part of these teacher education program.

During the course of researching and writing this book, I found that I needed two kinds of nourishment, nourishment for my mind and nourishment for my spirit. Luckily for me, there were individuals in my life who were able to provide me with one or the other, and sometimes both.

I want to first thank Ann Castel, my administrative editor. Ann and I developed a common vision for this book and during the sometimes bumpy road of writing and rewriting, I could always depend on her to guide me compassionately and gently in bringing this vision into clearer and clearer focus. I am grateful to Mary Irvin, my production editor, and Cindy Peck, my copy editor, who took my words and helped make them comprehensible and even enjoyable to the readers of this book.

I want to thank the reviewers for their time and their thoughts. Their comments provided me with a lens through which I could re-view the book as I sought to make my vision one that could be seen clearly by others. They are Richard L. Brodesky, Pima Community College; Victoria Deasy, San Francisco State University; B. Robert Gonzales, University of Northern Colorado; Jean Salisbury, Pacific Oaks College/U of Southern California; and Olga M. Welch, University of Tennessee Knoxville.

During the years that I have taught graduate students who are preparing to be teachers of deaf and hard-of-hearing children, I have learned that they examine and evaluate each bit of "wisdom" that I share with them. Every idea I present in this book has passed their careful scrutiny and I thank them for their substantial, though sometimes painful, feedback.

I have been involved in the education of deaf and hard-of-hearing children for more than two decades and during that time I have developed friendships with several valued colleagues, some who are college and university professors and some who are classroom teachers. From an outsider's point of view, many of our conversations might look like arguments, but these discussions over the years have crystallized my ideas about language and literacy development. I hope these individuals know how important they are in both my personal and professional life. I would like to publicly thank one of these persons, Dr. Frieda Hammermeister. From the moment I met her, when I accidentally called her Dr. Friedameister and she didn't bat an eye, I knew I had landed at the right place to learn how to teach deaf and hard-of-hearing children. It is a tribute to Frieda that her University of Pittsburgh graduates from various years find a common bond among themselves and always share "Frieda" stories whenever they meet.

I would like to take this opportunity to acknowledge the influence of my grandmother, Freda Schiller, who became deaf as a young child. She was a complex woman who was frustrated by her deafness and her lack of education. She didn't know my language and I didn't know hers, but we found a common language that I have always been unable to explain to anyone else.

It was obvious to me from the moment I decided to try writing this book that I would need a great deal of support from my secretary, Barbara McCormick. She has saved me countless hours through her willingness to word process and re-process hundreds of manuscript pages, to photocopy articles, to order reference materials, and to pick up and return library books. But her support has extended well beyond these mundane chores. From proposal to completed manuscript, she has constantly encouraged me, buoyed my spirits, patted me on the back, scolded me at times, and ignored my temper tantrums. I thank her for being the quintessential secretary and a wonderful friend.

I believe that when families function well, individual members feel safe enough to go out into the world and take risks. I dedicate this book to my husband, Jack, and my children, Alison and Todd, who take care of me so well that I feel secure enough to put my ideas on paper.

Contents

1

LANGUAGE DEVELOPMENT AND THE GOALS OF LANGUAGE INSTRUCTION   2

2

LANGUAGE DEVELOPMENT WITHIN THE CLASSROOM SETTING   48

3

LITERACY DEVELOPMENT   106

4

APPROACHES TO PROMOTE READING AND WRITING DEVELOPMENT   142

5

LEARNING THROUGH READING AND WRITING IN THE CONTENT AREAS   194

6
MONITORING THE LEARNING PROCESS IN READING AND WRITING   216

7
LANGUAGE AND LITERACY DEVELOPMENT THROUGH PARENT-CHILD-TEACHER PARTNERSHIPS   236

Language and Literacy Development in Children Who Are Deaf

1

Language Development and the Goals of Language Instruction

NATURE AND STUDY OF LANGUAGE ACQUISITION

COGNITIVE DIMENSIONS OF LANGUAGE ACQUISITION

DEVELOPMENTAL SEQUENCE IN LANGUAGE ACQUISITION
Gesture and Early Language Development
Syntactic and Semantic Development
Development of Language Use
Role of Parents in Language Development
Later Language Development
Metalinguistic Awareness

GOALS OF LANGUAGE INSTRUCTION

APPROACHES TO LANGUAGE ASSESSMENT
Nature and Role of Assessment
Informal Approaches to Assessment
Formal Approach: Standardized Assessment Instruments

ANALYZING THE CHILD'S DEVELOPMENTAL LANGUAGE STAGE
Analyzing a Language Sample
Using Results from Standardized Tests

IDENTIFYING APPROPRIATE LANGUAGE GOALS

FINAL COMMENTS

For many years, descriptions of child language acquisition consisted of lists of developmental milestones. These were basically simple catalogues of sequential steps observed in the developing child's language. For example, Menyuk (1971) described the sequence of development from babbling during the first year of life to single-word utterances to short sentences by the third year. Another example is the 1970 Denver Developmental Screening Test which used developmental milestones as an evaluation technique.

Beginning with Roger Brown's seminal study (1973) of Adam, Eve, and Sarah, the last two decades of child language research have demonstrated a complexity of the language acquisition process not evident in these earlier descriptions. More important for teachers of youngsters who are deaf, we can learn to use information from this relatively recent body of research to improve the language learning opportunities for the children in our classrooms.

In this chapter, I will begin by discussing what is currently known about the acquisition of linguistic knowledge in all children and specifically in the child who is deaf and what this information means for our goals for classroom instruction. I will then discuss the role of language assessment and describe methods and techniques for using informal approaches as well as formal instruments. Finally, I will explain how the classroom teacher or language specialist can use assessment information to determine each child's language development stage and to identify appropriate individualized language goals for children who are deaf.

NATURE AND STUDY OF LANGUAGE ACQUISITION

The first known study of child language acquisition was conducted by Psammetichus I, a pharoah of ancient Egypt. According to Herodotus, a Greek historian who lived at the time of Sophocles, Psammetichus I wanted to prove that the Egyptians were the original human race by showing that the Egyptian language was the natural language of humans. He gave two infants to a shepherd to raise, ordered the shepherd to use no speech with the children, and told the shepherd to take notice of the children's first spoken words. Psammetichus I found that the children did not spontaneously use the Egyptian language and he unhappily concluded that Egyptians were not the original human race.

Through the centuries, individuals continued to be intrigued with child language acquisition but systematic study did not begin until the late 19th century. Between the 1870s and 1920s, child language was usually studied from the perspective of parents, and data was recorded in the form of diaries. Indeed, most of these studies were conducted by psychologists, and the diaries they kept were observations of their own children. Ingram (1989) noted that interest in child language acquisition at this time was part of a larger interest by psychologists in child development.

Between the 1920s and 1950s, while diary studies continued, studies designed to sample language behaviors became very popular. These studies were strongly influenced by the behavioral theory of learning. Language studies based on behavioral theory had several characteristics in common. The researchers who conducted these studies examined the language of relatively large numbers of children who were chosen in a way that they could be considered representative of even larger numbers of whole populations. These researchers also chose particular language behaviors to test or observe, the procedures they used were precise and consistently followed, and the data they gathered lent itself to quantitative analysis. The researchers of this era were particularly interested in the average sentence length of children at different age levels, acquisition of speech sounds, and vocabulary development.

From the late 1950s through the 1960s, language acquisition studies using longitudinal language sampling procedures came into prominence. In these studies, language samples of a small number of children were systematically collected over a long period of time. Most of these studies were strongly influenced by the transformational theory of grammar and so focused on the child's acquisition of syntax.

In the 1970s, researchers shifted their attention away from syntax and toward semantics. In the 1980s, there was again a shift as attention was directed to the study of language use, particularly on the development of pragmatics and conversation. In the 1970s and 1980s, there was also an explosion of research interest into the relationship between language acquisition and the child's linguistic and nonlinguistic environment.

In the 1990s, language acquisition study encompasses a broad range of topics and the methodology used includes an array of quantitative and qualitative techniques. Some of the areas of study that continue to have important implications for teachers of children who are deaf are investigations into adult-child interaction, second language learning, sign language, language and cognition, metalinguistics, language and literacy, and development of language throughout the life span.

We know a great deal more today about child language acquisition than the ancient Egyptians did. Each study has added new information to a constantly increasing body of knowledge. It is my intent in this chapter to use information from this rich body of knowledge that I believe is most pertinent to the teachers of youngsters who are deaf and apply it in a way that will enable the classroom teacher to develop a multifaceted picture of the language development abilities of each child in their classrooms.

I want to emphasize that much of the information in this chapter comes from research in linguistics and child language acquisition. Some studies have been conducted with children who are deaf, and I have tried to cite each of these whenever appropriate. However, it is undeniable that most of the research on this topic has been focused on children who can hear. I include this body of research because it tells us a great deal about the process of language development, and as teachers of children who are deaf, we can rely on our experiences and intuitions when applying this body of knowledge to the children we are teaching.

COGNITIVE DIMENSIONS OF LANGUAGE ACQUISITION

Considerable discussion has taken place in the literature regarding the relationship between language acquisition and cognitive development. A thorough explanation of the issues involved in this discussion would go considerably beyond the purview of this chapter. Instead of giving equal emphasis to competing theories, I have decided to present a brief conceptualization of the cognitive dimensions of language acquisition.

According to Reed (1988), cognition is defined as the acquisition and use of knowledge. With this definition in mind, the relationship between cognition and language acquisition can be seen as an interdependent one. In this view, language acquisition occurs as a result of the interaction between the child's innate cognitive abilities, cognitive strategies, and conceptual knowledge.

This interaction can be illustrated with the analogy of the growth of a plant. The seed of the plant is the child's innate cognitive abilities. It provides the child with the cognitive capacity to make sense of linguistic information. The root system is the child's developing conceptual knowledge as he or she interacts with the environment. This root system, or conceptual knowledge, supports language acquisition and grows as language develops. The plant seeks out nourishment by sending its roots in the direction of water and its leaves in the direction of light. These movements by the plant can be likened to the child's own cognitive strategies that nourish language acquisition such as focusing, analyzing, organizing, classifying, and problem solving.

Rice and Kemper (1984) described language growth in the following way:

> The child draws upon the conceptual roots and the innate kernel to establish the first green shoots of language. As the roots develop, they provide further nourishment to strengthen the delicate young conceptual roots. In turn, as the roots firm and expand, they provide support and nourishment for the developing plant. The initial kernel continues to contribute to growth, perhaps through the timed release of growth hormones that stimulate root and leaf development. The stem, branches, and leaves of a plant are shaped by the plant's ecology and evolution. So, too, the syntactic structures, semantic content, and pragmatics of language are responsive both to the child's environment and heredity. . .Plant growth is governed by geotropic and heliotropic responses to gravity and light. In the same way, the growth of language is shaped by general cognitive strategies and heuristics. These strategies

interrelate previous experiences and knowledge with present and future situations. (p.121)

The child who is deaf begins life with a language seed that is full of cognitive potential. This child needs a fertile environment that will enable the language seed to grow into a mature language plant.

DEVELOPMENTAL SEQUENCE IN LANGUAGE ACQUISITION

Brown (1973) considered the order of progression in knowledge of a first language to be approximately invariant across children learning any language. Is there evidence that the developmental sequence observed in children with normal hearing is applicable to the child who is deaf?

The child with a hearing impairment has the same cognitive potential for learning the meaning, structure, and use of language as the hearing child. Through the child's interaction with fluent speakers and signers, language is learned. So it seems logical that children who are deaf would internalize language in the same order of progression as hearing children, and for more than a decade educators (Holmes & Holmes, 1981; Kretschmer & Kretschmer, 1979) have been recommending that the language of deaf children be compared to the developmental regularities observed in normally hearing children and that the results of these comparisons be used to create language curricula. Evidence to support this recommendation can be found in the literature.

A number of researchers have examined the language development of children who are deaf along dimensions of syntax, semantics, and pragmatics. They have found stages and sequences of language development comparable to those found in hearing children (Caselli, 1983; Christensen, 1988; Curtiss, Prutting, & Lowell, 1979; Petitto, 1987; Prinz & Prinz, 1985; Schirmer, 1985). The implication is that as teachers of youngsters who are deaf, we need to understand the universals of language development.

Gesture and Early Language Development

Much of the traditional research in prelinguistic development has focused on the child's perception and production of speech sounds. Studies of the relationship between babbling and language acquisition were interesting but not very illuminating to those of us teaching children who are deaf. Research that holds the promise of helping us understand prelinguistic development in deaf children centers on how prelinguistic children use gestures symbolically to represent functions and meanings and how gestural development is related to language acquisition. An example of a symbolic gesture is the young child pointing to an object that is out of reach while looking at mother.

At this point, conclusions from the research on the expression of communicative intent through the symbolic use of gesture in children who are hearing and deaf are tentative (Acredolo & Goodwyn, 1988; Bates, Bretherton, Snyder, Shore, & Volterra, 1980; Bates, Thal, Whitesell, Fenson, & Oakes, 1989; Bretherton, Bates, McNew, Shore, Williamson, & Beeghly-Smith, 1981; Carroll & Gibson, 1986; Goldin-Meadow & Morford, 1985; Mohay, 1982; Thal & Bates, 1988; Volterra, 1981; Volterra & Erting, 1990). My review of this literature found some support for the following views:

1. Both infants who are hearing and infants who are deaf use symbolic gestures to communicate.
2. Symbolic gestures appear approximately at the same time as spoken words in hearing children.
3. Symbolic gestures seem to be used for requesting before they are used for labeling.
4. Gestures and words are both used first in routinized activities.
5. Gestural communication is an important stage in the acquisition of language.

Syntactic and Semantic Development

Much of what is known about the development of the structure and meaning of language has come from observations of children communicating with adults and with each other. Children acquire language by moving through predictable stages of syntactic and semantic development. A thorough discussion of all the issues involved in normal language development is beyond the scope of this book, but the reader is encouraged to explore this topic by examining other texts (for example, Franklin & Barten, 1988; Gleason, 1989; Menyuk, 1988; Owens, 1992). I will, however, discuss in detail these predictable stages of development because they are pertinent in understanding the language acquisition process in children who are deaf.

Syntactic Development

What is typically referred to as syntactic development really involves *morphology* and *syntax*. As children learn the form of language, they are discovering the rules that govern how morphemes (the smallest meaningful unit of grammatical form) are combined into words (morphology) as well as how words are combined into sentences (syntax).

Stages of syntactic development have been well documented (Brown, 1973; deVilliers & deVilliers, 1979; Tager-Flusberg, 1989; Wells, 1981) and have been used to examine the deaf child's acquisition of spoken English and American Sign Language (Schirmer, 1985; Wilbur, 1987).

Framework of language development   The framework presented in Figure 1–1 represents an order of language development that has been found to be fairly constant across children. The stages are divided by mean length of utterance in morphemes rather than by chronological age because, while the rate at which children acquire language has been found to be highly variable, almost every new kind of language knowledge increases length of utterance. Children whose mean length of utterance is the same tend to do the same things with the morphemes they use. Indeed, the young child seems cognitively limited in the number of morphemes per utterance and uses this limit in consistent syntactic, semantic, and pragmatic ways to get meaning across. Beyond four morphemes per utterance, the child is able to make constructions of such variety and complexity that length is no longer a good indicator of development.

The following are the six stages of language development in the framework. The mean length of utterance (MLU) divisions are based on Brown's stages (1973) with the addition of a single morpheme stage that Brown did not include. (Mean length of utterance is defined as the average number of morphemes the child produces per utterance. The procedure for calculating MLU is provided later in this chapter.)

Stage 1: 1.00 MLU in morphemes

Stage 2: 1.00–1.99

Stage 3: 2.00–2.49

Stage 4: 2.50–3.12

Stage 5: 3.13–3.74

Stage 6: 3.75+

Within each stage is a developmental order of syntactic forms. The framework does not encompass all aspects of syntactic development. Furthermore, development of specific forms and relations does not start and stop within the boundaries of each stage. However, these processes appear in child language most strongly at the particular stage identified in the framework. The child may begin to use a particular form at an earlier stage and may not gain mastery until a later stage. (For a complete description of the framework, the reader is directed to Schirmer, 1989.)

Semantic Development

Semantics is defined as the meaning or content of language. As children learn the content of language, they are discovering the rules that govern the meaning of words, phrases, and sentences.

Researchers have focused on the semantic properties of words and morphemes and on the semantic roles that each word plays in a phrase or sentence in order to examine children's development of meaning (Bloom & Lahey, 1978; Brown, 1973; Luetke-Stahlman, 1988).

FIGURE 1–1
Framework for Assessing Early Syntactic Development

Identifier	Descriptor	Verb	Adverb
			here
			there
			in
			on
Personal pronouns (first & second person)	Number	Present progressive without auxiliary	
Plural (regular) *a* *the*		Imperative	
Personal pronouns (third person)	*some*	Present progressive with auxiliary	
Indefinite pronouns (*it, this, that*)		Copula	
	many	Past (irregular)	*now*
	all	Third person present indicative (regular and irregular)	*too*
Personal pronouns (plural)	Possessive (*'s*)	Past (regular)	
Indefinite pronouns (*something, somebody, someone*)	*more* *another* *other(s)*	Embedded sentences —infinitive —*wh-* —relative clause	

FIGURE 1–1
continued

Negative	Question	Conjunction	Stage	MLU
	Intonation		1	1.00
not *no*	*what* *where*		2	1.00–1.99
	who *when*	*and*	3	2.00–2.49
	how *why*		4	2.50–3.12
can't *didn't* *don't*	Yes/no question		5	3.13–3.74
		and then *because* *so* *but* *or*	6	3.75+

The ways in which children combine semantic categories within sentences become more complex as they are able to produce longer utterances. At the same time, they are able to create utterances of increasing syntactic complexity as well as to add new semantic categories to their repertoires. In Figure 1–2, a taxonomy of semantic categories and their definitions are given. Examples are provided in Figure 1–3.

Development of Language Use

When authors use the term *language use* they often use it interchangeably with the term *pragmatics*. However, I view pragmatics more narrowly as only one component of use. When we examine how children are acquiring language, we need to recognize that children are learning three different but related areas of use: functions, context, and conversation (Prutting, 1982; Roth & Spekman, 1984a). I will discuss pragmatics within the topic of language functions, as it is the function language serves for relating to others.

As the reader considers the information in this section, it will become obvious that considerably less is known about how children acquire the ability to use language than what is known about children's acquisition of syntax and semantics. Yet it is clear that if use is the overall organizing aspect of language (Owens, 1992), then it is at least as important for children who are deaf to learn the rules governing the use of language within communicative contexts as it is for them to learn the content and form of language.

Functions or Communicative Intents

Language functions   *Language functions* refer to the individual's intentions and expectations of the linguistic act. The function of language for individuals to relate to others and satisfy their own needs is called the interpersonal or *pragmatic*. The function of language within individuals for learning about the world is called the intrapersonal or *mathetic*.

In a study of his son's language acquisition from the age of 9 months through 24 months, Halliday (1975) found six early developing functions and one later developing function. These functions and their definitions can be found in Figure 1–4. He observed that these functions fell into two distinct groups, with the pragmatic intent arising most directly from the instrumental and regulatory functions and the mathetic intent arising from a combination of the personal and heuristic. The seventh function, the informative, was found to emerge considerably after the others.

Dore's (1975) research led him to identify a set of nine communicative intents which he called primitive speech acts. These intents and their definitions can be found in Figure 1–5.

James (1990) found that the categories developed by Halliday and Dore could be combined into three categories of communicative intents: *regulating others' behavior* (Halliday's *instrumental* and *regulatory*; Dore's *requesting action* and *protesting*), *establishing joint attention* (Halliday's *heuristic*

FIGURE 1–2
Taxonomy of Semantic Categories

Entity—any thing or person having a distinct, separate existence

Nonexistence—the child makes reference to the disappearance of an object or the absence of an object or action in a context in which its existence might be expected

Recurrence—the child either comments on or requests the recurrence of a thing, person, or process

Rejection—the child opposes an action or refuses an object that is in the context or imminent within the situation

Demonstrative—the child introduces an entity using *a, the, that, it, here, there*

Object—someone or something either suffering a change of state or receiving the force of an action

Denial—the child negates the identity, state, or event expressed in another's utterance or in his or her own previous utterance

Attribution—property, characteristic, distinctive feature, or quality of something or someone

Possession—objects within the domain of specific persons

Action—perceived movements

Locative—the place or locus of an action

State—the child makes reference to a state of being

Quantity—the child designates the number of objects or persons

Notice—the child refers to attention to a person, object, or event, and must include a verb of notice such as *see, look, listen, watch, hear*

Time—the child makes reference to time (ongoing, imminent, future, past)

Coordinate—the child refers to two events or states that are independent of each other but are somehow bound together in space or time

Causality—the child expresses an implicit or explicit cause and effect relationship (that is, one event or state depends on another event or state for its occurrence)

Dative—the child designates the recipient of an object or action (e.g., with *for, to*)

Specifier—the child specifies a particular person, object, or event

Epistemic—the child describes a relationship between two states, or one event and one state, that refers to certainty or uncertainty about an event or state (e.g., "seems like")

Mood—the child expresses an attitude about an event (e.g., with *can, must, should*)

Antithesis—the child expresses a dependency between two events or states and the dependency is a contrast between them

Source: Bloom & Lahey (1978) and Luetke-Stahlman (1988).

FIGURE 1–3
Examples of the Semantic Categories

Entity:	baby/(holding a doll) ball chair/(looking at the ball on the chair) what's this ↑
Nonexistence:	all gone/(bird lands then flies away) no/(turns picture over so he can't see it) there's no pocket in this jacket/
Recurrence:	more/(holding up an empty glass) can I have another cookie ↑
Rejection:	no/(mom wants her to put her toys away) don't touch my papers/
Demonstrative:	the man fell down/ I have a VCR at home/
Object:	push me/ drink juice/ dad is washing his car/
Denial:	no/(child is holding a toy telephone and is asked, "Is that mommy's telephone?") I'm not tired/(in response to an adult comment, "You're just tired.")
Attribution:	hot/(eating soup for lunch) my pants are dirty/
Possession:	mommy/(holding up mommy's book) that's my truck/ Ann's room is big/
Action:	run/(watching her sister running) she's riding her bike/

and *informative*; Dore's *labeling* and *requesting*), and *interacting socially* (Halliday's *interactional*; Dore's *calling* and *greeting*).

Although I discuss pragmatic development as if it were separate from syntactic and semantic development, these components are in reality interrelated. Children's acquisition of questions is an example that highlights the relationship between syntactic, semantic, and pragmatic development. Several researchers have found the order of acquisition of wh- question forms to be related to the child's increasing ability to understand semantic concepts (Bloom & Lahey, 1978; Brown, 1973; Lee, 1974). As Schwabe,

FIGURE 1–3
continued

Locative:	book table/(looking at the book on the table) the kids are swimming in the pool/
State:	you have none/ I feel sick/
Quantity:	two cow/(pointing to 2 animals) I have a lot of friends/
Notice:	watch me/ did you see that ↑/
Time:	I going home now/ Lisa will join us later/
Coordinate:	give me the ball but not the bat/ I got a sweater and earrings and money for my birthday/
Causality:	I fell down and hurt my knee/ Bobby can't go because he's being punished/
Dative:	I saved this seat for you/ give some juice to Christa/
Specifier:	I don't want that cookie/ Addie picked this one for Karlita/
Epistemic:	it's getting cloudy so I think it will rain/ Joe fell off the bleachers...is he hurt ↑
Mood:	I can do it/ Lori should give back the money/
Antithesis:	my feet are cold but I have socks and slippers on/ you go to the movies and I'll stay home with Lindy/

Olswang, and Kriegsmann (1986) noted, "The consistent sequence of acquisition of wh- forms reflects the child's ability to request information about increasingly abstract semantic notions" (p. 42). Questions, however, don't exist in a semantic-syntactic vacuum; they serve as functional linguistic devices for the child, such as Halliday's heuristic or "tell me why" function.

It has been observed that the ability to use pragmatic functions increases with age and stage of language development, and that children use new forms to express old functions and old forms to express new functions (James & Seebach, 1982).

FIGURE 1–4
Definitions of Halliday's Language Functions

Instrumental—"I want" or requesting; the function that language serves of satisfying the child's material needs, of enabling him or her to obtain the goods and services that he or she wants

Regulatory—"Do as I tell you" or controlling; the function of language for controlling the behavior of others

Interactional—"Me and you" or interacting with others; the function language serves for the child to interact with those around him or her, particularly with individuals who are important to the child

Personal—"Here I come" or communicating feelings; the function of language for expressing the child's own uniqueness, to express his or her awareness of self as distinct from the environment, and to ultimately develop personality

Heuristic—"Tell me why" or questioning; the function language serves for exploring the environment

Imaginative—"Let's pretend" or creating; the function of language whereby the child creates an environment of his or her own through story, make-believe, let's pretend, and ultimately poetry and imaginative writing

Informative—"I've got something to tell you" or declaring; the function of language for communicating information to someone who does not already possess that information.

Source: Halliday (1975).

Inner speech and sign   The difference between pragmatic and mathetic functions of language is most clearly captured by Vygotsky's concept of *inner speech*. Vygotsky (1962) viewed external speech as speech for others, the turning of thought into words. He viewed inner speech as speech for oneself, speech turned into inward thought. Vygotsky's conceptualization of inner speech is frequently contrasted with Piaget's (1926) concept of egocentric speech. Piaget believed that young children engaged in egocentric speech because they were incapable of taking the perspective of others. According to Piaget, this type of speech disappeared as the child became able to engage in more socially oriented speech. In contrast, Vygotsky believed egocentric speech was a stage of development preceding inner speech; thus one changed into the other.

The research on inner speech, particularly on its purpose for cognitive self-guidance and self-communication, has been reviewed by a number of researchers (Berk & Garvin, 1984; Diaz, 1986; Frauenglass & Diaz, 1985; Frawley & Lantolf, 1986; Pellegrini, 1984). They have found some support for Vygotsky's theory of inner speech, though great individual variation in both the development and production of inner speech. It seems that if

FIGURE 1–5
Definitions of Dore's Communicative Intents

Labeling—uses word while attending to object or event, does not address adult, and does not wait for a response

Repeating—attends to adult utterance, repeats part or all of the adult utterance, and does not wait for a response

Answering—attends to adult utterance and answers adult's question

Requesting an Action—attends to object or event, addresses adult and waits for a response. (The adult response is the performance of an action that helps the child complete his or her activity.)

Requesting Answer—addresses adult, asks a question, and waits for a response. (The adult response is an answer to the question.)

Calling—addresses adult by calling his or her name emphatically and waits for a response

Greeting—greets adult or object upon first seeing it

Protesting—resists or denies adult's action

Practicing—uses word with no object or event in evidence, does not address adult, and does not wait for a response

---

Source: Dore (1975).

hearing children experience inner speech then deaf children who use sign language would experience inner sign. There is currently no research on inner sign among individuals who are deaf but the concept of inner sign as a corollary to inner speech is an area of investigation worth pursuing because it may relate to both cognitive and language development.

Context or Presuppositions

Context refers to the environment of the linguistic act, both situational cues and information about the communication partner. (Much of the literature refers to the communication partner as the listener. However, the term *listener* has a connotation that excludes individuals with hearing impairments, so the term *communication partner* will be used.) As children are acquiring the ability to use language, they are learning how to use information from context to determine appropriate linguistic forms. Context includes information learned from situational cues and about the communication partner.

Situational cues   When children use *situational cues* to determine the form of their message, they are taking into account how formal or informal the communication setting is. For example, a conversation with a teacher during an I.E.P. meeting would be more formal than a conversation with the same teacher during recess.

Situational cues also refer to the child's need for perceptual support. Perceptual support is the extent to which the child needs to have direct experience about a topic in order to communicate about it. It includes the ability to communicate about objects not present and events in which one was not a participant.

The communication partner   If the child is to be able to adapt the message to the needs of the *communication partner*, the child must know and be able to use two kinds of information about the partner, prior knowledge and social status.

First, the child makes assumptions about what the partner knows and doesn't know (in terms of world knowledge, specific knowledge, and prior experiences) about the topic. Based on these presuppositions, the child decides what information to include and what information to leave out because the partner would find it redundant.

Second, the child draws conclusions about the partner's social status. The child learns to consider the partner's gender, age, and role in the child's life. The child may also learn to consider the partner's ethnic background, dialect, and degree of hearing. Based on this information, the child will vary his or her communication style.

At this point, it might be helpful to clarify the terminology being used. Warren-Leubecker and Bohannon (1989) referred to *language* as variation between countries, *dialect* as language variation between regions, *register* as language variation between social situations, and *style* as language variation distinctive of individual speakers. "While most speakers will spend their lives speaking a single language and often a single dialect, they must master several registers in order to be socially acceptable" (p. 330).

Learning to look for and use information about the communication partner's prior knowledge and social status enables children to become more skilled at adjusting the politeness markers they use and their linguistic forms for conveying formal versus informal register. Warren-Leubecker and Bohannon found that the ability to vary register develops well into childhood, and possibly into adulthood.

Conversation

Conversation depends on the child's ability to learn the discourse rules that speakers/signers and partners use for introducing, maintaining, and terminating a conversation.

To introduce or initiate a conversation, the child must know how to solicit the partner's attention, greet appropriately, and establish eye contact.

To maintain a conversation, the child must be able to ask and answer questions, take turns appropriately, handle regressions, request more information, make repairs, offer new information, acknowledge the partner's information, use eye contact appropriately, and shift topics.

Finally, to terminate a conversation, the child needs to know how to close a topic and use conversational boundary markers such as "It's been great seeing you," "See you later," "I have to get going."

Conversation is a particularly critical area of research because it represents not only the medium of social exchange but the milieu of language acquisition. In studies of the discourse development of children, it has been found that children at the early stages of language development have already acquired incipient understanding of conversation; by the time they have completed preschool, they have acquired the basic rules of appropriate conversational behavior; and their knowledge becomes increasingly richer through their school years and into adulthood (Brinton & Fujiki, 1984; Foster, 1983; Howe, 1981; Miller, Lechner, & Rugs, 1985; Terrell, 1985; Wells, 1986; Wilcox & Webster, 1980; Wilkinson, Wilkinson, Spinelli, & Chiang, 1984).

In a study of the development of conversational discourse skills in profoundly deaf children between 3 years-10 months and 11 years-5 months of age and who communicated primarily in sign language, Prinz and Prinz (1985) found these youngsters used developmentally appropriate eye contact, conversational attention-getting devices, tactics for conventional turn-taking and for remediating interruptions, and appropriate strategies for initiating, maintaining, and terminating topics.

Role of Parents in Language Development

For children to learn language, they need to have a considerable amount of experience in conversation with adults. In the Bristol Study, a longitudinal study of the language development of a group of children over a 15-year span, Wells and his associates "found a clear relationship between the children's rate of progress in language learning and the amount of conversation that they experienced with their parents and other members of the family circle" (1986, p. 44).

The nature of the interactions between children and their parents has been examined by a number of researchers and some interesting findings have emerged.

Motherese

The particular modifications in the language of adults when they are communicating with young children is called *motherese*. Another common term used by researchers to describe this special language is *baby talk*, although baby talk tends to connote the use of "baby" vocabulary rather than the characteristics of motherese listed in Figure 1–6. Mothers' language directed to their young children is generally simple, well-formed, and clear. Mothers use higher pitch and more exaggerated stress and intonation than when they are communicating with their older children or with adults. And they typically ask more questions (DePaulo & Bonvillian, 1978; Garton & Pratt, 1989; Grieser & Kuhl, 1988; James, 1990; Snow, 1979).

FIGURE 1-6
Characteristics of Motherese

- Sentences simplified semantically and syntactically
- Sentences well-formed (syntactically "correct")
- Short sentences
- Redundant (i.e., more repetitious)
- About the "here and now" (i.e., talk is about shared perceptions)
- Refers to concrete objects
- Exaggerated stress and intonation
- Clear pauses between utterances
- Sentences simplified phonologically
- Higher pitch
- Greater number of interrogatives
- Greater number of imperatives
- More restricted vocabulary
- Selective use of content words and fewer function words
- Slower (i.e., fewer words per minute)
- Highly intelligible

Some researchers have considered the term *motherese* to be a misnomer because it is not only mothers who modify their language to young children but all caretakers, and even older children (McCormick & Schiefelbusch, 1990; Owens, 1992). Yet others have found differences between the language modifications of mothers, fathers, and older siblings. Results have indicated that mothers are more attuned to the developmental level of their children than are fathers (McLaughlin, White, McDevitt, & Raskin, 1983; Warren-Leubecker & Bohannon, 1984), and that children under the age of 5 do not adjust the characteristics of their language when addressing younger children (Tomasello & Mannle, 1985).

While there is general agreement about the characteristics of motherese, there is less agreement on whether motherese indeed facilitates language development. In the motherese hypothesis, it is proposed that the special properties of caretaker speech play a causal role in language acquisition (Gleitman, Newport, & Gleitman, 1984). Although some researchers support the motherese hypothesis and other researchers dispute it, there are two points of agreement. First, as Gleitman, Newport, and Gleitman state, in a general sense the motherese hypothesis must be so "for it is the only explanation for the fact that language learning is variable—that French children learn French and Turkish children learn Turkish" (p. 76). Second, language acquisition is an interactive process. The language input from the environment may, indeed, be critical to the process but the child also plays a crucial role. The child must take the initiative to interact with others and actively process the incoming language information (Fivush & Fromhoff, 1988; Furrow & Nelson, 1986; Garton & Pratt, 1989; Gleitman, Newport, & Gleitman, 1984; Hoff-Ginsburg, 1986, 1990).

Adult Responses to Ungrammatical Forms

One of the questions that has intrigued researchers is why children bring their language into closer and closer approximations to the adult model. Why should they learn more complex forms if their simpler language adequately serves their communicative needs?

In the 1960s, it was suggested that children are positively reinforced for correct and increasingly more sophisticated forms and "punished" for incorrect forms. Brown and Hanlon (1970) found, however, that parents seemed to pay no attention to incorrect syntax and approved or disapproved only on the "truth value" of the child's utterance or when the child used naughty words. More recent research has demonstrated that parents do exhibit sensitivity to their children's well-formed and ill-formed utterances, though whether children use this subtle feedback to modify their language remains unknown (Bohannon & Stanowicz, 1988; Demetras, Post, & Snow, 1986; Hirsh-Pasek, Treiman, & Schneiderman, 1984).

Context of Parent-Child Communication

Almost immediately after birth, mothers and their children begin to interact with one another in ways that are remarkably like conversations. Rosenthal (1982) found 3-day-old infants are more likely to start vocalizing in the presence of maternal vocalization than in its absence. Bloom, Russell, and Wassenberg (1987) observed that turn-taking with an adult caused qualitative changes in the vocal sounds made by 3-month-old infants. Rutter and Durkin (1987) found that by 2 years of age, children are playing an active role in maintaining the coordination of vocal interactions with an adult, and that by 18 months of age they are using gaze in ways that are much like adult turn-taking patterns.

It has been suggested that child language emerges from routines in the child's daily life in which form and content of the language being used is largely repetitive, such as during bath time and lunch time. Bruner (1983) called these routinized activities *formats* and found that they often had a playful, gamelike nature such as in peek-a-boo and hide-and-seek. The language used in these formats is called *scripts*. The active guidance and support the adult gives in these conversations is called *scaffolding*. There is some evidence to indicate that shared script knowledge contributes to language development (Furman & Walden, 1990; James, 1990; Lucariello & Nelson, 1987).

Children learn language through conversation, and use language in conversation to learn about the world. As Wells (1986) wrote:

> Almost every situation provides an opportunity for learning if children are purposefully engaged and there are adults around who encourage their attempts to do and to understand and, in collaboration with them, provide a resource of skills and information on which they can draw. In such situations, language provides a means not only for acting in the world but also for reflecting on that action in an attempt to understand it. (p. 65)

This reciprocal relationship between learning language and learning through language will be further discussed in Chapter 2.

Later Language Development

The emphasis that educators, speech and hearing specialists, and linguists have placed on early language development is self-evident in the amount of research and number of textbook chapters devoted to this topic. It is exciting to watch young children learn language. Their progress is relatively fast and what they are learning is fairly easy to observe and measure. Yet we know that children don't stop learning language when they have attained basic knowledge of its form, content, and use. And as teachers of youngsters who are deaf, we also know that the child's ability to continue developing in language is critically important to cognitive and literacy development.

Later Syntactic and Semantic Development

In the early stages of language development, children acquire most of the morphologic and syntactic rules of their language, and they develop the ability to express basic semantic relations. In later language development, children add new morphologic and syntactic structures, expand and refine the ones they already use, and express increasingly complex semantic concepts.

Syntactic development   The study of later syntactic development has probably received the least amount of attention by linguistic researchers. Based on available data (Lee, 1974; Menyuk, 1988; Owens, 1992; Scott, 1988), the syntactic structures that appear in later language development are listed in Figure 1–7. Currently, we know very little about later language acquisition in American Sign Language (ASL) although, as in early language acquisition, the course of development appears to be similar to English (Wilbur, 1987).

The *personal pronouns* that appear in early language development (see Figure 1–1) include *I, me, my, mine, you, your, yours*; followed closely by *he, him, his, she, her, hers*; and then *we, us, our, ours, they, them, their, these,* and *those*. In later language development the child gains use of *indefinite pronouns*. The first ones to appear are *it, this,* and *that*; followed by *something, somebody,* and *someone*; and then *nobody* and *no one*. Considerably later *any-*

thing, anybody, anyone, everybody, and *everyone* appear. The child also begins to use *reflexives* consistently: *myself, yourself, himself, herself, itself, themselves,* and *oneself.*

The child also adds to the kinds of *descriptors* he or she uses. *Another, nothing,* and *none* appear, followed later by the many different descriptors that express quantity, such as *any, every, both, few, each, several, least, much,* and place in time, such as *next, first,* and *second.*

Verbs emerging in later language development include *modals (can, will, may* + verb), *do* + verb, and *past progressives* followed by *could, would, should* + verb. The child then demonstrates the ability to use *passives.* Some of the last forms to appear are *must* + verb, *shall* + verb, *have* + verb, complex embeddings, gerunds, and *complex auxiliary combinations* such as modal + *have* + verb + *en* and modal + *be* + verb + *ing.*

Adverbial clauses become evident in later language development, along with other subordinate clauses. Adverbial clauses of *time* (for example, *when*), *reason* (for example, *because*), and *purpose* (for example, *to*) appear considerably earlier than adverbial clauses expressing *condition* (for example, *if*).

The child continues to gain mastery of the conjunctions that appear in the latter stages of early language development and does not usually begin to use other conjunctions to express finer modulations of meaning for quite a while. These later developing conjunctions include *while, when, until, before, after, for, as, as if, if, although, though, however, therefore,* and *unless.*

The new question form that appears in later language development is the *tag question* (for example, "You are going, aren't you?"). However, it should be kept in mind that the child is developing the use of yes/no questions commensurate with the use of more complex verb forms (for example, "Do you see it?" "Should we go to the movies?" "Have you been eating?").

Note that many of these syntactic and morphologic structures are English-specific. In the section on assessment, I will discuss how to use this information to analyze the language of a child whose first language is ASL. Some children are exposed to both English and ASL, and they are likely to demonstrate some mixing of the two languages at points in their development. Furthermore, many children are not exposed to a full language model in either English or ASL because the adults in their lives use speech only and the child receives limited information through speechreading and auditory training, or the adults in their lives use pidgin sign. In the section on assessment, I will also discuss issues involved in analyzing the language of these children.

In addition to these forms, the child should be able to recognize the "goodness" of sentences, that is, whether sentences are grammatical or ungrammatical. You would not necessarily expect the child to know what morphologic or syntactic rules were being violated, however, as even adults often have difficulty with this metalinguistic task. The child should also be producing utterances that more and more closely resemble adult models.

FIGURE 1–7
Syntactic Structure in Later Language Development

Identifier	Descriptor	Verb	Adverb
Indefinite *pronouns (nobody, no one, nothing)*		Modals *(can, will, may* + verb, noun)	Adverbial clauses (of time, of reason)
		Past progressive *do* + verb	
Reflexives			Adverbial clauses (of purpose)
	Quantity	*could, would, should* + verb	
	Place in time		
Indefinite pronouns (*anything*, *anybody*, *anyone*, *everything*, *everybody*, *everyone*)		*must* + verb	
		have + verb	Adverbial clauses (of condition)
		Complex embeddings	
		Complex auxiliary combinations	
		Gerunds	
		Passives	

FIGURE 1–7
continued

Negative	Question	Conjunction	Stage
isn't *won't*			7
	Tag questions		8
			9
Later developing contracted negatives (e.g., *wasn't,* *hasn't, aren't,* *couldn't*)			10
			11
	whose *which*	Conjunctions expressing finer modulations of meaning *(although,* *though,* *however,* *therefore)*	12

Semantic development   The child's continued semantic development largely involves the learning of new words, new meanings for words already known, elaborated meanings, and interrelationships between word concepts (vocabulary growth). It also involves changes in the child's ability to relate word concepts (word association), explain word meanings (word definition), and understand nonliteral language (figurative language).

Vocabulary Growth   Growth in vocabulary occurs throughout the individual's lifetime. One of the major sources of lexical learning is reading. Not only do children add words that are longstanding in the language, but throughout their life span they will add words that are new to the language. Children learn shades of meaning for words they already know and they learn how some word meanings can be consolidated into one word with an elaborated meaning. They gain full understanding of abstract concepts and subtle meanings of words gradually through their school years (Nippold, 1988a; Owens, 1992).

Word Association   The developmental change in the way that children associate words has been called the syntagmatic-paradigmatic shift. Until the age of approximately 7, in a word association task children will respond to a stimulus word with a word related in syntax. That is, they respond with a word that would likely follow the stimulus word in a sentence. For example, in a syntagmatic association, the child would answer "juice" to the stimulus word *drink*. After the age of 7 (usually between 5 and 9), the child becomes more likely to respond to a stimulus word with a word that is semantically related and of the same grammatical category. For example, in a paradigmatic association, the child would answer "cold" to the stimulus word *hot* (Owens, 1992; Pease, Gleason, & Pan, 1989).

Word Definitions   Defining a word involves metalinguistic processes. The youngster must be able to reflect on word meanings and use words to talk about words. When defining a word, young children are likely to describe its appearance or its function. Gradually, youngsters become able to produce synonyms, explanations, and categorical relationships. It is interesting to note that word definition tasks have been included in IQ tests for many years because of the research correlating the ability to produce word definitions with intelligence (Nippold, 1988b; Pease, Gleason, & Pan, 1989).

Figurative Language   Along with vocabulary growth in later language development, the child develops the ability to understand figurative or nonliteral language. We currently know a great deal more about children's comprehension of metaphors, similes, slang, and proverbs than we do about their emerging ability to produce figurative language. While children begin to understand and use simple figures of speech in early language development, the ability to analyze the meanings of figurative language does not occur until late childhood or early adolescence. This ability to interpret nonliteral language increases with age and seems at least partly dependent on the amount of experience the youngster has had with the various forms of figurative language. The youngster's skill in comprehending figurative language also appears to depend on how relevant the expressions are to the child's personal experiences and whether the expressions appear in isolation or in context (Menyuk, 1988; Nippold, 1988a; Owens, 1992).

Later Development of Language Use

Throughout their school years, children acquire a range of communicative abilities that allow them to interact socially with increasingly greater skill. As Cooper and Anderson-Inman (1988) noted, "To talk is to interact with the world. Through this interactive process, children make connections with the world and also with themselves" (p. 243).

Functions or communicative intents   In later language development, children learn to express many new communicative intents. Figure 1–8 shows how most of these new language functions (Lococo, 1985; Menyuk, 1988; Owens, 1992) can be conceptualized as growing out of the original seven

FIGURE 1–8
Language Functions in Later Language Development

Instrumental ("I want")
—express personal needs
—cajole
—persuade
—request a favor
—request help
—request permission

Regulatory ("Do as I tell you")
—direct the behavior of others
—dissuade
—threaten

Interactional ("Me and you")
—share problems
—express feelings for others
—describe anticipated reactions
  of others
—criticize
—disagree
—compliment
—promise
—express support
—offer help

Personal ("Here I come")
—express emotions

—complain
—justify
—express opinions
—blame

Imaginative ("Let's pretend")
—storytell
—role play

Heuristic ("Tell me why")
—request information
—request clarification
—probe
—problem-solve
—predict

Informative ("I've got something to tell you")
—describe
—compare/contrast
—discuss cause and effect
—instruct others
—suggest

Humor

Lying

Sarcasm

functions postulated by Halliday (1975). This list is not meant to be exhaustive and, undoubtedly, the reader will be able to add later developing functions to the ones included.

Context or presuppositions   The child's ability to take into account situational cues and information about the communication partner becomes more sophisticated over time. One example of this is the child's use of indirect requests (Wilkinson, Wilkinson, Spinelli, & Chiang, 1984). A young child, who is visiting a family friend, might just get up and play on the interesting-looking piano in the family room. This same child, who is now a little older, might ask, "Can I play your piano?" Several years later this same youngster, who is now an adolescent, might look longingly at the piano and comment, "What a beautiful piano. I bet it is wonderful to play." This last statement is an indirect request.

In later language development, children gain mastery over the special registers needed to relate to peers, to members of the same gender and to the opposite gender, to others who share hobbies or interests, to people with similar cultural backgrounds, and to close friends and intimates (Obler, 1989).

Youngsters also learn that school discourse is different from home discourse. One of the common types of classroom exchanges that we never see at home is *"question-answer-evaluate,"* sometimes called question-answer routines. For example, the teacher asks, "John, what is the capital of Oregon?" John answers, "Salem." The teacher responds, "That's right. Mary, where is the Columbia River?" As this exchange demonstrates, the teacher controls the dialogue, the child who is called upon is supposed to give a brief answer, and the teacher's next question does not necessarily follow logically from the child's answer (Stephens, 1988). Question-answer routines have been found to be particularly difficult for deaf children with learning problems (Bullard & Schirmer, 1991).

Another difference between home and school language is the contrast between the amount of language produced by the adult and the child. Classroom discourse is marked by a high proportion of teacher language and a relatively small proportion of individual child language. Furthermore, unlike dialogue with parents and peers, dialogue with teachers typically means that teachers control choice of topic, take longer turns, monitor who takes turns and how long their turns are, and determine when the topic should be changed or terminated (Wells, 1986).

Classroom discourse is a relatively recent area of research and the reader is encouraged to examine works by Cazden (1988), Heath (1983), Blank (1988), and Blank & Marquis (1987). The implications of findings regarding teacher-child discourse will be weaved into the discussions of learning environments in Chapters 2 and 4.

In adolescence and early adulthood, young people learn that work settings require a language register that is different from the registers used at home and in school. Furthermore, most work settings demand knowledge of a particular professional jargon (Obler, 1989). Each week in *Newsweek's* Periscope section, the magazine lists several "buzzwords" used by a given profession. These words, meant to be a cross between jargon and slang, are humorous examples of how professional terminology maintains exclusivity among members.

Conversation   Several factors contribute to children's conversational ability in later language development. First, conversational ability develops as children become more aware of the conversational norms of their culture (Menyuk, 1988). Second, children become more skilled at engaging in conversation when they are able to take another persons's perspective (Owens, 1992). Finally, parents seem to "teach" the rules of discourse by gradually allowing the child to take over responsibility for initiating, maintaining, and terminating conversations as the child's skills increase (Wanska & Bedrosian, 1985).

Clearly, many rules for introducing, maintaining, and terminating a conversation in ASL may be quite different from the rules in English. Children who are deaf need to develop the ability to use appropriate conversational rules in both languages.

Conversational ability develops gradually and continues throughout the individual's lifetime. And, as we all can attest, not all adults seem equally skilled at carrying on a conversation.

Metalinguistic Awareness

The ability to reflect upon language is called *metalinguistic awareness*. During the period of early language acquisition, children's knowledge of language is intuitive. Children's ability to think consciously about language and to use language to talk about language signals a shift in their cognitive abilities (Menyuk, 1988). Garton and Pratt (1989) explained metalinguistic awareness using the following analogy:

> Using language is analogous to 'using' glass in a window to see the view. We do not normally focus any attention on the glass itself. Instead we focus our attention on the view. The glass serves the purpose of giving us access to the view. But we can, if we choose, look at the glass and may indeed do so for intrinsic interest or for a particular reason. (p. 126)

Metalinguistic awareness develops gradually in most children, beginning in their preschool years. Initially, they demonstrate this awareness by spontaneously making repairs in their own speech or sign, noticing others' errors, and "playing with" words that sound the same or look alike on the hands. By the time children are in first grade, they usually are able to think about the properties of words, they can make grammaticality judgments about sentences, and they have a rudimentary ability to reflect on the basic components of effective communication (Garton & Pratt, 1989; Owens, 1992).

The development of metalinguistic abilities accelerates during the emergence of reading and writing (Menyuk, 1988). Garton and Pratt (1989) suggested that reading and writing foster attention to words and sounds, syntactic structures of phrases and sentences, forms of paragraphs and longer discourse, and meanings and intents.

The development of metalinguistic awareness in children who are deaf seems to follow the pattern observed in normally developing children who are hearing (Zorfass, 1981). As teachers of children who are deaf, we need to pay particular attention to metalinguistic development because of the relationship between metalinguistic awareness and the child's ability to benefit from our language teaching strategies. In some traditional approaches to teaching language, we ask children to learn sentence patterns. The child with well-developed metalinguistic abilities may be able to reflect upon language well enough to manipulate parts of sentences, but children at early stages of language development would find this a formidable task. I will elaborate on this issue in the next chapter.

GOALS OF LANGUAGE INSTRUCTION

When we think about goals of language instruction, we are really formulating two types of goals. One type is the set of yearly goals we create for individual children who are deaf. These goals are the specific language structures, meanings, and uses we expect the child to develop understanding of or use of by the end of the academic year. These goals are an outgrowth of our assessment of each child's current language abilities.

The other type of goal we formulate is a more encompassing goal because it represents our philosophy of child language acquisition. How we assess our children, how we choose our teaching strategies and methods, and how we measure their progress will all flow from our belief about the goal of language instruction.

The goal of language instruction for children who are deaf is to provide them with a learning environment rich in opportunities to use language for meaningful interaction with others, for reading and writing as well as speaking/signing and listening/receiving sign, and for thinking about the world. Deaf children are not cognitively or linguistically deficient. Their language does not need to be remediated unless they have concomitant learning problems. An environment abundant with linguistic experiences will enable them to figure out the underlying rules of language for themselves, which will ultimately give them power over their own linguistic systems.

APPROACHES TO LANGUAGE ASSESSMENT

Nature and Role of Assessment

Assessment has been described as a problem-solving process (Gearheart & Gearheart, 1990). When we assess the language development of children who are deaf, our task is to collect information about their current language abilities, interpret this information, and make instructional decisions based on this information.

Assessment can serve many purposes. Teachers and language specialists need to be able to assess the language of children newly identified as having a hearing impairment, children entering an educational program for the first time, children leaving a program, or children undergoing I.E.P. review. We also need to know how to use assessment to monitor children's progress, to evaluate the effectiveness of our language curriculum, and to make placement decisions.

Ideally, language assessment is a collaborative effort between the teacher, parents, and language specialist. It is my view that language assessments of children who are deaf should be led, whenever possible, by the child's teacher. When the teacher is responsible for carrying out the assessment, or part of the assessment, understanding of the child's language is significantly deeper than when the teacher is given all of the diagnostic information from others. I have observed that teachers who personally assess the language of the children in their classrooms are better able to embed language objectives into learning opportunities and are more aware of their children's ongoing language development.

Process of Language Assessment

Figure 1–9 presents a model of the process of language assessment. It gives teachers and clinicians a unifying structure for carrying out a cohesive and comprehensive language evaluation and provides leeway for determining which instruments and procedures will produce the needed information about specific children. (For complete information about the model, see Schirmer, 1984).

The assessment moves in a left to right progression:

1. Information about the child's background is obtained, if this information is not already known.
2. The child's intellectual functioning is evaluated to identify the child as at an above-average, average, or below-average level because language ability is correlated with intellectual ability. Again, this information may already be available in the child's records and need not be reevaluated. (In my experience, achievement scores predominate in the cumulative files of children who are deaf, but results of intelligence testing are considerably more rare.)

FIGURE 1-9
Model of Language Assessment

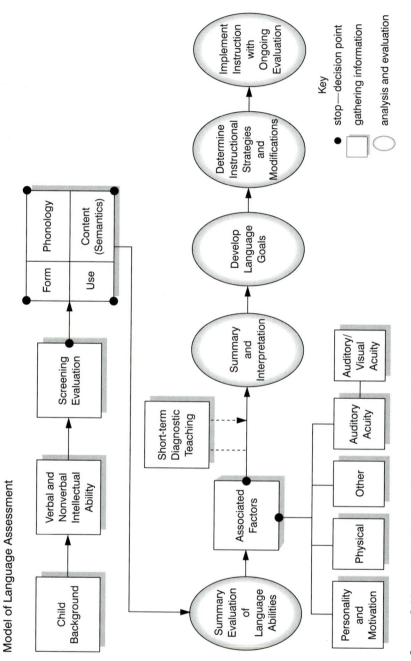

Source: Schirmer (1984). Reprinted by permission of the American Speech-Language-Hearing Association.

3. A screening evaluation is administered to determine overall language ability and to decide on the need and direction for further evaluation. This step is not necessary when the individual doing the assessment is already quite familiar with the child.

4. The next step involves the assessment of specific language abilities. The model lists the four areas of form, content, use, and phonology. However, the component skills within each area are not provided in the model. The reader is asked to refer to the discussion of component skills earlier in this chapter. Each test or procedure reveals information about the child's language abilities. It is up to the teacher or clinician to determine when enough information has been obtained or when a preceding evaluation has pointed to new areas that need further exploration.

5. When language evaluation is complete, a summary of the child's abilities should be prepared.

6. Factors that might be associated with the child's language should now be evaluated. Information regarding auditory acuity is almost always available; however, when other associated factors, such as visual acuity, seem to be impeding the child's language development, a referral for an outside evaluation may be needed.

7. At this point, it is often valuable to conduct diagnostic teaching. This allows the teacher to evaluate the child's language in a teaching situation and to try specific methods, techniques, and materials.

8. The information is summarized and interpreted, language goals are developed, instructional strategies and modifications are determined, and instruction is implemented with on-going evaluation.

The model provides a process for language assessment but does not tell the teacher or clinician which kinds of tests or procedures to use. In the next two sections, the two approaches to assessment, informal and formal, will be described.

Informal Approaches to Assessment

Informal assessment is defined as "any assessment that involves collection of data by anything other than a norm-referenced (standardized) test" (Salvia & Ysseldyke, 1991, p. 26).

Informal approaches offer the advantage of providing information about the child's understanding and use of language within natural communicative settings. Informal approaches have the best potential for providing a link between assessment and instruction. The disadvantage to these approaches is that the accuracy and completeness of information gathered about the child's language abilities depends heavily on the skill of the teacher or clinician.

Language Sampling

A *language sample* is a segment of a child's language performance regarded as representative of his or her linguistic ability. It has been argued that language sampling techniques should be used for assessing the language of children who are deaf because "language and intelligent behavior occur within a context; changes in context produce changes in language" (Ray, 1989, p. 38).

Obtaining a language sample   Obtaining a language sample from a child with a hearing impairment requires an interested, responsive, and minimally directive adult. For the sample to be considered representative, at least 50 utterances should be obtained and it is preferable to obtain 100. Of course, children at the very earliest stages of development may not be producing 50 utterances. For these children, I suggest collecting as much of their language as possible.

The following activities have been used with success to collect language samples. Some are more appropriate for younger children and some for older youngsters. A sample can be obtained in less than an hour with younger children and less than 30 minutes with older children, in one setting or over several days in a variety of settings. Classroom aides can do a wonderful job collecting language samples while the teacher is instructing the children. The reader will undoubtedly be able to add to this list of activities:

1. Use toys, such as a doll house, to play with a young child.
2. Show the child a wordless story book or a set of sequential pictures and ask him or her to describe the action.
3. Tell the child a story and ask him or her to retell it.
4. Place a brown paper bag in front of the child and have him or her ask questions to find out what is inside.
5. Have all the ingredients for a sandwich available and ask the child to tell you how to assemble it.
6. Engage the child in conversation about his or her weekend, vacation, or trip to a store.
7. Record the child's language during instructional activities.

Using videotape provides a record so that an accurate transcription can be made later. However, sometimes it is not possible to use videotape, and in these instances two other strategies can work fairly well, although the transcription will not be as accurate as one obtained through video. One strategy is to keep an ongoing written transcription, though this approach clearly influences the nature of the teacher-child interaction unless a third party is doing the writing, such as an aide during instruction. A second strategy is to subvocalize into an audio tape recorder, which is only possible if the teacher or aide is hearing.

Transcribing the language sample   When transcribing the language sample, I suggest using the form in Figure 1-10. This form was based on one developed by Bloom and Lahey (1978). The following conventions for recording child language data also rely heavily on Bloom and Lahey.

1. Utterance boundary is signified by a slash /. I don't use a period because a period is a convention for written language, and it is important to distinguish an oral or sign utterance from a written sentence. It is sometimes difficult to determine when a child has completed one utterance and started another. Linguists use the guideline that the boundary is

FIGURE 1–10

Form for Transcribing a Language Sample

Page No. _____

Student's Name _____ Age _____ MLU _____ Stage _____

Teacher's Name _____ Date(s) _____

Activity/ Context	Teacher's Utterance	Student's Utterance	Student's Behavior/Meaning	Analysis

determined by the length of a pause before the next utterance and by its apparent terminal contour. I also often encounter the problem of the child who connects every utterance with *and* or some other conjunction. Lee (1974) used the rule that one *and* (or any other overused conjunction) connecting two independent clauses was allowed per sentence. Her example was:

> I came home and my dad was there. . ./
>
> (and) he saw my dog and he started laughing. . ./
>
> (and) the dog got scared and he started to bark. . ./
>
> (and) my dad made me take him out/ (p. 75)

2. Questions should be followed by a rising arrow instead of a question mark [↑].
3. An unintelligible utterance or part of an utterance should be indicated by enclosing it in brackets.
4. When a child repeats an adult utterance, the child's utterance is written in full even if the repetition is exact.
5. Conversational route can be indicated through arrows or by leaving space between participants' utterances.
6. ASL glosses should be written in all capital letters with complex glosses connected by hyphens (e.g., WENT-AROUND-THE-BLOCK).
7. Symbols should be designated for distinguishing between sign, oral, simultaneous, and gestured utterances. These symbols should be explained in a key on the first page of the transcription.

Follow the guidelines listed here in creating the final transcript to be used for analyzing the child's language:

1. Maintain the integrity of the child's sentence unit, or utterance boundary, as nearly as possible. Since mean length of utterance is used to measure language growth, it is important to determine when the child has completed an utterance.

2. Record the child's exact utterance. This is often difficult because, as adults, we tend to reformulate an utterance into appropriate grammatical form.

3. Make a note of the utterances that are elliptical. Grammatical ellipsis is an omission of one or more words redundant with the prior utterance. For example, if the teacher asks, "How old are you?" and the child responds, "Five," the child's utterance is elliptical. The child may have knowledge of the full structure, "I am five," but is not required or even expected to use it in this context. Thus, the single-morpheme *five* may not be representative of the child's linguistic ability. (When you count the number of utterances the child has produced, do not include elliptical utterances or utterances that are identical to previous utterances toward the total of 50 or 100 that you will use in the analysis.)

4. Include the context or activities in which the child is engaged, the child's behaviors, and adult utterances in the transcription. This is particularly important when the child is at the one- and two-morpheme stages because much of the child's actual meaning at these stages of development is inferred. Notations regarding behavior and context can be extremely valuable when analyzing the child's utterances. Also, if the adult's utterances are not notated, you can't be sure when the child's utterance is elliptical.

Formats Used to Analyze Spontaneous Child Language

Numerous formats have been designed for analyzing language obtained in naturalistic settings. Authors have used various terms to describe their format including matrix, system, paradigm, taxonomy, checklist, protocol, framework, and model. It is interesting to note that more of the formats which I found in the literature were designed to assess pragmatic abilities (Hasenstab, 1983; Johnson, Johnston, & Weinrich, 1984; Luetke-Stahlman, 1989; Moeller, Osberger, & Eccarius, 1986; Prutting & Kirchner, 1987; Roth & Spekman, 1984a, 1984b), than semantic abilities (Luetke-Stahlman, 1988), semantic and syntactic abilities (Schirmer, 1989), or a combination of semantic, syntactic, and pragmatic abilities (Arwood, 1983; Wing, 1982).

In a forthcoming section, I will describe the steps involved in analyzing a language sample using my own formats, and I will discuss how to use data regarding the child's current language abilities to identify appropriate language objectives and goals. First, however, I want to discuss the role of standardized language testing.

Formal Approach: Standardized Assessment Instruments

Assessment that involves the use of formal procedures and strategies, especially standardized tests, has been referred to as *formal assessment* (Gearheart & Gearheart, 1990). In *standardized tests*, which are also called *norm-referenced tests*, the child's performance is compared to the performance of peers (that is, a large group of children at the same age or developmental level). Norm-referenced tests are similar in nature to criterion-referenced tests in that test answers are predetermined and strict standards for scoring have been set forth. However, in *criterion-referenced tests*, the child's performance is compared to an absolute level of mastery.

Standardized assessment instruments offer the advantage of providing objective information about the child's language, that is, information that has not been particularly influenced by the skill or bias of the examiner. Also, standardized tests provide data regarding reliability, validity, representativeness, and standard error of measurement that the teacher can consider in evaluating the accuracy and usefulness of the child's test results. One of the major drawbacks to using standardized assessment instruments is that they measure the child's comprehension or use of decontextualized language. Many tests measure children's metalinguistic abilities more than their linguistic abilities (Ray, 1989). Another drawback is the poor validity and reliability found in many standardized tests of language (McCauley & Swisher, 1984).

Special Considerations in Using Standardized Tests with Youngsters Who are Deaf

Relatively few standardized tests of language have been developed specifically for youngsters who are deaf or have included deaf youngsters in the normative sample (Abraham & Stoker, 1988). We clearly, then, need to be very careful about choosing and administering a norm-referenced language test.

One of the problems we encounter is the verbal directions. Standardized tests are meant to be administered exactly according to directions. If they are not, the norms are rendered useless (Salvia & Ysseldyke, 1991). However, the verbal directions may be confusing to the child who is deaf or it may not be possible to interpret them into sign word-for-word, particularly for the ASL child. As Ziezula (1982) stated, "If the individual being tested cannot fully comprehend the tasks required of him/her, the validity of the results must be questioned" (p.2).

Another problem with standardized tests, noted by Ziezula, is that test items can discriminate against an individual with a hearing impairment, although these items appear to be more prevalent in tests of intelligence, personality, and vocational interest.

These previous considerations all relate to the test. We also need to consider the child. During testing, the child should be benefitting from the kind of amplification he or she uses daily in school. The child should be in good health, with no allergic condition or middle ear infection influencing hearing level. The testing environment should be comfortable, with lighting that enables the child to clearly see the speaker/signer. In addition, the examiner should be fluent in the child's native language (Thompson, Biro, Vethivelu, Pious, & Hatfield, 1987).

Choosing a Standardized Language Test

Beginning with the first Binet-Simon intelligence scale developed in 1916, there has been widespread interest in psychological and educational measurement. Thorum (1981) found that the period between 1920 and 1940 was marked by rapid development of assessment methodology and the publication of achievement, intelligence, aptitude, interest, and personality tests. During World War II, the focus was on developing standardized tests to measure individual aptitudes, potentials, and skills. The 1950s brought standardized tests firmly into the public schools, with language assessment instruments becoming popular in the 1960s. The explosion of language tests in the 1970s and 1980s, and presumably this trend will continue in the 1990s, leaves us with a seemingly endless number of tests to sort through.

It is a challenge for most of us to choose appropriate standardized tests of language for the deaf children we teach. Unless we have the resources and time to actually read and personally evaluate the hundreds of tests on the market, we need to rely on other sources of information regarding these tests.

One of the oldest and most prestigious resources is the Buros Institute of Mental Measurements which publishes *Tests in Print* and the *Mental Measurements Yearbooks*. *Tests In Print* (the most recent one was published in 1983) lists and briefly describes every commercially available test published in English. *The Mental Measurements Yearbook* (the most recent one was the *Eleventh Mental Measurements Yearbook* published in 1992) lists and provides evaluative reviews of tests that are new or revised since publication of the last yearbook. These references are available in most libraries.

Textbooks on assessment provide us with a second resource. In recent years, a number of texts have been developed specifically to describe the process of assessment and to evaluate the most widely used tests. Two texts on special education assessment are Gearheart and Gearheart (1990) and Salvia and Ysseldyke (1991). Ziezula's text (1982) focuses specifically on assessment of individuals with hearing impairments, and the text by Thompson and her associates (1987) deals solely with language assessment of school-aged children with hearing impairments.

Our professional journals provide a third resource for test information. Many of our journals such as the *American Annals of the Deaf, The Volta Review, Journal of Childhood Communication Disorders, Journal of Speech and Hearing Disorders*, and *Language, Speech, and Hearing Services in Schools* include examinations of test use, evaluations of testing procedures, and reviews of tests.

In the Appendix, Standardized Tests, I have listed, described, and briefly reviewed the language assessment instruments I found to be most commonly used with youngsters who are deaf.

ANALYZING THE CHILD'S DEVELOPMENTAL LANGUAGE STAGE

Once the teacher or clinician has obtained a language sample and administered selected standardized tests, the data needs to be analyzed. My suggestion is first to analyze the information gained through informal approaches, formulate tentative conclusions, and then use the results from formal testing to modify findings and to reach final conclusions.

Analyzing a Language Sample

As discussed previously, numerous formats have been created for analyzing spontaneous child language. Following are the steps in my own formats that illustrate the process of analyzing a language sample.

As shown in Figure 1–10, Form for Transcribing a Language Sample, you leave one column open for analysis of syntactic and morphologic forms and semantic categories.

Start by calculating the child's mean length of utterance. First, count free and bound morphemes. A *free morpheme* such as *man* or *play* can occur alone, whereas a *bound morpheme* such as the *ly* in *manly* and the *ed* in *played* must be attached to another morpheme. Compound words, proper names, ritualized reduplications (for example, *trick or treat*, *thank you*), irregular past, catenatives (for example, *wanna*, *gonna*), and internal word changes to indicate plural (for example, *feet*, *people*) are counted as single morphemes. Auxiliaries, plural (*-s*), possessive (*-s*), third person singular present indicative (*-s*), regular past (*-ed*), present progressive (*-ing*), contractions, participles and gerunds (*-ing*), and comparative forms (*-er*, *-est*) are counted as separate morphemes.

The rules for counting morphemes in ASL would obviously follow somewhat different rules than the preceding rules for counting morphemes in English. For a thorough discussion of sign morphology, the reader should examine works by Isenhath (1990) and Wilbur (1987). As a general rule, however, a separate morpheme is counted each time a handshape, location, or movement signals a unit of meaning.

Once you have counted the child's morphemes, mean length of utterance is calculated by dividing the number of morphemes by the number of utterances. You should also note the child's upper bound, which is the longest utterance the child produces. The *upper bound* tells you about the child's willingness to take risks, to try new language features that add to the length of an utterance.

The mean length of utterance gives you an expectation about what forms and meanings the child will likely be expressing.

Now turn to the two formats for syntactic and morphologic development. Figure 1–1 presents a framework for early syntactic development and Figure 1–7 for later syntactic development. You know that the acquisition of forms does not stop and start within the boundaries of each stage, so no matter how long the child's mean length of utterance is, you need to use both frameworks for analyzing the child's utterances.

Each utterance is analyzed separately for forms the child is using. The analysis is written next to the utterance on the transcription. For example, if the child produced, "doll falling," *present progressive without auxiliary* (for "falling") would be written in the analysis column.

When you have completed the analysis for syntax and morphology, use Figure 1–2 to analyze the child's semantic development. Again, each utterance is analyzed separately, but this time you are analyzing the child's use of semantic categories. For example, the child's utterance, "doll falling," is now analyzed as *entity, action*. In the analysis column, *entity, action* is written below *present progressive without auxiliary*.

When all utterances have been analyzed, forms and meanings appearing in the language sample are tallied. It is helpful to write the tallies directly onto enlarged photocopies of the frameworks and the taxonomy.

The tally provides a picture of the child's current syntactic, morphologic, and semantic abilities. At each stage of development, it is clear which forms and meanings the child is using consistently, inconsistently, and not at all.

The next step in the analysis is to examine the child's abilities in the area of language use. Figure 1–11 presents a checklist of language functions, presuppositions, and conversational rules. The checklist simply offers a column for checking whether the child demonstrates, doesn't demonstrate, or sometimes demonstrates a particular skill or whether there was no opportunity to observe the skill. It is valuable, however, to include comments in this column regarding your impressions of the child's abilities.

Using Results from Standardized Tests

The child's performance on a standardized test should be interpreted according to the directions set forth by the publisher. This interpretation, along with any additional information gained from probing test answers with the child, can then be consolidated into the body of information already available from the informal assessment.

As McCormick and Schiefelbusch (1990) stated, "When used as an integrated part of an assessment protocol, standardized testing can provide extensive information regarding the comprehension of language content (vocabulary and basic concepts) and language form (phonology, morphology, and syntax) in elicited conditions. Comparable data are needed in less structured situations to complete the diagnosis" (p. 130).

IDENTIFYING APPROPRIATE LANGUAGE GOALS

Language goals are identified by comparing the child's current language abilities with the forms, meanings, and uses you would expect to appear at the child's stage of development. In other words, language goals are developed based on what has already appeared and what would be expected to appear in the child's language.

The following case study of a child who is deaf illustrates how information from the assessment and analysis procedures previously discussed can be used in creating appropriate language goals.

FIGURE 1–11
Checklist of Language Functions, Presuppositions, and Conversational Rules

(Scale is from 1 to 5, with 1 representing "not observed" in the child's language, 3 representing "uses sometimes" or "uses appropriately some of the time," and 5 representing "uses appropriately at all times.")

	1	2	3	4	5

Language Functions

Instrumental—requests, expresses personal needs, cajoles, persuades, requests a favor, requests help, requests permission

Regulatory—controls, directs the behavior of others, dissuades, threatens

Interactional—interacts with others, shares problems, expresses feelings for others, anticipates reactions of others, criticizes, disagrees, compliments, promises, expresses support, offers help

Personal—communicates feelings, expresses emotions, complains, justifies, expresses opinions, blames

Imaginative—creates, pretends, storytells, role-plays

Heuristic—questions, requests information, requests clarification, probes, problem-solves, predicts

❏   **A Case Study**   ❏

Courtney is a profoundly deaf child, 7 years-3 months old. Her MLU (mean length of utterance) was calculated to be 5.71. I will not try to show the full analysis of Courtney's language but I will highlight a few of the major goals I developed and discuss how I decided on them.

When I examined Courtney's use of questions, using Figures 1–1 and 1–7, I found that she used *what, who,* and *when* questions consistently. She used no *where* questions, no *how* questions, and 2 *why* questions. She asked many *intonation* questions, such as "You play basketball?" but no fully formed *yes/no* questions. She also used no *tag* questions in the language sample. Her MLU placed her well beyond Stage 6, so I had expected her to be consistently using the Stage 2 and 3 forms, using at least a few of the

FIGURE 1–11
continued

	1	2	3	4	5
Informative—declares, informs, describes, compares/contrasts, discusses cause and effect, instructs others, suggests					

Presuppositions

Situational Cues—takes into account how formal or informal the context is, needs perceptual support, makes indirect requests

The Communication Partner—takes into account the partner's background knowledge, is able to use different language registers

Conversational Rules

Introducing a Conversation—solicits conversational partner's attention, greets appropriately, establishes eye contact

Maintaining a Conversation—asks questions, answers questions, turn-takes appropriately, handles regressions, requests more information, makes repairs, offers new information, acknowledges the partner's information, uses eye contact appropriately, shifts topics

Terminating a Conversation—closes a topic, uses conversational boundary markers

Stage 4 and 5 forms, and perhaps starting to use the later-developing form, tag questions. When I compared her development of questions with other forms on the frameworks, I found a similar pattern. She was consistently using the syntactic and morphologic forms from Stages 2 and 3, but her use of forms beyond Stage 3 was sporadic.

I chose the goals with this pattern of development in mind. Since Courtney's stage of language development seemed to be clearly beyond Stage 2, the Stage 3 question form *where* became an important goal and one I would target for classroom emphasis. I also considered it appropriate to add *how* and *why* questions, since she was already using a few *why* questions, and *how* questions typically appear in child language at about the same time. My last goal for question forms was *yes/no* questions because this form usually appears next in child language, and Courtney gave evidence of being ready to begin using this form through her consistent use of intonation questions. I did not include *tag* questions because at this point they seemed considerably beyond her stage of development. When she began to develop the use of *yes/no* questions, I would probably add tag questions as a goal.

I identified goals for Courtney from each of the other categories (Identifier, Descriptor, Verb, Adverb, Negative, and Conjunction) in the same way.

When planning language goals, the teacher first concentrates on the forms from stages earlier than the child's stage of development (as determined from the child's mean length of utterance) that do not appear or do not appear consistently in the language sample. These become the first and most important goals. The next step is to look at the forms in the child's current stage of development that he or she is using inconsistently or not at all. These also become language goals. The final step is to determine which of the forms from the later stages of development would be expected to appear next in the child's language, and these are added as appropriate goals.

If Courtney was acquiring ASL as a first language, I would need to use the frameworks a little differently. Instead of looking for the English inflections and word order, I would be looking for the syntactic and morphologic structures in ASL that express the same grammatical intent. For example, when analyzing Courtney's language for her use of questions, I would examine the ways she expressed wh- questions, *yes/no* questions, and tag questions in ASL, and I would expect these forms to appear in the approximate order presented in the frameworks.

If Courtney was acquiring both ASL and English at the same time, it would be important for me to be aware of the possibility that she might mix the languages, utterance to utterance or within the same utterances, by alternating between ASL and English. Research on bilingualism indicates that this mixing is normal. In assessing her language, I would need to analyze the ASL features and English features within each utterance. The language goals I created for Courtney would include goals for ASL and goals for English.

If Courtney was exposed to incomplete models of English or ASL, she might produce a mix of English, ASL, home signs, and gestures. I would, first of all, need to analyze the English features and ASL features she expressed and use this analysis to develop appropriate goals in both English and ASL. Second, I would look at Courtney's home signs and gestures in terms of what she was trying to express semantically and pragmatically. The goals for syntax that I chose for Courtney would include forms in ASL and

English that are used to express these meanings and functions that Courtney was already expressing in her home signs and gestures.

Once I had analyzed Courtney's syntactic and morphologic development and created goals for these areas, I analyzed her semantic development. I used Figure 1–2 to determine which semantic categories she used with consistency and which she used inconsistently or not at all. When I identified semantic goals for her, I not only included those categories she used inconsistently, such as *time*, and those she seemed ready to begin using, such as *mood*, but I also included goals related to vocabulary growth within the categories she was already expressing.

When I analyzed Courtney's development of language use, I found she demonstrated many skills appropriate to her age and language development level. One of the goals I identified was in the area of conversational turn-taking. Courtney was able to participate in short conversational turns but had some difficulty giving more than brief responses to her conversational partner. I included extended turn-taking as an appropriate goal, realizing also that this particular goal would provide the teacher an instructional context (that is, conversational role-playing) for many of Courtney's syntactic, morphologic, and semantic goals.

The goals for Courtney that I have discussed represent just a few of the ones identified for her. I used information from the other sources in the assessment, such as standardized test results, to modify and extend the goals initially identified through the language sample.   ❑

FINAL COMMENTS

Using a model of language acquisition based on what is currently known about normal language development, the language abilities of a child who is deaf can be analyzed and described. Individual language goals are based on the discrepancies found between forms, meanings, and uses currently appearing in the child's language with those expected to appear according to the child's language development stage. These individual language goals can include both English and ASL. Language goals can then be used to provide a learning environment that enhances the child's cognitive capacity to create for him or herself a deep-level, abstract, and complex language or languages. In the next several chapters, I will be describing aspects of this learning environment.

SUGGESTED READINGS

Cazden, Courtney B. (1988). *Classroom Discourse: The Language of Teaching and Learning*. Portsmouth, NH: Heinemann.

Franklin, Margery B., & Barten, Sybil S. (1988). *Child Language: A Reader*. New York: Oxford University.

Gearheart, Carol, & Gearheart, Bill. (1990). *Introduction to Special Education Assessment: Principles and Practices*. Denver: Love.

Gleason, Jean Berko. (1993). *The Development of Language (3rd ed.)*. New York: Merrill/Macmillan.

Salvia, John, & Ysseldyke, James E. (1991). *Assessment in Special and Remedial Education (5th ed.)*. Boston: Houghton Mifflin.

Wells, Gordon. (1986). *The Meaning Makers: Children Learning Language and Using Language to Learn*. Portsmouth, NH: Heinemann.

Wilbur, Ronnie B. (1987). *American Sign Language: Linguistic and Applied Dimensions (2nd ed.)*. Austin, TX: Pro-Ed.

Language Development
Within the Classroom Setting

TEACHING MODELS AND STRATEGIES THAT
ENCOURAGE LANGUAGE GROWTH
Direct Instruction
Inquiry
Role Playing and Simulations
Cooperative Learning
Peer Tutoring
Discussion
Computers and Related Technology
Incidental Teaching of Language Goals

DEVELOPING LANGUAGE THROUGH CONVERSATION

Features of Conversation that Promote Language Development
A Conversational Approach

INTERDISCIPLINARY CURRICULUM:
INTEGRATING LANGUAGE INTO THEMATIC UNITS

Models for Developing an Integrated Curriculum
Procedure for Developing a Thematic Unit
Example of a Thematic Unit

INCORPORATING STRATEGIES OF SECOND LANGUAGE LEARNING
Factors in the Development of Bilingual Proficiency
Bilingual Education: Considerations and Perspectives
Language and Culture
Bilingual Education Models
Bilingualism and the Education of Children Who Are Deaf:
Issues, Problems, and Prospects

FINAL COMMENTS

The teacher of deaf youngsters who has taken the time to assess each student's current language abilities is confronted with the question of how to encourage each child's continued language development. In the past, teaching methods developed for use with youngsters who are deaf relied heavily on the notion that their language needed to be straightened out. Teachers were therefore advised to use strategies that focused almost exclusively on English syntax, such as the Fitzgerald Key (Fitzgerald, 1949; Pugh, 1955) and Apple Tree (Caniglia, Cole, Howard, Krohn, & Rice, 1975). (See McAnally, Rose, and Quigley, 1987, for a thorough description of traditional language methods.)

Current knowledge of language acquisition has led to dramatic changes in the way language instruction in the classroom is viewed. It is widely recognized that labeling and drilling the deaf child on surface structure features has no lasting or significant influence on the child's internalization of the language itself, whether that language is English or ASL. The alternative is to create an environment replete with opportunities to interact with others using the language for meaningful communication. As Harrison, Layton, and Taylor (1987) noted, developmental language "programs must be constructed around the notion that the acquisition of language and the concurrent understanding of the function of language occur through topical communicative exchanges which are the product of shared activities" (p. 230).

In this chapter, I will discuss language as a curricular foundation on which the full school day is built and not as a subject area that comprises one class period per day. It is hoped that this chapter will help the reader to take the language goals that he or she carefully and explicitly developed for each child and embed those goals within a myriad of daily learning experiences.

TEACHING MODELS AND STRATEGIES THAT ENCOURAGE LANGUAGE GROWTH

The terms *model* and *method*, often used interchangeably in the literature on teaching, both refer to a design for a particular kind of teaching activity. The design is described in terms of its theoretical underpinnings, goals, procedures, and strategies for carrying it out. The term *model* implies that the description is a somewhat idealized version that is open to interpretation. The term *method* implies that the description is actually a prescription to be followed relatively closely.

I have chosen to use the word *model* because I believe that the terminology should emphasize the teacher's self-efficacy, flexibility, and reason. I agree with McNergey, Lloyd, Mintz, and Moore (1988) who wrote that a teacher is a professional "who decides how to apply his or her specialized knowledge and skills to solve particular problems and does so with a reasonably high degree of self-determination" (p. 37).

In this section, several models will be described. The reader will be familiar with most, if not all, of these models from course work in educational psychology and methods of teaching school subjects. The purpose of discussing these models is neither to repeat the information in those courses nor to discuss the research supporting or not supporting the effectiveness of any model for teaching subject matter and for encouraging the development of thinking skills. The purpose, instead, is to present these models in light of how well each one can encourage the development of language in children who are deaf.

Teaching strategies will also be discussed with the same purpose in mind. A *strategy* is a careful plan for meeting teaching objectives and overcoming obstacles. According to this definition, a number of strategies are used within any teaching model.

The models and strategies discussed here are either commonly used or are relatively new models or strategies that offer exciting opportunities for language development. The reader can use these particular models and strategies as seeds for creating a mixed garden of classroom learning activities. As Joyce (1987) observed, "A highly skilled performance in teaching blends the variety of models appropriately and embellishes them. Master teachers create new models of teaching and test them in the course of their work, drawing on the models of others for ideas that are combined in various ways" (p. 420).

For each of the models, actual scenarios of teaching lessons are provided. Note that for the purpose of readability, dialogue in all scenarios is written in English although many of the teachers and youngsters use ASL or pidgin sign. Indeed, all of these models can be used for encouraging the development of both ASL and English. Whether the teacher uses ASL, spoken English, simultaneous speech and sign, or pidgin sign with or without voice, it is hoped that the teacher recognizes the importance of providing a consistent language model to the child who is deaf.

Direct Instruction

The term *direct instruction* has come to have both a broad and a narrow definition. In the broadest sense, direct instruction is any form of structured teaching. Gersten, Woodward, and Darch (1986) referred to this definition of direct instruction as little "d" little "i." When defined narrowly, as Direct Instruction with big "d" big "i," it consists of the following features:

1. Teach an explicit step-by-step strategy. (When this is not possible or necessary, model effective performance.)
2. Develop mastery at each step in the process.
3. Develop strategy (or process) corrections for student errors.

4. Gradually fade from teacher-directed activities toward independent work.

5. Use adequate, systematic practice with a range of examples.

6. Use cumulative review.(p. 19)

    For some teachers, direct instruction denotes the even narrower definition of scripted lessons developed for the commercially available DISTAR programs in reading, math, and language.

    As a teaching model, the definition developed by Baumann (1988a) is appropriate. According to Baumann, in direct instruction the teacher tells, shows, models, demonstrates, and explains the skills, processes, and strategies to be learned. What are the opportunities for language development within a direct instruction lesson? On one level, it would appear that direct instruction provides a lot of opportunity for receptive language but limited opportunity for expressive language. After all, the teacher dominates the interaction between teacher and child, and virtually no child-to-child interaction is built into this model. However, providing frequent student opportunity to respond is a vital component of the model. Although responses can be brief, teachers of deaf youngsters with language goals in mind can encourage responses that require the youngsters to express themselves in elaborated ways. The following scenario illustrates some of the ways that language development can be nurtured within a teaching lesson implementing a direct instruction model.

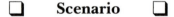

❏   Scenario   ❏

Ms. Bond was teaching a lesson on state capitals to a group of fifth grade students in a self-contained classroom for students with hearing impairments in a public elementary school. She began by orienting the students to the topic.

Ms. Bond: What have we been discussing in social studies?

Jill: United States.

Ms. Bond: Tell me more. What about the United States?

Jill: We learned about the fifty states. . .different states.

Ms. Bond: Right, we've discussed the names of the fifty states and where they are on a map. What else did we learn?

Jane: Parts of the country. You know.

Ms. Bond: I do? Tell me what you know. Tell me about parts of the country.

Jane: You mean like New England, like that?

Ms. Bond: Yes.

JANE: Okay. Well, there is New England states. They're in the northeast part of the United States. I think Maine, Vermont, New Hampshire, Massachusetts, Rhode Island, Connecticut. . .

This orientation phase went on a bit longer while Ms. Bond activated the youngsters' background knowledge by reviewing previous learning. She could have asked closed questions, questions requiring one- or two-word answers, and accomplished this phase in less time. But by asking open-ended questions, questions requiring elaborated answers, and expanding on the children's responses, she combined her content goals with language goals. After she obtained answers from all four youngsters, she continued her introduction of the lesson by telling the students what they would be learning that day.

Ms. BOND: Today we'll learn something new about the states. We'll be learning the capitals for each state. Here's a map of the United States. The capital is marked with a star. Sometimes the capital is the biggest city in the state. Sometimes it's the most well-known city. But sometimes it's a small city. Let's start with Oregon. The capital of Oregon is Salem. Here it is on the map. Jodi, what's the capital of Oregon?

JODI: Salem.

Ms. Bond continued the presentation phase of the lesson by explaining the new information, using the map as a visual representation of the information, and frequently checking for understanding. But because Ms. Bond was just as interested in the children's language development as she was in their subject matter knowledge, she modified her procedure sometimes and asked questions requiring longer responses and discussions between students. These responses encouraged particular syntactic forms, semantic categories, and functions that were language goals for individual children.

Ms. BOND: Jack, you said the capital of Washington is Olympia. But I think Seattle is the biggest city in Washington.

JACK: I think Seattle is bigger than Olympia.

Ms. BOND: I think so, too. But why is Olympia the capital?

JACK: Sometimes the capital is a small city.

JODI: Olympia is close to Seattle.

JANE: Maybe the capital is a small city. But near a big city.

MS. BOND: Look at the ones we already found on the map. Tell me about them.

JACK: Salem is a small city. But near Portland. Sacramento is a small city. Near San Francisco.

JILL: No it's not. Sacramento is a big city.

JACK: Not big like San Francisco. . .

When Ms. Bond finished presenting 10 state capitals in this way, she provided the students with practice on the new information.

MS. BOND: Take out your white boards and markers. I'll fingerspell the name of the state. You write the capital. When I given the signal, hold up your board. . . .

When the students completed this activity, Ms. Bond gave each one a blank map of the United States. She then listed 10 states on the chalkboard. For seatwork, the students were supposed to write the names of the capitals in the appropriate places on their individual maps.

During the practice phases, first guided practice and later independent practice, Ms. Bond recognized that there was less opportunity to incorporate language goals. But whenever the chance arose, she encouraged the youngsters to discuss the characteristics of the state capitals as well as to memorize their names, thus nurturing the development of semantic categories such as attribution and causality and functions such as description and compare/contrast.   ❑

Inquiry

As a model of teaching, inquiry provides students with a learning experience similar to the kind of investigation scholars and scientists engage in when they are exploring phenomena, generating principles and theories, and organizing knowledge (Joyce & Weil, 1986). It is generally agreed that inquiry involves five major steps:

1. Identifying and defining the problem. Often this step involves generating a question. When the teacher presents the students with a puzzling occurrence, Orlich and associates (1990) refer to the model as guided inductive inquiry. In guided inquiry, the teacher plays "the key role in asking the questions, prompting the responses, and structuring the materials and situations" (p. 294). In unguided inquiry, the teacher

"introduces situations that are still predicated on inductive logic but are more open-ended in that the students must take more responsibility for examining the data, objects, or events" (p. 294).

2. Forming hypotheses. In this step, the students propose educated guesses regarding the answer to the question they generated in step 1.

3. Gathering data. This step can involve experimentation, reading, surveying others, or other methods of collecting evidence relevant to the problem.

4. Analyzing and interpreting data. In this step, the students examine the data, organize it in a way that makes sense, and use it to test their hypotheses.

5. Formulating conclusions and making generalizations. Based on their results, the students determine whether the hypotheses are supported or not. They then construct an explanation and, if possible, generalize their results to other situations or events.

A sixth step in the inquiry model is added by some authors. Joyce and Weil (1986) call this step an *analysis of the inquiry process*. Pasch, Sparks-Langer, Gardner, Starko, and Moody (1991) describe this step as one in which the students examine, analyze, and discuss their own thinking processes.

What are the opportunities for language development within an inquiry lesson? Inquiry clearly provides abundant opportunity for receptive and expressive language not only between the teacher and the students but also among the students. The following scenario demonstrates some of the ways that an inquiry lesson can incorporate language goals.

❏   Scenario   ❏

Ms. Parmelee has been teaching a unit on the physical properties of matter to a class of high school juniors at the state school for the deaf. For today, she planned an inquiry lesson on the concept of specific gravity.

Ms. Parmelee: I brought in two cans of pop, one diet and one regular. I have two containers of water. I'm going to drop a can into each container of water. Watch carefully. . .

Ms. Parmelee dropped the cans into the water and much to the surprise of her class, one can floated and one can sank.

Ms. Parmelee: Do you have any questions?

Minnie: Why did one can float and one can sink?

Anna: Are they different? What's different?

GEORGE: One is diet. Why did the diet pop float? Look at the weight on the can.

MS. PARMELEE: They're both twelve ounces.

AL: Let me hold them. Okay. They look the same size. Something's wrong. . .

Ms. Parmelee let them discuss the possibilities a few more minutes and then she wrote "Problem" and "Question" on the overhead projector.

MS. PARMELEE: What's our problem?

ANNA: Two cans of pop look the same but one floats and one sinks in water.

MS. PARMELEE: What question do we want to answer?

GEORGE: Why does the diet pop float and the regular pop sink in water?. . .

Ms. Parmelee wrote "Hypothesis" under George's question.

MS. PARMELEE: We've talked about hypothesis before. What hypothesis do you want to make?

AL: My hypothesis is I think that the aluminum for the diet can is less than the aluminum for the regular can.

MINNIE: But they weigh the same.

AL: Maybe not. The weight on the can is the pop. It tells how much pop is inside.

MINNIE: Okay. I agree. That's my hypothesis, too.

ANNA: My hypothesis is that the regular pop has sugar in it so it sinks. The diet pop has no sugar so it floats.

AL: But diet pop has something in it.

GEORGE: I don't remember the name but it's not the same as sugar.

ANNA: Okay. Wait a second. My hypothesis is that the regular pop has sugar in it so it sinks. The diet pop has that weird name in it but it's not so much inside. There's less inside. So it floats.

GEORGE: I have the same hypothesis as Anna.

MS. PARMELEE: How do we find the answer to our question?

MINNIE: We need a scale. I want to weigh the two cans.

ANNA: I think we need to get some sugar and some of the other sweetener. Then we can compare them. Like how much you need to make a drink sweet. . .

The students developed several more ideas and then gathered the materials they needed. During the experiments, they discussed their findings. They ultimately figured out that aspartame, an artificial sweetener, weighs less than sugar.

Throughout this lesson, Ms. Parmelee encouraged the youngsters to discuss their questions and possible solutions and to pay careful attention to what the other students were contributing to the discussion. Sometimes she rephrased a statement or expanded a comment, not only to provide clarification or further information but also because she wanted to emphasize specific language goals regarding syntax, semantics, and use. Because she had analyzed each student's language earlier in the year, she had these goals in mind and was able to encourage the development of particular language features within the context of this science discussion. For example, she was able to embed into the dialogue several indefinite pronouns and adverbial clauses, the semantic categories epistemic and antithesis, and the heuristic functions of problem solving, probing, and predicting, which were language goals for several youngsters in the class. ❑

Role Playing and Simulations

Simulation has been defined as "a representation of a real-world event in a reduced and compressed form resulting in a dynamic process that is safe and efficient" (Rockler, 1988, p. 94). It has its roots in the pretend play of young children.

Yawkey and Hrncir (1983) noted that "pretend play provides a basis for using objects and situations 'as if' they are other things" (p. 265). These two researchers found that for the preschool child, imaginative play serves an important function in language development. They observed four links between role playing and language development:

1. Role playing encourages the use of various forms of communication because "the child uses language to become the chief observer, participator, and actor" (p. 265).

2. Role playing encourages the development of social language because in pretend play children re-enact social situations from their own world. They learn not only to express many of the functions of language, such

as the instrumental and interactional, but also the "words flowing among and between the child actors expand social relationships with others" (p. 266).

3. Role playing encourages creative expression because the activity itself is free of real-world constraints. Thus, children can use a box for a car and describe to one another the features of the car.

4. Role playing encourages concentration. Yawkey and Hrncir found that children's increased concentration and attention to the actions, situations, and ideas they developed in their pretend play required extended communication among themselves.

Role playing in preschool and kindergarten classrooms is usually used spontaneously by the children rather than planned by the teacher. However, some children rarely engage in role playing. Levy, Schaefer, and Phelps (1986) conducted a study in which they encouraged role playing by all the children in a preschool classroom by (a) centering the curriculum around a common theme, (b) stocking the housekeeping center with props that supported the theme and having the teacher explain the use of the props to the children, and (c) having the teacher model appropriate play behaviors by assuming one of the roles at first and later facilitating the children's play within the housekeeping center.

Levy and her associates found that the language of the boys in the study increased significantly beyond the growth that would be predicted through maturation alone. The lack of significant difference in the girls' language was explained by the investigators' observation that before intervention, the children who engaged in pretend play in the housekeeping center were primarily girls and rarely boys. The implication of this finding is that teachers can create an atmosphere conducive for pretend play among children who would not otherwise normally engage in pretend play and that, furthermore, the pretend play for these children encourages the development of their language.

When used as a model of teaching for children beyond the kindergarten level, role playing consists of nine basic steps:

1. The teacher introduces the problem and explains role playing.

2. The teacher analyzes and assigns the roles.

3. The teacher decides how the situation will be acted out.

4. Concurrent with the third step, which involves the actors, is the fourth step, which involves the observers. In this step, the observers determine what they will look for during the role play.

5. The problem is actually enacted.

6. The simulation is discussed, analyzed, and critiqued. This step also involves decisions regarding the next simulation.

7 & 8. Steps 7 and 8 are the same as steps 5 and 6 with new participants and revised action. Steps seven and eight can be repeated several times.

9. All the students participate in a discussion of the problem and make plans for ways they can solve similar problem situations in their own lives.

What are the opportunities for language development within a role-playing and simulation lesson? The discussions that take place prior to and after the simulations and the actual role play itself obviously provide much opportunity for the use of expressive and receptive language. The following lesson provides some of the ways that role playing and simulations can incorporate language goals.

❑   **Scenario**   ❑

Mr. Esch has been spending quite a lot of time discussing feelings with his class of seventh grade students at the state school for the deaf. He has decided to try a role-playing lesson on two emotions with which all of the youngsters are having difficulty.

MR. ESCH: We've been talking about different emotions. What are some of the feelings we've discussed?

RONI: One was jealousy.

JANET: A different one was disappointment.

LAURA: I think we talked about frustration.

MR. ESCH: Right. Today I want to discuss anger. . .

Mr. Esch went on to ask the students what anger meant to them, what situations made them angry, and how they handled their anger. Then he set the stage for the role playing.

MR. ESCH: I've noticed that when one of you gets angry, it's hard on you and it's hard on the people around you. You need to figure out how to control your own anger, and you also need to figure out how to deal with someone else's anger. We can discuss our feelings and then you know in your head how you're supposed to behave. But when something makes you mad, you forget and just blow up. Another way is to role-play. In a role play, each person takes a role, pretends the situation is real, and practices how to behave in the situation. Patrick, what's a role play?

PATRICK: I don't know.

MR. ESCH: Roni?

RONI: Role play means that we make-believe a situation that makes us angry. Then we try not to blow up.

MR. ESCH: Right. You practice how to react to the situation. For the first role play, I'll be one person and I need one other person. Patrick? Okay. Patrick and I will decide on a situation. But the rest of you have an important role, too. You need to watch us carefully and figure out if our behavior is helping or hurting. These are the two emotions we're working on. . .

Mr. Esch wrote "Handling My Own Anger" and "Dealing With Someone Else's Anger" on the chalkboard. Then he and Patrick stepped outside the classroom and decided on a simulation. Mr. Esch came into the room, sat in a chair, and pretended to write. Patrick walked up to him.

PATRICK: Mr. Esch. I want to talk with you about my test.

MR. ESCH: I'm very disappointed, Patrick. You didn't study and got an F.

PATRICK: (Becoming angry) I tried to study but I didn't understand the math. It's not fair. I missed two days of class.

MR. ESCH: (Becoming angry) If you didn't understand the math, you should have come to see me. You have to take responsibility.

PATRICK: (Very angry) It's not my fault. (He crumples the test paper and throws it in the trash. Then he stomps out of the room.)

MR. ESCH: Okay. That's the end of the role play. What do you think?

JANET: Was that a real situation?

PATRICK: It happened one time to me. Not with Mr. Esch.

JANET: Both of you got mad.

MR. ESCH: What went wrong?

LAURA: First, I think you made Patrick mad because you said he didn't study. But he did. He didn't understand the math. But he did try.

MR. ESCH: That's a good point. And then Patrick got mad.

RONI: I noticed that Patrick got mad. Then you got mad. Then Patrick got madder.

MR. ESCH: What would be a better way to behave?

PATRICK: I don't know. Maybe I could explain more. Why I didn't understand the math.

MR. ESCH: That would probably help. I felt you were blaming me.

LAURA: Take responsibility for yourself.

MR. ESCH: (Pointing to the chalkboard) We've talked about "Handling My Own Anger." But how did I deal with Patrick's anger?

JANET: Not good. You got angry.

MR. ESCH: What would be a better way to behave?

LAURA: I think you should have explained and not got angry.

MR. ESCH: Laura, you can be Mr. Esch in the next role play. Then you can show how Mr. Esch should behave. Who wants to be Patrick?. . .

The students complete two more simulations, alternating roles and trying out different solutions. After the last simulation, they discussed situations in their own lives and how they could handle them in the future.

The discussions inherent in this teaching model provide the same opportunities for infusing language goals as other models in which discussion is used. The actual role play itself can provide the teacher with a fairly structured setting for encouraging the appearance of particular language features. Even though the simulation is not scripted, by setting the stage for the role play the teacher can make it necessary for the players to use specific syntactic forms, semantic categories, and language functions. For example, if Mr. Esch asks Patrick during the role play, "What will you do for the next test?" Patrick is encouraged to use a verb form expressing future tense, to express time and mood semantically, and to use the heuristic function.   ❏

Cooperative Learning

Cooperative learning involves a set of teaching strategies that are designed to structure student-to-student interaction in the classroom in a way that fosters cooperation rather than competition or individualization. In every classroom, learning goals are established. How students view these learning goals marks the difference between competitive learning, individualized learning, and cooperative learning.

According to Johnson and Johnson (1986), in competitive learning, the goals can be achieved by one or only a few students so some students work hard to do better than the others in the class and some work relatively little because they feel they have no chance at all. In individualized learning, students work in isolation to achieve learning goals that have no relationship to the goals of anyone else in the class. In cooperative learning, the goals are shared by classmates and they can only be accomplished if everyone works equally hard.

Cooperative learning looks like traditional group work but cooperative learning is distinguished by the following essential elements, according to Johnson, Johnson, and Holubec (1986):

1. Positive interdependence. In cooperative learning, group work is structured so that students need each other to complete the group's task. In traditional group work, one member can do most of the work and make most of the decisions, and some members can do relatively little. In cooperative learning, the performance of each group member is the concern of every group member and responsibility for leading the group is shared.

2. Face-to-face interaction. In cooperative learning, students must interact with one another. In traditional group work youngsters in the same group can work on separate parts of a project and never interact with other members of the group.

3. Individual accountability. In cooperative learning, every member of the group is responsible for learning the information at a level of mastery appropriate to the individual student. In traditional group work, only the final product is assessed, and individual students are not held accountable for how much they contributed or for how much they learned.

4. Interpersonal and small-group skills and group processing. In cooperative learning, the social skills needed to work harmoniously with others in a group are taught by the teacher, and the students are given opportunities to analyze how effectively they are using these skills to work together. In traditional group work, it is assumed that students already know how to work with others.

What are the opportunities for language development when using cooperative learning strategies? The face-to-face interaction essential to cooperative learning provides children extensive opportunity to use language expressively and receptively with peers. The following lesson illustrates how language goals can be incorporated within cooperative learning.

❏   Scenario   ❏

Mrs. Twiss teaches a multiage group of elementary level students with hearing impairments in a public school classroom. As part of a science unit on animal species, she decided to divide the class into groups of three and assign one species to each group.

She set up the groups heterogeneously so that within any group at least one student was at a lower ability level and at least one was at a higher ability level.

She developed one set of questions and discussed the questions with the whole class. She gave each student material about the species written at a level that the student could read independently. For one child, this meant that the material was largely in picture form. Mrs. Twiss then assigned roles to group members. In each group of three, one student was a summarizer-checker whose responsibility was to make sure every person in the group understood the information, one student was a recorder whose responsibility was to write the answers to the questions, and one student was an encourager-observer whose responsibility was to encourage each group member to contribute to the process and to monitor how well the group was working together.

Mrs. Twiss explained to the students that when they finished writing their answers to the questions, every group would make a report to the class. She told them that each student in the group would be responsible for delivering part of the report. She also explained that the class would probably have extra questions to ask and that each member of the group needed to be able to answer any question. Finally, she told them that the group would receive a grade based on the group's presentation.

When Mrs. Twiss finished her explanation, the groups moved their desks together and started to work. One of the groups consisted of Sydney, Lori, and Susan.

SYDNEY: I have the questions. Our species is kangaroo.

LORI: Wait. I'm the recorder. I need a pencil.

SYDNEY: Okay. Right. I'm the summarizer-checker. Susan's the encourager-observer.

SUSAN: Good job!

SYDNEY: What's the first question?

LORI: What does the species look like?

SUSAN: I have a picture. It has short front legs and big back legs.

SYDNEY: In my paper it calls them limbs. The front ones are called fore limbs. The back ones are called hind limbs.

LORI: What do you want me to write?

SYDNEY: Short fore limbs and big hind limbs.

LORI: Let me see how that's spelled.

SUSAN: It has a long tail.

LORI: So I'll list three things, right?

SUSAN: It has a pouch, too.

MRS. TWISS: You need to make sure each person adds information. I don't think Lori has contributed.

SYDNEY: Look in your paper Lori and see if it says anything different.

LORI: That's all I can find. I guess I can say it has fur.

MRS. TWISS: Susan, you should encourage Lori to find more information in her paper.

SUSAN: What else does it say?

LORI: That's all.

MRS. TWISS: Sydney, you should summarize what you found out and make sure everyone knows the information.

SYDNEY: Okay. A kangaroo has two short fore limbs, two big hind limbs, a long tail, a pouch, and fur. What's the next question?

LORI: Where does this species live?. . .

The face-to-face interaction between students in cooperative learning groups, such as in the preceding scenario, provides the same kinds of opportunities for language development as discussion provides in the other teaching models. It also provides a particular opportunity to focus on language goals that relate to conversational skills. For example, the student-to-student interaction in cooperative learning groups allows youngsters to practice turn-taking, asking and answering questions, requesting more information, acknowledging someone else's information, and shifting topics appropriately.   ❏

Peer Tutoring

Peer tutoring is "one child teaching another child of approximately the same age and skill level" (Cooke, Heron, & Heward, 1983, p. 1). It is similar to cross-age tutoring in which older and more knowledgeable students tutor younger students, but peer tutoring is easier for classroom teachers to manage because they can set it up within individual heterogeneous classes whereas cross-age tutoring requires the cooperation of several teachers across grade levels whose schedules may differ considerably (Kauchak & Eggen, 1989).

Peer tutoring is typically used for drill and practice on functional academic skills such as spelling words and math facts (Delquadri, Greenwood, Whorton, Carta, & Hall, 1986). However, it has also been used successfully in learning activities that require lengthy student responses. For example, peer tutoring can be used in answering comprehension questions, as the following scenario illustrates.

❏   **Scenario**   ❏

In Mrs. Twiss' class, the students have been studying about Australia. Mrs. Twiss has divided the class into student pairs and given each pair the same set of eight questions.

MRS. TWISS: I have given you eight questions. Each person has to pick four questions. You need to find the answers and then teach the answers to your partner.

WILLIAM: Do we write the answers?

MRS. TWISS: You should write notes to yourself but you don't need full sentences.

LINDA: How do we divide the questions?

MRS. TWISS: You need to cooperate. Maybe Diane wants to answer number one. But you want to answer number one. You have to look at the other questions and decide. Diane can answer number one but you want number five. So Diane says okay. Now set up your desks with your partner. You have twenty minutes to answer your questions, then twenty minutes to teach the answers to your partner. At eleven o'clock you'll have a quiz.

LIZ: (To Karen) I think first we need to read all the questions.

KAREN: Okay. I'm going to mark the ones I like. You mark the ones you like.

After reading the questions, Liz and Karen decided that Liz would find the answers to numbers 1, 5, 6, and 8 and Karen would answer 2, 3, 4, and 7. They spent the next 15 minutes finding the answers and making notes to themselves.

MRS. TWISS: It's time to start teaching your partner the answers.

LIZ: I have number one so I'll start. What is the size of Australia and where is it located? It's 2,948,366 square miles. It's southeast of Asia. It's between the Pacific Ocean and the Indian Ocean. I'm not sure if we need to know this, but it's a continent.

KAREN: Do you think it's fine to write three million square miles?

Liz: I don't know. In the book it says the exact amount. You have number two.

Karen: What is the population, where do most people live, and what languages do they speak?. . .

Peer tutoring allows for the same kind of student-to-student interaction as in cooperative learning, and the same kinds of language goals can be incorporated into peer tutoring lessons. In particular, alternating between being tutor and tutee allows for the development of skills involved in extended turn-taking and taking into account the communication partner's background knowledge.   ❏

Discussion

One of the strategies used in many teaching models is discussion. Wilen (1990) made the observation that discussion "should mean an educative, reflective, and structured group conversation with students," but that, realistically, to teachers it "generally means a recitation or review of basic information about a content-related topic" (p. 3).

Pasch and associates (1991) pointed out that many teachers confuse having a discussion with asking questions. In questioning, "communication travels from teacher to student, back to teacher, and is redirected to another student, forming a pattern like a many-armed spider. In a discussion, the patterns of communication are much more diverse. While the initial stimulus may come from the teacher, additional comments may travel from student to student, with students adding questions or comments as desired" (p. 141).

Orlich and associates (1990) found the following elements to be essential to discussion:

1. A small number (preferably four to eight) of students meeting together.
2. Recognition of a common topic or problem.
3. Introduction, exchange, and evaluation of information and ideas.
4. Direction toward some goal or objective (often of the participants' choosing).
5. Verbal interaction—both objective and emotional.(p. 232)

It is this last point, verbal interaction, that makes discussion a rich language milieu. Virtually all of the language functions, presuppositions, and conversational rules can be incorporated as language goals within discussion, as the following scenario demonstrates.

❏   **Scenario**   ❏

Mrs. O'Hara has been teaching a unit on the neighborhood to a class of second graders at the school for the deaf. The children are sitting in a semicircle on the floor and Mrs. O'Hara has put photographs on a portable easel.

MRS. O'HARA: Let's look at the pictures of our school and the neighborhood around it.

PATTY: Dorm. Sleep in the dorm.

SHIRLEY: Cafeteria. School building. Playground.

STEVE: Track. PE building. Library.

MRS. O'HARA: Great. You found lots of places in our picture. Now, what if Dr. Finn, the superintendent, had enough money to buy something new for the school like a building or a special classroom? What suggestion would you give him?

SHIRLEY: I think a new dorm.

MRS. O'HARA: Tell us why.

SHIRLEY: The girls dorm is old and smells and small and the bathroom, you know, old.

JOANNIE: My room is nice. My mom bought me posters and I put them on the wall. She got them at Saturday Market.

MRS. O'HARA: That's interesting but you're off the point, Joannie. What about using the money to build a girls dorm? What do you think?

JOANNIE: I think that's a good idea because then they could build apartments. I visited my cousin and at her school they have apartments not dorms.

MRS. O'HARA: A girls dorm is a good idea. What's another?

STEVE: Pool outside.

PATTY: That's dumb.

MRS. O'HARA: It's not a dumb idea, Patty. But maybe you don't like the idea. Why not?

PATTY: Because in October, November, December, January, February, March, April, it's cold.

MRS. O'HARA: Patty thinks that the outside pool wouldn't be used much. Because in the summer you go home. And when you're at school, it's usually cold.

STEVE: I want a pool outside.

MRS. O'HARA: That's fine. That's our second idea. What's another?

PATTY: Computers.

ANN: We have computers. Look.

PATTY: One.

ANN: But we have a computer room. Upstairs.

PATTY: I want computers. In the classroom.

MRS. O'HARA: How many in each classroom?

PATTY: One, two, three, four, five.

MRS. O'HARA: Oh, you want a computer for each person.

JOANNIE: Not me. I hate computers.

MRS. O'HARA: Computers for each classroom is a third idea. . .

Mrs. O'Hara continued the discussion for a few more minutes, encouraging each child to contribute at least one idea. During this discussion, as well as other discussions in which the students engaged, Mrs. O'Hara incorporated goals of language use for each child. For example, knowing that one of the children's goals included complains, justifies, expresses opinions, and blames, which are language functions from the personal category, Mrs. O'Hara encouraged this particular child to express these functions within the discussions.   ❑

Computers and Related Technology

Educational technology has been defined as the systematic application of knowledge to solve an instructional problem (Seels, 1989). Traditionally, educational technology has included media such as filmstrips, slides, 16mm films, overhead projectors, models and kits, and games as well as audio cassettes and records. In the 1980s, educational technology included all of these things plus computers and video cassette recorders (Nelson, Prosser, & Tucker, 1987; Seidman, 1986). The schools of the 1990s have added interactive systems such as interactive videodisc systems (a linking of videodisc, which is a combination of audio and video signals on a disc, with computer) and hypermedia (information from video and audio sources that are accessed by a computer) (Blanchard & Rottenberg, 1990; Buttery & Parks, 1988; Colman, 1989; Hansen, 1989; Hosie, 1987; Howe, 1985).

While much has been written about the potential of technology to transform classrooms, studies have shown that teachers are slow to assimilate media into their instruction. In 1986, Seidman conducted a review of the literature on classroom use of media and a survey of 545 teachers in one school district. He found that "schoolteachers do not use much of the media equipment and materials at their disposal. When they do employ media, the simplest and most accessible are selected usually: overhead transparencies, book and magazine illustrations, games and simulations, phonograph records, and models. More complex technologies—computer and video equipment—are avoided" (p. 20).

Ainsworth (1987) observed that schools "make use of these technological appliances rather like a mother may use telephone directories to boost a child at the dinner table. They serve a function, but not the one for which they are best suited" (p. 26). In other words, teachers may be using the equipment but not the technology.

It is not my objective to discuss the capabilities of currently available technologies and the applications of these technologies to classroom instruction. The literature is replete with articles and texts on this topic. My objective here is to look at how the media have been used to help develop the language and literacy of children who are deaf.

Our field has always viewed media as a critical component of teaching deaf children because we have recognized the importance of supplementing the amount of informational input to the child with a hearing impairment, particularly through the visual channel. Indeed, from 1965 to 1985, a conference on educational media and the deaf was held yearly, with the exception of 1975, 1976, and 1977. It was sponsored by the University of Nebraska in Lincoln for the first 16 years and by the Texas School for the Deaf and Gallaudet for one year each. In 1965, the symposium was titled "An Overview of Audiovisual Research Affecting Deaf Education" and in 1985, it was titled "The Classroom Computer: An Agent for Change." For each of those years, proceedings were published in a fall issue of the *American Annals of the Deaf*.

Financial difficulties forced the discontinuation of the conference until 1992, but interest in the topic never wavered among teachers, administrators, media specialists, college and university faculty, and others concerned with the education of youngsters who are deaf. The conference was reestablished in 1992 in Rochester, New York, under the sponsorship of the National Technical Institute for the Deaf and the Rochester School for the Deaf with the theme "National Symposium on Educational Applications of Technology for Deaf Students." The topics addressed in this conference demonstrate the breadth and depth of influence that technology has on instruction:

❑ the VCR as a teaching tool
❑ computer applications in the classroom
❑ interactive applications of television

❏ distance learning
❏ captioning: language learning/literacy
❏ desktop publishing
❏ computer graphics
❏ video production
❏ computer networking (e.g., E-Mail, Bulletin Board systems)
❏ TDD/assistive devices
❏ records management with computers
❏ computers in program administration and counseling
❏ real-time speech to print
❏ assistive listening devices

Technology and Language Development of Children Who Are Deaf

One way to organize the research on the use of technology in the education of youngsters who are deaf is with the five-point classification system devised by Kinzer (1986). For this system, he divided classroom uses of microcomputers into five categories: (a) learning about microcomputers, (b) learning from microcomputers, (c) learning with microcomputers, (d) learning about thinking with microcomputers, and (e) managing learning with microcomputers. This classification system is appropriate for looking at instructional technology in general.

Learning about the technology   This category includes activities that involve learning about the nuts and bolts of the equipment, such as how it works and how to take care of it. It might also include rules and procedures for using the equipment. From the point of view of language development, the new terminology involved in learning about the technology provides opportunity for increasing the deaf child's vocabulary.

Learning from the technology   This category includes activities that are designed to increase the child's skills and knowledge of a subject area. Computer tutorial programs and drill-and-practice programs are examples of activities in this category. Although such programs have been developed in the area of language, by their very nature they teach language in isolated skills segments. This may be appropriate for children who are already competent language users because the programs can be designed to show them how to analyze the language they are already using. For example, it can be very valuable for a youngster to be able to explore the syntactic differences between ASL and English. However, for children whose language is developing, these types of programs are of limited value.

The use of video for the purposes of learning ASL is an activity that also fits into this category, although this particular use of the technology is more common with individuals who are hearing than with children who are deaf.

Learning with the technology   This category includes activities in which the technology is one aspect of the overall learning environment. In the previous category, learning from the technology, the media is the teacher. In this category, the media provides an opportunity to learn. One example is the use of word processing. The word processor does not teach the child who is deaf to write but because of the ease with which children can revise their writing with the use of this technology, it provides a learning environment conducive to the development of children as writers. (I will discuss more about the writing process in Chapter 4.)

Captioned films are films in the areas of education and entertainment that have subtitles specifically created for audiences of persons with hearing impairments. *Closed captioned television* is the captioning of TV shows. In closed captioned television, the subtitles appear only on the screens of sets equipped with a decoder. Film, television, and video captioning offers the potential for encouraging the reading development of youngsters who are deaf. Two research studies on the influence of captioning illustrate this potential.

Hertzog, Stinson, and Keiffer (1989) conducted a study in which they showed a technical film captioned at approximately the 8th- and 11th-grade reading levels to hearing impaired college students. Greatest comprehension was achieved when viewing the film was supplemented by teacher instruction at several stop-points during the film. Students identified as "high" readers comprehended more information from the film, with or without supplementary instruction, than students identified as "low" readers. Students identified as "low" readers not only comprehended less information from the film without supplementary instruction, but benefitted from instruction when the film was captioned at the 8th-grade level but not at the 11th-grade level.

Hertzog, Stinson, and Keiffer concluded that when a "class is mixed in terms of reading ability, the teacher should try to select captioning that matches the reading level of the poorer readers to ensure that the film will reinforce instruction" (p. 66). While this conclusion seems to follow logically from the results of the study, it also seems logical that numerous opportunities to watch captioned films on subjects with which the youngsters are familiar will likely result in increased reading ability. In other words, the technology of captioning can provide a medium for the reading of highly motivating material which in turn will help children who are deaf to become better readers.

Koskinen, Wilson, and Jensema (1986) conducted a study on the use of closed captioned TV programs for reading instruction. Eight teachers, with hearing impaired students between the ages of 13 and 15 (reading at levels from first to third grade), were given 10 one-half hour captioned TV programs on videocassettes, scripts of the programs' captions for each child in their reading groups, and reading lesson suggestions. The investigators compared student retention of sight vocabulary, teacher perception of student comprehension, and teacher perception of student interest for the teachers' regular reading lessons and the captioned TV lessons. Although statistical data were not reported, the investigators reported observing that the students showed improvement in all areas when closed captioned TV was used for reading instruction. They concluded that "the combination of an entertaining picture with written words appears to be a powerful tool for reading instruction" (p. 46).

TDDs, telephone communication devices for the deaf, were developed to provide telephone access to individuals with speech or hearing impairments. TDDs can be used to enhance the language development of children who are deaf, but relatively few articles have been written on this topic. TDD conversations between teenagers who are deaf have been used as the context for examining conversational behaviors (Geoffrion, 1982; Johnson & Barton, 1988; Rittenhouse & Kenyon, 1987), however no references are available on studies that used TDDs to teach conversational skills and other aspects of language use. Yet, as Rittenhouse and Kenyon noted, "One could hypothesize that improved TDD language in deaf children would lead to improved reading and language ability" (p. 212).

Much of the new technology available today is *interactive*, which means that the individual interacts with the system by being able to input data and that components of the system interact with one another. One of these systems is the computer-mediated text (CMT) system. According to MacGregor and Thomas (1988), in CMT systems "the computer manipulates and presents text and permits interactions between the reader and text which are not possible with the printed page. Text mediations utilized in CMT systems include such adjuncts as electronic dictionaries, paraphrases of text, concept mapping and reciprocal questioning" (p. 280).

MacGregor and Thomas investigated the effects of a CMT system on the reading and writing performance of 45 hearing impaired children in grades four through six. The researchers were particularly interested in studying the influence of (a) the electronic dictionary that the students could access at any time during their reading of passages on the CMT system, (b) extrinsic motivation in the form of post-passage vocabulary and comprehension questions, and (c) intrinsic motivation in the form of a vocabulary game. They found that vocabulary knowledge was facilitated with this CMT system and that post-passage questions were more motivational than the games. The investigators concluded that the strengths of the CMT system were "its interactive nature, the capability for immediate feedback, and the provision of student-controlled vocabulary knowledge acquisition" (p. 284).

Videodisc-computer systems are another example of technology that is interactive. One of the first interactive videodisc systems developed specifically for use with students who are deaf was produced by the Media

Development Project for the Hearing Impaired at the University of Nebraska in the late 1970s. The first system they developed included a videodisc of a captioned film, teacher guide materials, vocabulary instruction, filmstrip-type sequences, and interactive quiz sections that students could respond to by manually writing the answers on paper or by using a computer keyboard (Propp, Nugent, Stone, & Nugent, 1981).

Tomlinson-Keasey, Brawley, and Peterson (1986) studied the effectiveness of an interactive videodisc system to teach English language skills to hearing impaired students in junior high school. Although the investigators found no significant differences between the progress of students using the system and students engaged in regular classroom instruction, the investigators believed that the system was motivating to hearing impaired students learning English syntax.

"HandsOn" is an interactive videodisc system developed as a bilingual approach for teaching English to deaf students who are fluent users of ASL (Copra, 1990; Hanson & Padden, 1989). In this system, stories signed in ASL were recorded on videodiscs. By using the computer, the child can access the ASL story alone, access English text above the video simultaneously with the ASL story, or access the English text without the ASL story. At any point, the child can move back and forth between the ASL video and English text. Research on this system is ongoing but the researchers believe it holds much promise for supplementing bilingual instruction.

Prinz (1991) conducted a study on the combined use of a computer program, called the ALPHA Interactive Language Program, with videodisc still and action pictorial sequences. The system was designed so that the language lessons presented by the ALPHA program on the computer could be supplemented with real-life pictures on the videodisc player. Furthermore, the youngster using the system was supposed to be accompanied by a teacher or speech-language pathologist who interacted with the child in speech and/or sign. The adults' role was to comment on, clarify, and expand on the child's language during the sessions. Prinz reported that the 5- to 20-year-old hearing impaired subjects in the study demonstrated significant gains in reading and writing new words and sentences. He also reported that there was some evidence to support the observation that the youngsters showed strong gains in general language skills.

Learning about thinking with the technology   This category includes activities designed to engage children in creating the technology. When children learn to program computers themselves or produce their own videos, they are learning about thinking with the technology.

The use of video in classrooms of children who are deaf is not a new idea. Children have been videotaping their own plays, news programs, and speeches for many years. In the last several years, captioning equipment that is not prohibitively expensive has been purchased by some school programs to enable youngsters to caption their own productions.

Learning to program computers or to create interactive systems is, to use the words of Kinzer (1986), "an area that is as yet relatively unexplored but has great potential" (p. 230). In the following example of part of a teaching lesson on cause and effect, the teacher is demonstrating the relationship between computer language and a reading concept to a group of students:

> In our program, we said that IF something happens, THEN something else happens. In the story we just read, there were also things that happened first. We can think of the IF statement as a cause that made something else (an effect) happen. (Kinzer, 1986, p. 230)

Managing learning with the technology   This category includes technology used by the teacher but not directly by the students. Test construction, files of student progress, and newsletters to parents are only a few examples of activities that teachers can perform more quickly and easily with personal computers. Furthermore, testing and grading can be simplified with spreadsheet software.

Although this category of technology use does not relate directly to strategies that can enhance the language development of children who are deaf, indirectly there are possible benefits. For example, word processing software can allow the teacher to construct classroom newspapers, books, and stories that the children have written.

Incidental Teaching of Language Goals

When the term *incidental* is used, it generally means that two events are occurring concurrently, one is major and one is minor, and the minor event is fortuitous. I use the phrase "incidental teaching of language goals" similarly but with a deemphasis on the "minor" aspect. To me, incidental teaching of language goals means that the teacher of youngsters who are deaf always has a double agenda—content and language. Every instructional event is an opportunity to develop language. The content goal might be the "major" one but the language goal is never really "minor."

Warren and Kaiser (1986) defined incidental language teaching as "interactions between an adult and a child that arise naturally in an unstructured situation and are used systematically by the adult to transmit new information or give the child practice in developing a communication skill" (p. 291). The difference between incidental language teaching and direct language teaching is the difference between participating in real conversation and practicing language pattern drills. As Staab (1983) noted, "Learners must engage in meaningful activities with other speakers [or signers] who model the appropriate language functions and forms. A meaningful activity is defined as any activity in which speakers [and signers] concentrate on doing something rather than on language. The rules are learned by observation and participation in these activities, while competent language users model the process" (p. 165).

Figure 2–1 presents several learning activities that involve the incidental teaching of language goals. These examples were created by graduate students preparing to become teachers of deaf children. As part of their practicum and course work, they had each obtained a language sample from a child who is deaf, analyzed it, and determined appropriate language goals for the child in the areas of syntax, semantics, and use. They were then asked to create instructional activities that incorporated the child's language goals. Each graduate student worked with a different child, so the instructional activities they developed were for children from preschool through high school.

It was explained that the activities would be evaluated on the basis of (a) how whole, meaningful, and relevant the language was to the child, (b) how appropriate the activities were to the child's age, language development stage, and conceptual level, and (c) whether the activities reflected the importance of function over form. Finally, they were told that the only unacceptable activity would be a grammar lesson.

These activities are examples. They are not meant to encompass the range of possibilities but only to demonstrate that if a teacher has a language goal in mind, the learning situation can be structured in a way to encourage the receptive or expressive communication of that form, meaning, or use. Creating, adapting, and modifying an activity to meet the unique needs of an individual deaf child is the role of the teacher.

DEVELOPING LANGUAGE
THROUGH CONVERSATION

Two lines of reasoning support the use of conversational strategies for teaching language to children who are deaf. First, because language develops within conversational contexts, strategies that come as close as possible to replicating natural conversational interactions between parent-and-child and child-and-child can provide deaf children with an authentic environment for learning language (Clarke, 1983; Clarke & Stewart, 1986; Stone, 1988).

Second, because children who are deaf often demonstrate problems in developing conversational competence, language teaching strategies that incorporate conversational skills are needed by many deaf children (Griffith, Johnson, & Dastoli, 1985; Newton, 1985; Weiss, 1986). Based on these two lines of reasoning, one could make the observation, as Holdgrafer (1987) did, that "in effect, conversation is a goal of language intervention as well as a general strategy for teaching language" (p. 71).

FIGURE 2–1

Examples of Learning Activities Incorporating Incidental Teaching of Language Goals

Goal	Grade Level	Activity
Conjunction *and* Coordinate	Preschool/ kindergarten	This is a "memory game" activity. The teacher arranges at least six items on the activity table such as empty food containers with labels. The teacher asks the children to pretend they went shopping. The children study the items on the table, then all close their eyes. The teacher takes two items and puts them in a grocery bag. The children open their eyes and raise their hands if they know what's been purchased. The teacher watches for and guides the use of *and* in the answers.
Imperative verb form	High school	The class has been learning how to fix an auto engine. During a review, the teacher gives the name of an engine problem and the student has to list the steps involved in fixing it. Each student takes a turn.
Plural Number Quantity	Early elementary	The child is learning the concept of set in math. As the child divides various colored items into sets, the teacher asks questions such as, "How many _____ s are in this set?" and "Tell me about this set."

Features of Conversation That Promote Language Development

Conversation has been defined as "the initiation and maintenance of topics while interchanging reciprocal roles of speaker and listener in smooth and coordinated turn-taking" (Holdgrafer, 1987, p. 71). Given that conversation is crucial to language development, it is important to ask if certain specific features of conversation are considered to be particularly critical and so should be integrated into a conversational teaching strategy.

Prinz and Masin (1985) found that adult recasting of deaf children's utterances facilitated their language development. Prinz and Masin defined *recasting* as a particular kind of adult response to a child's preceding utterance. Recasting occurs when the adult response is signed or spoken in a

FIGURE 2–1
continued

Goal	Grade Level	Activity
Question forms: *who, what, how, where, why, when*	Junior high school	As part of a deaf studies unit, the students interview a deaf adult. The students have to develop a list of questions prior to the interview.
Possession	Preschool/ kindergarten	For show-and-tell, the children drop their items into a box held by the teacher. The teacher reaches into the box, takes out an object, and asks, "Whose is this?" The child will probably answer "mine" or another child might answer "Susie's."
Mood	Junior or senior high school	Once each week, the class reads a newspaper or news magazine article and has a discussion. The teacher encourages the youngsters to express their feelings about events that can effect their lives.
Instrumental: persuades	High school	During a civics class, the students have been examining issues involved in the upcoming November election. They now have to persuade classmates to vote for a particular candidate or a ballot measure.

different syntactic structure than the child just used but the response maintains the central meaning expressed by the child.

Prinz and Masin conducted their investigation with six children from 9 months to 6 years of age at the outset of the study. Two children had deaf parents who primarily used ASL in the home, and the other children had hearing parents who used manually coded English or pidgin sign. Their teachers used pidgin sign, which the authors described as "combining semantic and syntactic aspects of both ASL and signed English" (p. 360). Parents and teachers were given training on how to recast the children's utterances into the specific syntactic structures that the researchers had targeted. The study lasted for five months and during that time each child received at least 20 hours of intervention. Prinz and Masin found that the targeted syntactic-semantic structures in ASL and English appeared in the spontaneous communication of the children in the study. The implication of this finding is that recasting is one of the conversational features between adult-and-child that supports language development.

Wood and associates (Wood & Wood, 1984; Wood, Wood, Griffiths, Howarth, & Howarth, 1982) found that several conversational features worked in combination to encourage deaf children to be conversational partners with their teachers. Personal contributions, in the form of comments or statements, and phatics (phrases such as "Oh, that's interesting" and "I see," head nodding in response to the child's contribution, or repeating the child's comment) by the teacher resulted in greater conversational participation, elaborated answers, and greater asking of questions by the child. Asking questions, particularly stringing questions together, and requiring the child to repeat phrases resulted in little spontaneous conversational participation by the child.

Wood and associates also found, however, that simply asking teachers to become more responsive to the deaf children's responses produced better conversations but not the lively or purposeful discussions the researchers had observed in other classrooms. The reason seemed to be that the teachers these researchers observed had some difficulty always understanding the children's meaning. Wood and associates concluded that "a very great strain is put on the teacher's conversational skills as she struggles to interpret short, ambiguous utterances. If she goes straight into repair to 'sort things out', she may be increasing the problems facing both her and the child. In such a situation it is perhaps not surprising that a teacher's reaction to such a high degree of uncertainty may be to keep control through questioning whence she can judge the appropriateness of the child's responses" (p. 61).

A Conversational Approach

The teacher of deaf children who wants to encourage language development through conversation can choose from two currently available approaches. With the first approach, the teacher would use naturally occurring opportunities during the school day to have conversations with the children. Clarke and Stewart (1986) suggested that teachers of hearing impaired children exploit opportunities for short and meaningful conversations with individual children throughout the school day and orchestrate opportunities for longer conversations with small groups of children.

Rogers, Perrin, and Waller (1987) found that naturally occurring opportunities for conversation are the result of a special kind of relationship between teachers and students. They observed that children become enthusiastic conversational partners over time when their teacher consistently responds with interest to the topics they initiate, encourages them to share their thoughts, and allows them time to complete what they wanted to discuss without interruption.

The second approach the teacher can use is the one developed by Stone (1988) for use with children who are deaf. At the center of this approach are *conversational scenarios*. Conversational scenarios are "role-playing situations which contain appropriate dialogue. They are planned by the teacher and presented to the child in such a way that a realistic conversation takes place between teacher and child. The child's part in the conversation requires the use of a specific conversational skill which has not been mastered. Acquiring this skill is the teacher's objective" (p. 28).

Unlike the first approach in which the teacher capitalizes on opportunities during the school day to engage the children in conversation, Stone's approach requires careful planning and a setting aside of time for the scenarios to be role-played. There are five essential elements to any scenario:

1. The situation and topics are familiar to the student.
2. The teacher makes sure that the student understands the situation before beginning.
3. As the dialogue proceeds there is a conversational need for the targeted conversational skill to arise.
4. The teacher does not tell the child what to say, rather the situation and conversation bring about a need for use of the targeted skill.
5. The situation and conversation are carried to a logical conclusion. (Stone, 1988, p. 29)

Scenarios begin with the teacher "setting the stage." For example, the teacher might provide the following description to a child who is working on the skill "initiating a conversation":

> Let's pretend that your grandmother came for a visit last weekend. She took you to the zoo. On Monday, you come to school and tell your friend Valerie about it. I'll be Valerie and you be yourself.

The teacher and child then role-play the scenario. But what happens when the child makes a mistake? Stone considered it important that the teacher intervene only when the mistake is related to the specific skill targeted for the scenario. Errors involving other conversational objectives can be noted by the teacher for future scenarios. But when the mistake is pertinent to the scenario's objective, the teacher should intervene. The following four intervention strategies are recommended by Stone:

1. Teacher clarification. In this strategy, the teacher offers a statement that clarifies what the child just expressed. The following dialogue is one example of teacher clarification. The teacher and student are role-playing the scenario just described; the teacher is the friend, Valerie, and the student is herself, Lillian.

LILLIAN: Hi, Valerie.
VALERIE: Hi, Lillian.
LILLIAN: I saw different animals at the zoo with my grandma.
VALERIE: (Pauses, looks confused, then smiles). Oh, you mean your grandma visited and took you to the zoo?
LILLIAN: Yes. My grandma visited and she took me to the zoo.

2.   Role switching. In this strategy, the teacher and student switch roles so that the teacher can demonstrate the conversational skill. They then switch back to their original roles. Using the same scenario, role switching might look like this:

TEACHER: Let's switch. I'll be Lillian and you be Valerie.
TEACHER (as Lillian):   Hi, Valerie.
CHILD (as friend):   Hi, Lillian.
TEACHER: My grandma visited last weekend. She took me to the zoo.
CHILD: Neat.
TEACHER: Okay. Let's switch back. You be yourself and I'll be Valerie.

3.   Requesting clarification. In this strategy, the teacher makes a comment or looks at the child in a way that makes it obvious to the child that his or her utterance was not appropriate. The teacher then pauses, giving the child time to clarify it. In the scenario, instead of using teacher clarification or role switching, the teacher could have used requesting clarification in the following way:

LILLIAN (the child):   Hi, Valerie.
VALERIE (the teacher):   Hi, Lillian.
LILLIAN: I saw different animals at the zoo with my grandma.
VALERIE: Excuse me? What did you say?
LILLIAN: My grandma visited. She took me to the zoo.
VALERIE: Oh, your grandma visited. That's neat. Tell me what you saw at the zoo.

4.   Prompt. This strategy is used in conjunction with role switching. The difference is that the teacher steps out of the role play and points out to the child the place in the conversation where the child is making a mistake. Using the scenario with Lillian and Valerie, prompting would look like this:

LILLIAN (the child):   Hi, Valerie.
VALERIE (the teacher):   Hi, Lillian.
LILLIAN: I saw different animals at the zoo with my grandma.
TEACHER: That was ok but there's another way to say it. Let's switch. I'll be you and you be Valerie.
TEACHER (as Lillian):   My grandma visited last weekend. She took me to the zoo.

CHILD (as Valerie):   Neat.

TEACHER (as Lillian):   Okay. Let's switch back.

Role switching and prompting obviously interrupt the flow of the conversation, and Stone recommended they be used only when the other two strategies do not give sufficient feedback to the child.

Whether teachers use naturally occurring opportunities to have conversations with their students, the conversational scenarios proposed by Stone, or a combination of both approaches, engaging in meaningful conversations is vitally important to the language development of children who are deaf.

INTERDISCIPLINARY CURRICULUM: INTEGRATING LANGUAGE INTO THEMATIC UNITS

Interdisciplinary curriculum, as defined by Jacobs (1989a), is "a knowledge view and curriculum approach that consciously applies methodology and language from more than one discipline to examine a central theme, issue, problem, topic, or experience" (p. 8). Depending on one's perspective, interdisciplinary curriculum is referred to in the literature as "integrating the language arts," "language across the curriculum," "webbing," and "theming" (Donaldson, 1984; Wagner, 1985).

Although the concept of interdisciplinary curriculum did not originate in our field, it would seem that youngsters who are deaf would benefit greatly from this curriculum design for several reasons. One reason is that the common set of concepts that are explored in an interdisciplinary curriculum are expressed through a common set of vocabulary, and the learning of this vocabulary becomes deeper as the nuances of meaning are examined and applied to a variety of contexts. Dillon (1990) noted that "language across the curriculum implies that we focus on what meaning learners make and how that meaning is made, how learners come to know their experience by placing a shape on it through their language, how learners structure their experience by 'languaging' it" (p. 8).

A second reason that interdisciplinary curriculum is particularly beneficial to youngsters who are deaf is that it avoids the fragmentation and lack of connection that a typical curriculum fosters. Deaf students can miss much incidental information, particularly when they are in classes with hearing students, and after a unit of instruction they may have learned bits and pieces of knowledge but be unable to connect one area of learning with another. The use of common terminology and concepts within an integrated curriculum makes it more likely that youngsters who are deaf will be able to access fully the information presented and draw the connections between bodies of knowledge.

A third reason that interdisciplinary curriculum makes sense in educational programs for students who are deaf is that it is a way to deal with the expansion of knowledge in all areas of study and the difficulty in making parts of the curriculum relevant to the youngsters. As Jacobs observed, "Knowledge will not stop growing, and the schools are bursting at the seams" (1989a, p. 4). Thematic study allows youngsters to explore a few topics in depth. Obviously, hard choices are needed to determine which topics to study and which to leave out, but those decisions are being made anyway by state curriculum departments, program curriculum specialists, and classroom teachers.

Fourth, thematic study encourages youngsters to see real-life applications of the information they are learning. Jacobs noted that "only in school do we have 43 minutes of math and 43 minutes of English and 43 minutes of science. Outside of school, we deal with problems and concerns in a flow of time that is not divided into knowledge fields" (1989a, p. 4). Interdisciplinary curriculum provides youngsters a context for seeing associations between bodies of knowledge and making associations to issues in their own lives.

Models for Developing an Integrated Curriculum

How an interdisciplinary curriculum is designed depends largely on how many teachers and classrooms are involved. If one teacher with a class of students who are deaf is the only person in his or her school building who believes in using this approach, the model used will undoubtedly look quite different from the one used by a group of teachers across grade levels who are equally committed to the approach. The models briefly presented here are based on a continuum of designs developed by Jacobs (1989b).

Parallel Disciplines

Parallel Disciplines is a model in which topics taught in different subject areas are chosen to parallel one another. The content that has been taught in each of the subject areas is not changed but only resequenced. For example, in social studies the teacher has always taught about Middle Eastern countries in the spring but decides to teach this unit in the fall to parallel the science unit on fossil fuels. According to Jacobs, "Teachers working in parallel fashion are not deliberately connecting curriculum across fields of knowledge; they are simply resequencing their existing curriculum in the hope that students will find the implicit linkages" (p. 15).

For the teacher of children who are deaf, this model provides a relatively easy way to move toward an interdisciplinary curriculum. In the parallel disciplines model, vocabulary development is encouraged because the same vocabulary is taught in each subject area discipline.

Complementary Disciplines

Complementary Disciplines is a model in which a topic is explored from the perspective of two or more disciplines that complement one another. For example, a high school teacher might decide to combine the subject areas of health and history for a unit on AIDS and the history of communicable diseases, which would include information on the transmission of AIDS as well as an exploration of how societal attitudes toward AIDS are similar to or different from attitudes in the past toward other communicable diseases.

This model provides the teacher of youngsters who are deaf with an opportunity to help students see relationships between concepts in both subject areas and, of course, to express these relationships in class discussions and in their writing.

Thematic Units

Thematic Units is a model in which each school subject focuses on the same topic for a unit of study and approaches the topic from the unique perspective of the discipline. Thematic units can be taught periodically throughout the school year and can last from a few days to a quarter or semester, though they generally are three to five weeks in duration. An example of a thematic unit is provided in Figure 2–2.

Because terminology and concepts cut across the subject areas in thematic units, this model helps to build deaf youngsters' vocabulary and knowledge structures and provides them opportunities to explore the relevance of ideas to their own lives.

Complete Interdisciplinary Study

Complete Interdisciplinary Study is a model in which all school learning is themed around common topics. The school day is flexible to allow for more or less amounts of time to be spent on any activity on any given day. Topics chosen are ones that capitalize on student interest and motivation. This model requires enormous flexibility on the part of teachers and administrators, and it carries some risk that state-mandated curricular areas would not be covered. However, this may be the most nurturing curriculum for language and cognitive development because it is based so directly on the child's own interests, concerns, and questions.

Procedure for Developing a Thematic Unit

The steps presented in a procedure for developing a thematic unit are based on approaches developed by Jacobs (1989c) and Norton (1982). This procedure can be used by teachers at all levels of instruction, and it can be used by one teacher working alone or a group of teachers working as a team, although it would undoubtedly work most successfully with a team of teachers.

Step 1. *Identify a Topic.* The teachers agree on a topic for the thematic unit. The topic should be broad enough to cut across several subject areas yet narrow enough to be explored in depth within the time frame of the unit. According to Jacobs (1989c), topics can be themes, subject areas, events, issues, or problems.

Step 2. *Brainstorm Ideas.* Using the topic as a focal point, the teachers brainstorm questions or subtopics that are associated with the topic. One way to do this is by creating a web. In the center of the web, the topic is written. On lines emanating from the center, subject areas are written such as social studies, science, math, art, health, and reading. As ideas are generated, they are placed under the most appropriate subject area heading.

Step 3. *Organize Ideas and Add Pertinent Subtopics.* The web that was created from the brainstorming activity is looked at critically at this point. Redundant subtopics are combined, final decisions are made regarding where to place subtopics, and obvious gaps are filled in with new ideas.

Step 4. *Establish Topic Questions to Guide the Unit.* The teachers develop four to five questions that serve to guide the unit as a whole. These questions provide a common purpose for the unit. Jacobs (1989c) viewed these questions as a kind of scope and sequence for the unit. She noted that "the questions are cross-disciplinary in nature and are analogous to chapter headings in a textbook" (p. 59).

Step 5. *Develop Learning Activities That Correspond to the Subtopics in the Web.* These learning activities also need to provide ways to explore the questions developed in step 4. The activities should include a multitude of opportunities to use language in face-to-face communication, in reading, and in writing.

Example of a Thematic Unit

The example in Figure 2–2 was created by a group of teachers who developed this thematic unit for middle school level youngsters who are deaf. In the past, only the social studies teacher would have taught this unit as part of her government curriculum while the science teacher might have been teaching a unit on the solar system and the health teacher a unit on drug awareness.

The teachers who implemented this unit were still able to teach significant concepts in their own subject areas but the concepts were complemented as the students went from class to class. The teachers were also able to build on the students' vocabulary by presenting new words for the new concepts being taught in the unit, but now the learning of these new words was reinforced because they were used in a variety of subject area contexts. These teachers were able to offer the students many experiences in writing

FIGURE 2–2
Example of a Thematic Unit

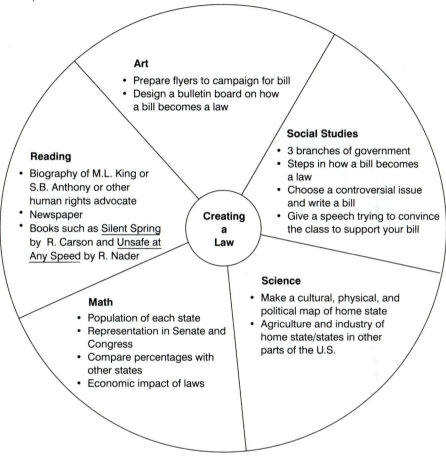

Art
- Prepare flyers to campaign for bill
- Design a bulletin board on how a bill becomes a law

Reading
- Biography of M.L. King or S.B. Anthony or other human rights advocate
- Newspaper
- Books such as Silent Spring by R. Carson and Unsafe at Any Speed by R. Nader

Creating a Law

Social Studies
- 3 branches of government
- Steps in how a bill becomes a law
- Choose a controversial issue and write a bill
- Give a speech trying to convince the class to support your bill

Math
- Population of each state
- Representation in Senate and Congress
- Compare percentages with other states
- Economic impact of laws

Science
- Make a cultural, physical, and political map of home state
- Agriculture and industry of home state/states in other parts of the U.S.

Guiding Questions:
1. What is a law?
2. What is the purpose of laws?
3. Why do some bills succeed and some bills fail to become laws?
4. What is the impact of laws on citizens?

and reading about the topic. And they were able to encourage face-to-face communication during small-group and whole-class discussions, student speeches, and class presentations. All in all, thematic units such as this one on "creating a law" can provide teachers of youngsters who are deaf with a curriculum design that makes sense both for language learning and content learning.

INCORPORATING STRATEGIES OF
SECOND LANGUAGE LEARNING

No discussion of language teaching methods for children who are deaf is complete today without a review of current bilingual/bicultural education approaches and the theories that underlie these approaches. Within just a few years, bilingual/bicultural education has moved from idea to implementation in many programs across the United States and Canada.

What is bilingualism? Most of us would respond to this question with an answer such as, *bilingualism* is being able to converse in two languages. We might then be asked, what do you mean by converse? Face-to-face? Reading? Writing? Does conversing mean that the individual is able to have an equally thoughtful conversation about abstract concepts in both languages? The problem in defining bilingualism is that there is no precise point of mastery at which a person is bilingual. Rather, most linguists view bilingualism as being on a continuum from native-like control of two languages at one end and being able to produce meaningful utterances in two languages at the other end.

A person's placement on this continuum certainly depends on his or her proficiency in the language syntactically, semantically, pragmatically, and phonologically but it also depends on his or her ability to vary registers, to think in the language as well as to comprehend and produce it, and to read and write in the language as well as to engage in face-to-face communication (McCollum, 1981).

Factors in the Development of Bilingual Proficiency

Age of Acquisition

One of the factors that influences bilingual proficiency is age of acquisition. Harding and Riley (1986) observed that there are four major points at which individuals become bilingual—infancy, childhood, adolescence, and adulthood. They defined infant bilingualism as the simultaneous acquisition of two languages, childhood bilingualism as the successive acquisition of two languages, adolescent bilingualism as the acquisition of a second language after puberty, and adult bilingualism as the acquisition of a second language after age 19. It is generally believed that the earlier a second language is introduced the easier it is learned, although some evidence indicates that unless two languages are introduced simultaneously in infancy, the second language should be introduced only after the child has developed fluency in a first language (Cummins, 1979; Saville-Troike, 1979a).

Family and Community Languages

Infant and childhood bilingualism are the result of a combination of influences that include language used by the mother, language used by the father, language used in the community at large, and the parents' strategy in communicating with the child. The following six types of bilingual families have been described in the literature (Harding & Riley, 1986; Romaine, 1989).

In a Type 1 family, the parents have different native languages but have some degree of competence in each other's language. One parent's language is the dominant language of the community. The parents each use their own native language to communicate with the child from birth. The child in this family is bilingual from infancy.

In a Type 2 family, the parents have different native languages and the language of one parent is the dominant language of the community. However, the parents both use the nondominant language to communicate with the child. The child is only fully exposed to the dominant language outside the home, particularly in school. Romaine (1989) noted that in this type of home, the child is generally not exposed to the second language until after infancy.

In a Type 3 family, the parents share the same native language and use this language in communicating with the child. The parents' language is not the dominant language of the community. As in a Type 2 family, the child is generally not exposed to the second language until after infancy.

In a Type 4 family, the parents have different native languages and they each use their own native language to communicate with the child. The dominant language of the community is not either of the parents' languages. The child in this family is bilingual from infancy and adds a third language in childhood.

In a Type 5 family, the parents share the same native language and this language is also the dominant language of the community. However, one parent communicates with the child in a language that is not native to him or her (that is, the language is a second language for this parent). The child in this family is bilingual from infancy.

In a Type 6 family, the parents are bilingual, the community or parts of the community are bilingual, and the parents code-switch and mix languages (that is, each parent does not consistently use one language at home and sometimes even mixes the two languages in the same utterance).

Research on all of these family types demonstrates that any of these configurations can result in children learning and retaining two languages. For example, it used to be thought that "one language-one source" was an essential attribute for any linguistic environment. To put this another way, it was believed that children could successfully learn two languages only if there was consistency regarding which language came from which adult. Yet Romaine reported studies of children who became bilingual from mixed language backgrounds, such as in family type 6. However, she also noted that when a home language is a minority language, children often show preference for using the language that is dominant in the community. "Sociolinguistic studies of minority languages have shown that it is usually very difficult for children to acquire active command of a minority language, where that language does not receive support from the community" (1989, p. 169).

Individual Differences

Children show individual differences in their ability to learn a second language just as they show individual differences in all areas of learning. As McLaughlin (1990) recognized, even when the environment is the same, "two children can differ in their acquisition of bilingual proficiency because of native ability" (p. 172). Native ability includes language aptitude and general intelligence (Gardner, 1979; Romaine, 1989).

Children also differ in the ways that their families encourage them to use effective language learning strategies. McLaughlin (1990) observed that "children from some homes learn how to ask questions and keep a conversation going, how to practice and develop routines, how to use memory aids, and how to plan and set goals" (p. 172).

A third aspect of individual differences involves motivation. Baker (1988) considered motivation to be a key reason that individuals become, stay, or reject being bilingual. For example, he noted that the need to have and maintain close friendships can be a strong motivation for being bilingual. A second motivation is the need to preserve one's minority language. When these two motivations are combined, it can be a powerful draw toward bilingualism or a powerful rejection of bilingualism. Baker found that "when friendships operate through minority groups, such groups will be reinforced in their existence. When friendships evolve outside the minority group, language erosion may be more probable" (p. 151).

Yet another motivation involves an individual's need to achieve. If bilingualism carries social and economic advantages, the individual may be highly motivated. If one of the languages is considered to be inferior by the dominant community, the individual may see negative social, economic, and educational consequences in being bilingual and so be motivated to be monolingual (Baker, 1988).

Family and Community Attitudes

Children grow up in a family and community that convey beliefs about language and culture. These attitudes significantly influence children's success or lack of success in becoming and remaining bilingual (Cummins, Harley, Swain, & Allen, 1990).

Communities can frame bilingualism in a positive light, and this attitude can result in increased motivation by citizens to learn a second language. However, bilingualism can also be viewed negatively by a community, and this attitude can result in the disinclination of its members to learn a second language. Baker (1988) observed that "in many white communities in England, the transmitted belief is that bilingualism is unnecessary, difficult to achieve and, if achieved, is at the expense of other areas of achievement. Such communities also tend to share the traditional United States philosophy of assimilation of minority cultures and language. In some Canadian communities, opposite beliefs about French-English bilingualism and biculturalism exist, thus allowing the establishment, evolution, and extension of bilingual schooling" (p. 183).

Societal attitudes certainly can influence families indirectly in terms of the value placed on bilingualism in the community and the pressure placed on families to conform to the community's value system. But the influence can also be quite direct. Romaine (1989) reported that parents are often advised not to bring up their children bilingually because, as they are told by school professionals, mixing languages will confuse the children and will retard their learning of the dominant language. Romaine commented that there is no research to support either of these assertions.

Sometimes society maintains an outwardly positive attitude toward a minority language because the language is a symbol of ethnic heritage. However, a dichotomy exists between the public and private attitude. Privately, individuals recognize that the minority language is not well accepted since it is not used in the workplace, in schools, by individuals in positions of power, or by the media. In this situation, Baker (1988) found that use of the minority language diminished because "goodwill stops when the personal pay-off is not great" (p. 133).

Parental attitude toward bilingualism has a particularly strong influence on children's acquisition of a second language. When the attitude of the community and the attitude of the parents are in conflict, parental attitude has been found to enable children to resist the negative pressure of the community. Gardner's (1979) research on the role of attitude and motivation in second language learning demonstrated to him that truly successful students gain their motivation from the home. He concluded that children's motivation "appears to derive from the attitudinal characteristics in the home and must be fostered by an accepting attitude, by the parents, concerning the other language group" (p. 327).

Attitudes are learned and unless attitudes are modified by experience, they tend to remain unchanged over time. How to change attitudes is, thus, an issue in bilingualism and certainly in bilingual education. Baker (1988) observed that attitudes toward bilingualism can be changed in several ways, though some involve major societal shifts in behavior.

One way to changes attitudes is for use of the minority language to be rewarded and not punished by society. When an individual in public uses a minority language and the result is obvious dismay by others, the individual experiences punishment. When a teacher encourages the use of a minority language in the classroom, the individual experiences reward. Realistically, it is difficult for any individual to have an impact on changing societal attitudes. Baker noted that "where everyday events of perceived high status are almost entirely in the majority language, there is little hope of attitude change" (p. 135).

Another way to change attitudes is through advancing knowledge about the language and culture. Knowledge increases one's enjoyment of the unique characteristics and qualities of a language and culture, and this enjoyment is likely to carry over into respect and admiration. Based on several research studies of grade 1 through 11 English-speaking students enrolled in French immersion programs in Quebec, Lambert (1987) concluded that "learning thoroughly another ethnic group's language and learning about that group through a teacher who is a native informant has a favorable impact on pupils' attitudes toward that group and the associated culture" (p. 217).

Attitudes can also be changed by increasing the esteem with which individuals using the minority language are held. This can happen when someone from the minority culture rises to a position of importance in the community at large. According to Baker (1988), these individuals "need to be highly regarded, respected, admired, and credible in what they say and do" (p. 138).

Finally, individuals are more open to change their attitudes toward a minority language when they do not feel threatened by the minority culture. The current popularity of talk shows and the topics that are discussed on these programs is a measure of the kinds and amounts of insecurity that human beings are experiencing today. For many people, bilingualism raises anxiety regarding their own importance and role in the lives of their children, their peers, their community, and perhaps the universe.

Ultimately, attitude is at the heart of bilingualism. And attitude change is at the heart of a bilingual education program. Lewis (1981) asserted that "any policy for language, especially in the system of education, has to take account of the attitude of those likely to be affected. In the long run, no policy will succeed which does not do one of three things: conform to the expressed attitude of those involved; persuade those who express negative attitudes about the rightness of the policy; or seek to remove the causes of disagreement" (p.262).

Bilingual Education:
Considerations and Perspectives

Bilingualism and Cognitive Development

For a number of years it was thought that bilingualism had a negative effect on intelligence. It was believed that there was only so much room in the brain and if too much room was needed to sort out languages, there was simply less room for other kinds of knowledge. In addition, it was believed that bilingual education resulted in lower academic achievement.

The relationship between bilingualism and cognition has been extensively studied and the results are, well, mixed. Baker (1988) found that the history of research into the relationship between bilingualism and intelligence could be divided into three overlapping periods: the period of detrimental effects from the early 19th century to the early 1960s, the period of neutral effects from the late 1950s to the early 1960s, and the period of additive effects from the early 1960s to the present. Unfortunately, the methodological problems inherent in much of the research make any clear cut statement regarding a relationship almost impossible, although Baker argued that the available evidence indicates that bilingualism results in cognitive advantage. Harding and Riley (1986) made the following observation about the research:

> Most studies reporting that bilingualism had 'negative effects' were carried out on children from minority language groups who have to learn the majority language whether they like it or not and who, very often, have not reached a very high degree of proficiency in their mother tongue when they start the second language in school. In contrast, most of the studies reporting 'positive effects' were made in societies where bilingualism is encouraged, where the languages concerned are both high-status languages and where the parents of the children tested have relatively high socio-economic class. (p. 68)

Based on their own review of the available literature, Palij and Homel (1987) concluded that bilingualism does not appear to have any major negative cognitive consequences and does seem to have beneficial cognitive consequences "in the form of enhanced language awareness and greater flexibility in its usage" (p. 146).

Several researchers contend that bilingualism can actually have great advantage for cognitive development but only under certain conditions. Lambert (1990) observed that this advantage is only realized when the two languages have "enough social value and worth that both can be permitted to flourish as languages of thought and expression" (p. 210).

Cummins (1979, 1984) argued that an interaction between sociocultural, linguistic, and school program factors underlies the cognitive advantage of bilingualism that some children experience. He hypothesized there are three broad levels of linguistic proficiency and each level has concomitant cognitive effects. At the level Cummins called "limited bilingualism," the child demonstrates low proficiency in both the first and second languages. He believed that negative cognitive effects are the result of limited bilingualism.

At the level he called "partial bilingualism," the child is at an age-appropriate level in one of the languages. He considered that neutral cognitive effects, that is, neither positive nor negative effects, are the result of partial bilingualism. Cummins referred to this level as the lower threshold level of bilingual proficiency and believed that its attainment is sufficient to avoid any negative cognitive effects.

At the level he called "proficient bilingualism," the child is at age-appropriate levels in both languages. He believed that positive cognitive effects are the result of proficient bilingualism. Cummins referred to this level as the higher threshold level of bilingual proficiency and considered that its attainment is necessary for long-term cognitive benefits.

He postulated that studies which reported to have found cognitive and academic advantages among bilingual children were conducted with children who had attained the upper threshold level of bilingual proficiency and that studies reporting negative cognitive effects were conducted with minority language children who had "failed to develop a sufficiently high level of proficiency in the school language to benefit fully from their educational experience" (1984, p. 60).

Relationship Between First and Second Language Acquisition

Much of the information available on child language acquisition is based on the learning of a first language. Teachers of bilingual children need to ask themselves if this picture of the language acquisition process is different for children learning two languages simultaneously in infancy or for the learning of a second language in childhood.

Research has demonstrated some striking similarities in the development of syntactic structures and the kinds of simplifications and overgeneralizations that are made early in the acquisition process for first and second languages (Hakuta, 1987; Kessler, 1984). Nevertheless, the two processes are not identical.

Although acquisition of two languages in infancy is called "simultaneous," Kessler (1984) found that there is often an uneven development in the two languages. One reason for this difference in development is that the child may actually be exposed to one language more than the other. This is likely to happen, for example, when each parent uses a different language with the child and the child spends more time with the mother than with the father. Uneven development can also occur when the community's attitude is more positive toward one language and so the child is motivated to use this language more often than the other language.

Some evidence indicates that children learning two languages simultaneously pass through a stage in which the two languages are undifferentiated; that is, they function as a single language system that is constructed from elements of both languages and therefore is distinct from either language presented to the child (Kessler, 1984; Lindholm & Padilla, 1978; Redlinger & Park, 1980; Vihman, 1982, 1985). However, Genesee (1989) argued that the same evidence used by researchers to support a unitary language system hypothesis can be reexamined and used to demonstrate that bilingual children are able to differentiate between the two language systems from the beginning and that they use their differentiated systems in context sensitive ways.

For children learning a second language after gaining proficiency in a first language, the process of acquiring the second language is similar but not identical to the stages involved in first language acquisition. According to Hakuta (1987), one aspect that changes the process is the environment.

In first language acquisition, the child is immersed in the language virtually all of his or her waking hours whereas in second language learning, the child may be exposed to the language for a few hours a day or less. In some instances, the setting is quite different from the natural conversational interactions between caretaker and child.

A second difference in second language learning is that at any given stage of development in the second language, the child is more cognitively advanced than he or she was at the same stage of development in the first language. As Saville-Troike (1979a) pointed out, "In general, a child learns his first language to express new meanings he perceives in his environment; in a second language, he usually learns new terms to express concepts he has already assimilated" (p. 116).

A third difference is that knowledge of a first language can cause some interference with learning a second language. Interference occurs when rules from the first language are applied inappropriately to the second language (Kessler, 1984; Saville-Troike, 1979a).

Language and Culture

Culture is a pattern of beliefs, values, behaviors, arts, customs, institutions, social forms, and knowledge that are characteristic of a community. Culture is transmitted to succeeding generations through material products, physical interaction with members of the community, and language. In the words of Saville-Troike (1979b), "Children learning their native language are learning their own culture; learning a second language also involves learning a second culture to varying degrees, which may have very profound psychological and social consequences for both children and adults" (p. 140).

Bilingualism presumes biculturalism, but how realistic is this presumption? According to Harding and Riley (1986), "Biculturalism refers to the co-existence of two cultures in the same individual" (p. 42). Yet even when individuals achieve proficiency in two languages, they tend to feel a connection predominantly to one of the cultures.

How culture is incorporated into a bilingual education program is, in large part, dependent on the dominant culture's attitude toward cultural diversity. Taylor (1987) identified four societal orientations to cultural diversity:

1. assimilation
2. integration
3. separation
4. deculturation

When the dominant culture takes an *assimilation* view, diversity is believed to be harmful because diversity fragments society by setting up group barriers. Although assimilation implies that each culture will add a dimension to the dominant culture, in reality the assimilation view encourages the abandonment of separate languages and cultures in favor of the dominant language and dominant culture. The traditional concept of the United States as a "melting pot" was based on an assimilation view.

In an *integration* view, the dominant culture encourages each minority culture to retain its identity, including its language. Taylor (1987) noted that Canada's multicultural policy is an example of this view. There is currently extensive discussion regarding whether the United States has shifted from an assimilation view to an integration view. For example, Erickson (1985) wrote that "salad bowl" is a more accurate reflection of American society today than "melting pot." Homel and Palij (1987) noted that "although the U.S. is a nation that primarily uses English as a language of communication, and there appears to be a distinct U.S. culture, the U.S. is neither linguistically nor culturally homogeneous" (p. 19).

Nonetheless, there is considerable difference of opinion within segments of society regarding the desirability of encouraging cultural pluralism through bilingual education. As Romaine (1989) recognized, "The antipathy to multiculturalism and multilingualism runs deep in the American ethos" (p. 225). This antipathy has led, according to Homel and Palij (1987), to considerable opposition to bilingual education from individuals and groups who cling to the concept of a linguistically and culturally homogeneous culture.

A *separation* view is the result of cultures fighting for primacy. In this view, there is no room for diversity because cultures threaten each other's existence. The dominant culture wants no relationship with any other culture or wants to subsume the other cultures, and the minority culture wants to be dominant. Examples include the White Supremacist movement in the United States and the Quebec Separation movement in Canada.

When the dominant culture takes a *deculturation* view, the minority culture is discredited to the point where its members lose their sense of identity. Deculturation takes place when the culture of the dominant community is not available to the group that has given up its own culture.

Connected to deculturation is Lambert's (1974) concept of subtractive and additive bilingualism. When an individual gives up his or her first language in favor of the second language, the language of the dominant culture, the individual is considered to be a *subtractive bilingual*. Lambert observed that only members of minority cultures have been observed to give up their first language. When an individual adds a language to an already prestigious language, the individual is considered to be an *additive bilingual*. Additive bilinguals enjoy the positive consequences of proficiency in two languages whereas subtractive bilinguals are faced with a loss of culture and first language along with potential lack of access to the dominant culture and low proficiency in the second language.

Bilingual Education Models

Bilingual education models tend to fall into two major categories—models based on the phasing out of the first language as the child gains proficiency in a second language, and models based on the development and maintenance of two languages throughout the child's schooling.

The bilingual education models described in the following sections are the three major paradigms discussed in the literature. It should be recognized that actual bilingual education programs involve a variety of permutations, variations, and alterations of these three patterns.

Immersion

In an immersion bilingual education model, all or most classroom instruction is in the second language (Aguirre, 1982). A number of researchers distinguish between immersion and submersion programs (Baker, 1988; Cummins, 1979; Romaine, 1989). Both programs look like an immersion model but the students in the two programs look quite different. In an immersion program, the students are from a dominant culture. The educational goal for these students is enrichment. By learning a second language, they become additive bilinguals. In a submersion program, the students are from a minority culture. The educational goal for these students is assimilation, not enrichment. By learning a second language, the language of the dominant culture, they become subtractive bilinguals. The term *submersion* is thus used by these researchers to describe what really happens to minority students in an immersion program.

Baker (1988) used the analogy of learning to swim.

> Immersion bilingual education paints a picture of moving gradually from the shallow to the deep end. Pupils are allowed to splash about in their home language while being taught the skills of swimming. Soon they move into deeper and deeper water, eventually acquiring the four basic strokes and skills to swim unaided in either language (listening, speaking, reading and writing). . . .Submersion contains the idea of a non-swimmer being thrown in at the deep end. (pp. 47–48)

One of the researchers who has expressed serious concern about submersion programs is Lambert (1990). It is his conviction that "immersion education conducted in a second or foreign language is not meant for the linguistic minority child. It fuels the subtractive process and places the minority child into another form of psycholinguistic limbo, where his/her infant language is suppressed and his/her cultural heritage and its language is subtly stigmatized as a handicap to be washed away" (p. 217).

According to Cummins (1984, 1987), two factors interrelate to make it extremely difficult for the minority language child to succeed in an immersion program. The first factor involves the amount of support the classroom context offers the child for communicating. In classrooms in which teaching involves meaningful and relevant explanations and discussions, language understanding is supported. However, most classrooms involve the kind of discourse described in Chapter 1—a high proportion of teacher language, question-answer routines that are quite different from conversational questions and answers, and movement between topics that are often unrelated to one another, such as from social studies to science.

In the typical classroom, understanding the language of the teacher well enough to comprehend the subject matter the teacher is explaining can be an enormous challenge to the minority language child. Cummins depicted this factor as a range of contextual support, with context-embedded communication at one end of the continuum and context-reduced communication at the other end.

> They are distinguished by the fact that in context-embedded communication the participants can actively negotiate meaning (e.g., by providing feedback that the message has not been understood) and the language is supported by a wide range of meaningful paralinguistic and situational cues; context-reduced communication, on the other hand, relies primarily (or at the extreme end of the continuum, exclusively) on linguistic cues to meaning and may in some cases involve suspending knowledge of the "real" world in order to interpret (or manipulate) the logic of the communication appropriately. (1987, p.62)

The second factor that influences how much the minority language child will benefit from an immersion program is the level of cognitive demand required in classroom communication. Cummins defined cognitive demand as "the amount of information that must be processed simultaneously or in close succession by the individual in order to carry out the activity" (1987, p. 63). He conceptualized cognitive demand as being on a continuum, with cognitively demanding communication at one end and cognitively undemanding communication at the other end. Since most classroom instruction involves the processing of information that is cognitively demanding, it can be surmised that the minority language child would be likely to have considerable difficulty benefitting from instruction in a second language.

Cummins pointed out that surface fluency in a language, a skill level he called "basic interpersonal communication skills," is adequate for context-embedded and cognitively undemanding communication, such as in informal conversations, but simply not sufficient for the context-reduced and cognitively demanding communication in most classrooms. He determined that classroom instruction requires a level of skill he called "cognitive academic language proficiency."

Baker (1988) noted that Cummins' theory could be used to explain why minority language children may seem ready for immersion when in reality they have acquired only enough ability in the second language to carry on informal conversations. "The theory suggests that such children are not in fact ready. Such children may fail to understand meanings and be unable to engage in higher order cognitive processes such as synthesis, discussion analysis, evaluation, and interpretation" (p. 179).

Two types of immersion programs have emerged for minority language students (Baker, 1988; Trueba, 1979):

1. Submersion. In a submersion program, the minority language child is placed in a classroom where the teacher and other students use only the second language. Teachers in these programs are typically monolingual in the dominant language.

2. English-as-a-Second-Language. In an ESL program, the minority language child receives formal English-as-a-second-language instruction for a period of time each day. This instruction is conducted in the child's first language. The rest of the day the child is in a classroom where the second language is used by the teacher and students for communication.

Transitional

In a transitional bilingual education model, classroom instruction is initially in the child's first language. The second language is gradually introduced and the goal is to mainstream the child full-time into classes where the second language is used for instruction. The educational goal of transitional programs is assimilation and children in these programs, as in immersion programs, often become subtractive bilinguals.

According to Trueba (1979), transitional programs typically are designed to last no more than three years and the concept of transition "refers to both the language use (from the home to the school language) as well as the nature of the classroom (from a 'special' to a 'regular' classroom)" (p. 56).

Two modifications to this model have emerged. In one type of transitional program, the second language is taught as a subject for part of each day (Paz, 1980).

Another modification of this model, structured immersion, is a combination of immersion and transitional (Baker & DeKanter, 1983). In structured immersion, students are grouped with others who use the same language and the teacher is bilingual. The students use their first language with each other and with the teacher but the teacher generally responds in the second language. Although instruction is in the second language in most instructional immersion programs, language arts is taught in the first language for one period each day.

Maintenance

In a maintenance bilingual education model, the child's minority language is given equal emphasis as a language of instruction throughout his or her schooling. The educational goal is integration and children in these programs are likely to become additive bilinguals.

Trueba (1979) noted that maintenance programs can take three forms. In one form, the minority language is used for face-to-face communication but the dominant language is the language of instruction in the subject areas, and it is used in reading and writing. In a second form of the maintenance model, reading, writing, and subject matter instruction are conducted in both languages but the dominant language is predominantly used for subjects except culture. In the third form of the model, there is an equal balance in the use of the minority and dominant languages.

One type of bilingual education program that is based on a maintenance model is the dual-language program. In a dual-language program, the class is taught by two teachers; one uses the minority language and the other uses the dominant language. The teachers employ a team-teaching approach. For approximately half the students in the class, the minority language is their first language. For the other half, the dominant language is their first language. Trueba (1979) commented that "the strength of this design is that each of the two teachers must maintain the role model of one language only and that both student populations have the opportunity to use both languages in the instructional context" (p. 71).

Bilingualism and the Education of Children Who Are Deaf: Issues, Problems, and Prospects

Bilingual/bicultural education for children who are deaf is a topic that is currently receiving a great deal of attention. For many educators in our field, this attention has been a long time coming. The impetus for implementing bilingual programs comes basically from two sources. The first is the deaf community who advocate for the right to pass on their language and culture to succeeding generations. The second is the overall disappointing academic achievement of youngsters who are deaf.

The preceding discussion of bilingualism and bilingual education will provide the reader with a structure for examining the issues involved in bilingual/bicultural education for children who are deaf. Many of these issues have been analyzed in depth whereas others have not yet been thoroughly addressed. Bilingual/bicultural education programs are currently being implemented throughout the United States and Canada and it is clear that some of the discussions surrounding decisions to implement these programs have been as impassioned as they have been reasoned. It is my hope that all of us involved in the education of deaf children can continue to look thoughtfully and carefully at all the questions surrounding bilingual/

bicultural education, those that are relatively easy to answer and those for which answers are difficult to find.

Stewart (1985) raised some of the questions that need to be addressed:

> How might the needs of certain subject areas be met best, by using English or ASL? How will teachers' and students' levels of competence in signing English or ASL be assessed? What bio/demographic characteristics of the students are indicators of candidacy in a bilingual program? At what age should English and ASL start to be used for communication? Should all teachers become conversant in both ASL and English, or should language specialization occur? Which language is to be recognized as a student's first language; and what student characteristics favor one language over the other? What are the effects of each language on comprehension and memory, and what perceptual features of language are involved? And what are some of the better methods for teaching English or ASL as a foreign language? (p. 376)

What Should Be the Deaf Child's First Language?

This is not a question asked in most bilingual education programs because most normally hearing children enter the educational system with a first language. And certainly some deaf children come to school with a first language that they learned from their parents without the intervention of education professionals. For example, some deaf children learn ASL from their deaf parents. Nevertheless, one of the primary goals of educating children who are deaf is to help them to acquire language and so educators of deaf children have traditionally been the ones to decide which language to teach.

In the past, the decision has been that English is the first language of children who are deaf. Oral/aural approaches, simultaneous communication, manually coded English systems, reading, and writing have all been employed to enable the deaf child to develop English as a first language.

Advocates of bilingual/bicultural education programs argue that ASL is or should be the deaf child's first language. One reason is that ASL is seen as the language of the deaf community because ASL developed through communication between deaf individuals over hundreds of years. Vernon (1987) noted that ASL "is a totally visual language which has evolved into its present grammar and hand configurations because generations of deaf people through trial and error have found these to be the best, that is, they are the easiest to form and to read" (pp. 159–160).

Another reason ASL has been promoted as the deaf child's first language is that compared to manually coded English systems, ASL is viewed as easier for the child who is deaf to learn. Vernon (1987) found that hand positions and movements from sign to sign in manually coded English were difficult to execute and read, largely because they were based on the grammar and vocabulary of spoken English and not based on the visual modality in which they were being used. He noted that by contrast, ASL's "structure is ideally suited to sight and to the motor and visual functions of human beings" (p. 159).

A third reason is that ASL gives the deaf child entrance into the deaf community. Reagan (1988) called ASL a language of "group solidarity." He observed that ASL "functions as both the deaf community's vernacular language and its principal identifying characteristic. Further, it has been, and remains, the sine qua non for membership in the deaf community" (p. 2).

Fourth, the importance of ASL to deaf individuals can be demonstrated by the fact that although ASL has not until quite recently been used as a language of instruction in the schools, it has flourished among deaf individuals. Unlike most languages that are passed on from parent to child, deaf children have usually learned ASL from peers, older deaf youngsters, deaf teachers, deaf houseparents, and deaf staff members at residential schools for the deaf (Reagan, 1985; Stewart, 1987).

If an educational program for children who are deaf decides to encourage the development of ASL as the child's first language, several issues need to be considered. One issue is that the language of the parents is probably English, the language of the dominant community. The literature is replete with studies on the effects of attitude on the acquisition of a minority language and studies examining the influence of parental attitude on the child's language acquisition. Therefore, bilingual education programs will need to deal directly with parental attitudes toward ASL. And, of course, the issue of parent-child communication when the child is learning a language that is foreign to the parent or a second language to the parent will need to be considered.

What Are the Characteristics of an Exemplary Bilingual/Bicultural Education Program?

There are three characteristics of an exemplary bilingual/bicultural education program:

1. ASL is viewed as the deaf child's first language.
2. Deaf individuals should be empowered within educational programs.
3. Deaf culture should be part of the curriculum.

ASL is viewed as the deaf child's first language   It has been suggested that fundamental to any bilingual/bicultural education program for children who are deaf is that ASL is considered as the first language of deaf children and English as a second language (Paul & Quigley, 1990; Reagan, 1988; Vernon & Andrews, 1990). There is some difference of opinion, however, regarding the role of pidgin sign.

Pidgin sign, which some individuals capitalize as in Pidgin Sign English or Pidgin Sign Language and which some individuals do not capitalize because they do not consider it the name of an actual language, is the term generally used to describe an individual's use of ASL signs in English word order and with some inclusion of English morphemes. Pidgin sign is often used simultaneously with speech or a mouthing of words with no voice.

Pidgin sign can serve important functions both within and outside the classroom. For example, pidgin sign provides a way for individuals who are fluent in ASL and individuals who are fluent in English to communicate with one another. It also allows teachers to present information in sign to their students when the manually coded English system they are using becomes cumbersome. Nonetheless, pidgin sign is not a language in itself and since it is neither ASL nor English, it cannot provide the deaf child with the richness of forms, functions, and uses from either of those languages. Stewart (1987) cautioned that "the time-honored manner of using whatever it takes to get a message across must be seriously reviewed in light of the goals of a bilingual program" (p. 68).

Yet some individuals suggest that pidgin sign has a place in a bilingual/ bicultural education program. Vernon and Andrews (1990) maintained that pidgin sign is more natural than manual codes of English and believed that its use would provide access to ASL. Vernon (1987) contended that realistically, it is the form of sign most likely to be used by hearing teachers and the goal should be to maximize the language input to the child through as many avenues as possible.

Deaf individuals should be empowered within educational programs   There is virtually no disagreement among advocates that bilingual/bicultural education programs will not succeed unless deaf individuals play a major role in design, implementation, and evaluation. However, it is recognized that it may take considerable time to change behaviors and attitudes to the point at which deaf individuals will be full participants in educational decision making.

Vernon and Andrews (1990) reported that discriminatory practices have kept deaf adults out of positions of importance in schools, colleges and universities, and the workplace. And there is certainly a relationship between the overall low academic achievement among students who are deaf and the limited number of deaf professionals. Even programs that are highly motivated to include deaf adults, such as the American Sign Language/English Studies Project at Pima Community College in Arizona, can find it difficult to recruit candidates with the necessary credentials. Brodesky and Cohen (1988) recounted that they had "not been able to find a qualified deaf educator to teach the ASL portion of the course" (p. 331) in the Pima Community College project.

Deaf culture should be part of the curriculum   For youngsters who are deaf to develop positive attitudes toward ASL and the deaf community, advocates consider it critical that deaf culture be a part of any bilingual/bicultural program. According to Reagan (1988), study of deaf culture should include the heritage and traditions of deaf people, the structure of the deaf community, social behaviors among deaf individuals, the history of deaf culture, and subcultures within the deaf culture such as Black deaf and Latino deaf. He also recommended the inclusion of cross-cultural study which should encompass the dominant Anglo-American culture, other minority cultures in American society, and the cultures of deaf people in other countries.

These three characteristics are discussed frequently in the literature on bilingual/bicultural education programs for deaf children. These are not the only important aspects of a bilingual/bicultural program. Indeed, throughout this book other teaching models and strategies for language and literacy development will be discussed that are crucial to any educational program for children who are deaf. But these three characteristics are somewhat unique to bilingual/bicultural programs. Not all educational programs regard ASL as the deaf child's first language. And while most educational programs welcome deaf adults into their midst and wish to incorporate deaf culture into the curriculum, they do not emphasize these areas as much as bilingual/bicultural education programs do.

Which Models for Bilingual/Bicultural Education Are Being Proposed and Implemented?

Any discussion of current bilingual/bicultural education models being proposed and implemented is tentative because so much growth is occurring and so many new ideas and programs are being developed. Therefore, realizing that the models available in the literature today may not capture the breadth of programs currently being developed, the following two models represent relatively recent conceptualizations.

Paul and Quigley (1990) depicted an ideal bilingual education program as one in which all instruction is conducted in ASL from preschool to approximately third grade. In grade three, English, in sign and with speech as an option, is gradually introduced as a language of instruction until ASL and English are used about equally throughout the school day. During the third grade, speech, speechreading, and auditory training activities are implemented. Reading and writing in English are also begun during third grade.

Johnson, Liddell, and Erting (1989) portrayed an ideal bilingual education program as one in which deaf children are taught by a team of two teachers from preschool through high school. One teacher is deaf and one teacher is hearing, and both use ASL for face-to-face communication. Class size is approximately 16 students instead of the more common 8 students to offset the cost of two teachers per class. Beginning in grade one, English is taught through reading and writing. Subject matter is taught through ASL and the reading of material written in English. Speech, speechreading, and auditory training activities are conducted on an individual basis. As part of this program, all children from the time of identification of hearing loss until the end of third grade attend a child development center daily. At the child development center, deaf adults fluent in ASL provide day care. The program proposed by Johnson, Liddell, and Erting also includes a family support program and a family-infant-toddler program.

As I mentioned at the beginning of this section, any bilingual/bicultural education program for students who are deaf will need to respond to a number of questions. To the excellent set of questions that I quoted from Stewart, I would like to add the following:

> How can hearing teachers develop fluency in ASL given what we know about learning a second language in adulthood?
>
> Can English be taught through the written form only, especially since spoken and written English are not identical?
>
> Where does emergent literacy fit in if English is postponed until grade one or grade three?
>
> Are there enough qualified deaf adults to staff all education programs?
>
> How can speech, speechreading, and residual hearing be developed if they are used for only a part of each day?
>
> What is the role of parents in the child's language development and how is this role reflected in the goals of the bilingual/bicultural education program?

FINAL COMMENTS

The teacher of children who are deaf must be able to create a classroom environment rich in opportunities for each child to develop the forms, meanings, and uses of language in face-to-face communication. This means that the teacher must be able to concurrently accommodate both language goals and academic goals. The agenda is two-fold. The first part involves being able to constantly remember each child's individual language goals and embed these goals daily into all learning activities. The second part involves teaching the child subject area information appropriate to the child's academic level, helping the child develop the ability to think critically and creatively, and enabling the child to learn how to learn.

In this chapter models and methods used by teachers of deaf children for actualizing this two-fold agenda were described. I also discussed issues involved in bilingual/bicultural education for children who are deaf. While this chapter concentrated on face-to-face communication, the next chapter will focus on the development of reading and writing in children who are deaf.

SUGGESTED READINGS

Harley, B., Allen, P., Cummins, J., & Swain, M. (1990). *The Development of Second Language Proficiency*. Cambridge, England: Cambridge University Press.

Jacobs, H.H. (1989). *Interdisciplinary Curriculum: Design and Implementation*. Alexandria, VA: Association for Supervision and Curriculum Development.

Joyce, B., Weil, M., Showers, B. (1992). *Models of Teaching (4th ed.)*. Boston: Allyn & Bacon.

Orlich, D.C., Kauchak, D.P., Harder, R.J., Pendergrass, R.A., Callahan, R.C., & Keogh, A.J. (1990). *Teaching Strategies: A Guide to Better Instruction*. Lexington, MA: D. C. Heath.

Romaine, S. (1989). *Bilingualism*. Oxford, England: Basil Blackwell.

Literacy Development

Holistic approaches to teaching and learning are based on the belief that the whole is different from and greater than its parts, and so they emphasize the wholes of subject matter and the integration of parts with wholes (Harris & Hodges, 1981). Currently, holistic approaches are the lens through which educators are philosophically, pedagogically, and theoretically viewing literacy development. The traditional basal reader, skills, and language experience approaches that have historically dominated reading instruction are being reexamined and reformulated to be compatible with holistic philosophy and theory. For teachers of youngsters who are deaf, the changes are profound and yet subtle. They are profound changes because they challenge our assumptions about the roles of teachers and students. They are subtle changes because, in our field, we have always recognized the importance of providing a classroom environment that reflects the value of relevant, meaningful, functional, and authentic learning experiences.

This chapter will define whole language and discuss the rationale for using whole language principles in teaching children who are deaf. Current views of reading and writing development and the kinds of reading materials that can enhance the development of literacy in deaf youngsters will also be discussed. Finally, the instructional implications of the relationship between language, literacy, and cognitive development will be examined. Teaching strategies that incorporate these principles will be presented in Chapters 4 and 5.

WHOLE LANGUAGE DEFINED

Defining whole language is akin to eating spaghetti with a knife. You think you've got it. No, you don't. Now you've got it. Carefully, carefully. No, it slipped again. One of the problems is that the terminology used to define whole language tends to be as ambiguous as "whole language." Another problem is that whole language is conceptualized in a number of ways, from a movement to a philosophy, a set of principles to a learning theory, types of materials to teaching strategies, and a curriculum focus to a political perspective.

As a movement, whole language began in the late 1970s and was originally built on the developmental theories of John Dewey, Jean Piaget, Lev Vygotsky, and Michael Halliday (Goodman, Y., 1989; McCaslin, 1989). Whole language theory evolved from these early influences in response to research in reading, writing, early childhood, and curriculum which, in part, explains the difficulty one has in capturing the essence of whole language. Whole language theory is as much psychological, philosophical, cognitive, and linguistic theory as it is educational theory.

Two types of whole language definitions are found in the literature, the short versions and the long versions. The short version I would like to share was K. Goodman's (1989), who stated, "The term whole language itself draws on two meanings of whole. It is undivided, and it is integrated and unified" (p. 210).

I would like to preface my longer version with a story. When my son was 3 years old and finishing a year of preschool, I knocked on his teacher's office door for my annual parent-teacher conference. The teacher greeted me with a smile and said, "Well, we can have a short or a long conference. I can tell you that Todd is great or we can sit and talk awhile about how great Todd is." I chose the long conference. The moral of this story is that the longer version can be more enjoyable but it is not necessarily more enlightening.

Principles of Whole Language

The following principles reflect the essential qualities of whole language. They are not meant to be rules, tenets, laws, or truths. These principles are compatible with Halliday's (1984) concept that three types of learning involving language occur simultaneously and interdependently: learning language, learning through language, and learning about language.

All Forms of Expressive and Receptive Language Work Together

It is a basic premise in whole language that reading, writing, speaking/signing, and listening/receiving sign are interrelated processes (Altwerger, Edelsky, & Flores, 1987; Brountas, 1987; Goodman, K., 1986; Goodman, Y., 1989; Harste, 1990; Shuy, 1981). As Pearson (1989) stated, "All are regarded as supportive facets of the same underlying cognitive and linguistic phenomenon" (p. 233).

The implication for instruction is that if development in one area enhances development in the others, then one form of language learning should not be emphasized at the expense of the other forms. Whole language advocates envision classrooms in which children are engaged in writing as much as reading and in speaking or signing as much as listening or receiving sign.

Focus is on Meaning of Spoken, Sign, and Written Language in Authentic Context

Much of the discussion about whole language revolves around this principle. It is believed that language and literacy develop as the child is engaged in the meaningful use of language for communicating (Altwerger, Edelsky, & Flores, 1987; Brountas, 1987; Dudley-Marling & Rhodes, 1987; Fountas & Hannigan, 1989; Goodman, K., 1986, 1989; Goodman, Y., 1989). The test of meaningfulness is how relevant the activity is to the child and how authentic the context is when compared to a real-life setting.

The major implication of this principle has been the promotion of literature-based reading programs (Fountas & Hannigan, 1989; Pearson,

1989; Pickering, 1989) though there are certainly other instructional implications involving the teaching of writing and spoken and sign language. Whole language advocates believe that children should be engaged in the reading of whole, real, predictable texts from the very beginning of instruction. In a recent position statement from the International Reading Association, it was concluded that "students need to be taught comprehension strategies using meaningful materials, not contrived selections written to focus on specific skills training" (Reading/Language Through The Years Subcommittee On Secondary Schools, 1990, p. 285). The goal of reading and writing instruction is viewed as comprehension of meaning for readers and expression of meaning for writers. Skills are not taught in a pre-set sequence of development but as they are needed within the context of reading and writing.

Classrooms Are Communities of Learners in Which Language and Literacy Are Acquired Through Use

This principle is based on the belief that children will learn to read by reading, and they will learn to write by writing. Both reading and writing are tools for learning, thinking, growing, and changing. This view of literacy development places the teacher as a co-learner in the classroom (Brountas, 1987; Dreher & Singer, 1989; Fagan, 1989; Fountas & Hannigan, 1989; Goodman, K., 1986; Harste, 1989c; Slaughter, 1988; Smith, 1978). As Wells and Wells (1984) stated, "Teaching and learning are collaborative enterprises in which the participants contribute, as far as possible, on an equal footing" (p. 196).

The implication for classroom instruction is the change from the traditional role of the teacher as leader to the teacher as facilitator. In this new role, the teacher fosters the children's natural learning abilities by providing numerous and varied opportunities for reading and writing. Furthermore, the teacher is a collaborator who learns from and with his or her students by watching, listening, and conversing with them.

Children Are Empowered When They Are Given Choice and Ownership

Respect for the learner is another basic principle of whole language. Literacy programs that build on each child's current language and literacy abilities, that provide the child choice and a sense of ownership over reading and writing activities, that encourage children to take risks with their language and support their successes, and that promote children's active use of language in personally and socially satisfying ways are programs that whole language theorists believe will ultimately empower children (Fagan, 1989; Fountas & Hannigan, 1989; Goodman, K., 1986, 1989; Harste, 1989b; Slaughter, 1988).

The implication for instruction is that in order to create learning opportunities that will meet these goals, teachers must become instructional decision makers and creators of their own curriculum.

Processes Should Be Emphasized, Not Products

Whole language advocates regard reading and writing as active, constructive, thinking processes. Becoming proficient at decoding words through phonic or structural analysis during reading, and spelling words correctly and punctuating appropriately during writing are only important insofar as they allow the reader and writer to create and communicate meaning efficiently (Brountas, 1987; Dreher & Singer, 1989; Dudley-Marling & Rhodes, 1987; Fountas & Hannigan, 1989; Goodman, K., 1986; Pearson, 1989; Pickering, 1989; Smith, 1978).

The instructional implication of viewing the products of reading and writing, such as how many stories the child completed reading in a month or how well the child can write a persuasive essay, as less important than the thinking processes involved in reading and writing has been the promotion of process-oriented teaching strategies such as writing workshop and reading workshop.

Literacy Development and Content Should Form an Integrated Curriculum

In whole language classrooms, curriculum is integrated in two ways. First, the literacy curriculum is not separate from the content curriculum. Reading, writing, speaking and signing, and listening and receiving sign are all used to learn and think about subject matter. Second, content subjects are taught around common themes or thematic units (Brountas, 1987; Fountas & Hannigan, 1989; Goodman, K., 1986; Harste, 1989c; Pearson, 1989; Pickering, 1989). For example, a unit on the solar system could be used as an umbrella for study in science, math, social studies, health, and literature.

The instructional implication is that each teacher must view himself or herself as a teacher of reading and writing as well as a teacher of subject matter, and that content curriculum encompasses the interrelations between subjects as well as the scope and sequence within individual subjects.

RATIONALE FOR USING WHOLE LANGUAGE PRINCIPLES

Whole language is based on the belief that youngsters have the cognitive capacity to make sense of reading and writing in much the same way that they have the innate ability to make sense of spoken and sign language.

Whole language principles will work only if we trust that deaf children do indeed have the cognitive ability to construct for themselves language in all its forms.

If we develop curriculum and build instruction on these principles, a number of outcomes are possible. When all forms of expressive and receptive language are seen as interrelated to each other and to the curriculum as a whole, the youngsters in our classrooms will have greater opportunities to be engaged in meaningful language use throughout the day. The richness of this learning environment will enable them to deduce the rules, meanings, and uses of these language systems. From the inception of language and literacy, our children can be creating and sharing meaning with speakers, signers, readers, and authors.

Because the current research on whole language is fragmentary, pertinent studies will be discussed as they relate to specific aspects of literacy development. Much of the difficulty in reviewing this body of research is the lack of an agreed-upon definition for whole language by the investigators. For example, while one researcher can state emphatically that "the practice of whole language is solidly rooted in scientific research and theory" (Goodman, K., 1989, p. 207), another finds that whole language proponents "seem too ready to support their claim that the basic premises of the whole language approach are theoretically well grounded with quick citation of a well-worn list of child-advocate theorists" (McCaslin, 1989, p. 225). At the present, I agree with Harste who commented that "the future of whole language is collaboratively ours for the creating" (1989b, p. 248).

READING DEVELOPMENT

I use the term *development* quite deliberately. Reading is developmental. It is part of the youngster's language development. Although in this section I arbitrarily separate reading from other forms of language for the purposes of describing how children learn to read, reading can no more be truly separated from the development of writing, speech, or sign than semantics can be separated from syntax and use.

In the last two decades the amount of research into literacy has exploded. Every year the International Reading Association publishes a *Summary of Investigations Related to Reading*. In the 1960s, the summary contained 2,758 references. In the 1970s, 6,001 references were annotated. And between 1981 and June of 1990, 8,750 references were already included.

In this section, I will describe what is currently known about the development of reading in children who are deaf, drawing as well on the research regarding reading development in all children.

The Reading Process

Reading involves an interaction between the reader and the text. The reader brings prior knowledge and experiences that shape expectations for the text. As these expectations are confirmed or disconfirmed, information is integrated and meaning is created. In this view of reading, meaning is not fixed by the author but is constructed by the reader (Dreher & Singer, 1989; Jones, 1982; Strickland, 1982; Wittrock, 1982). The reader's prior knowledge and experiences include general world knowledge, specific knowledge of the topic, past experience with the written genre, ability to understand the syntax and lexicon, and skill in decoding the words (Beck, 1989; Blachowicz, 1984; Hacker, 1980; Jones, 1982).

The complex interaction between reader and text has led some researchers to view this relationship as a transaction rather than an interaction (Chaplin, 1982; Probst, 1988; Rosenblatt, 1978; Weaver, 1988). "Transactional theory proposes that the relationship between reader and text is much like that between the river and its banks, each working its effects upon the other" (Probst, 1988, p. 378).

The reciprocal relationship between the reader and the text can be partly illustrated by the following example of a narrative passage.

> Alison's hair was white with snow in the few minutes she had been waiting for the bus. She checked her watch again, worried about her first day at work.

One reader might interpret this passage to mean that Alison was worried about being late to work on her first day because busses are often delayed during snow storms. Another reader, with less knowledge of public transportation but with more knowledge of human nature, might interpret Alison's worry to be related to her wet hair. Yet another reader might draw on personal experience to view Alison as being absorbed with worry over being able to learn her new job, and only abstractedly gazing at her watch.

To understand how readers construct meaning from text, it is essential to understand what kinds of knowledge they bring to texts. Schema theory provides a way to conceptualize these knowledge structures.

Schema Theory

Schema is a construct used in theories of perception, memory, and learning. According to schema theory, conceptual knowledge is organized cognitively into memory structures called *schemata* (*schemata* is plural, *schema* is singular). A schema can be thought of as a framework that interrelates one's knowledge and experiences about a topic. Schema are thought of as having hierarchical organization with more general concepts stored at the top. Some researchers view this framework as having slots or placeholders for the schema that fit within, or are embedded within, the lower parts of the hierarchy. It is through this framework that new information is interpreted, stored in memory, and retrieved when needed.

For a concept to be comprehended it must trigger a schema from the individual's memory. The person's prior knowledge and experiences which are organized in schema in turn influence how the new information and new experience will be understood. In essence, then, individuals store and arrange their knowledge and experiences as schemata that they then use in interpreting new information and experiences.

However, schemata are not static entities. They change as an individual processes new information and experiences. Learning can occur when new information or a new experience fits into an existing schema. This is referred to as *accretion, assimilation,* or *comprehension.* Learning can also occur when the new information or experience does not fit neatly into the schema and the schema changes, is modified, or is altered. This is called fine tuning or *accommodation.* Finally, learning can take place when schema is discarded and new schema developed to accommodate new information and experiences. This is called *restructuring.*

It is important to recognize that sometimes new information or a new experience that does not fit neatly into an existing schema can be ignored, considered irrelevant, unimportant, or even incongruent. (Psychologists have long recognized this phenomenon as denial.)

Perceiving, interpreting, and classifying new information and experiences into schemata is an active cognitive process as incoming information evokes associations with an existing schema. When new information or a new experience requires the reorganization of cognitive structures, schema undergoes qualitative change and cognitive development has taken place (Anderson, Spiro, & Anderson, 1978; Beers, 1987; Blachowicz, 1984; Hacker, 1980; Lange, 1981; Monteith, 1979; Pearson & Spiro, 1982; Richgels, 1982; Rumelhart, 1980; Thorndyke, 1977; Thorndyke & Hayes-Roth, 1979).

Readers use their schemata to create meaning from text. As Strickland (1982) stated, "Reading is a process that both develops schemata and depends on schemata" (p. 10). Two kinds of schema have been identified as particularly important in the reading process—content schema and textual schema.

Content schema   *Content schema* is the prior knowledge readers have about any given textual topic. Content schema includes the reader's general world knowledge, particular information, and personal experiences about a topic. Evidence suggests that background knowledge directly influences reading comprehension (Anderson, Spiro, & Anderson, 1978; Callahan & Drum, 1984; Gormley, 1981; Marr & Gormley, 1982; Ohlhausen & Roller, 1988; Recht & Leslie, 1988; Stevens, 1980) and, indeed, activating and expanding children's background knowledge prior to reading is conventional wisdom to teachers. As Beck (1989) commented, "The notion of enhancing comprehension by building background knowledge has been institutionalized in basal reading programs, the major vehicle for reading instruction in the elementary grades" (p. 55).

One of the problems faced by youngsters in reading a new story, chapter, article, poem, essay, or any text passage is *schema availability.* Do they already possess a rich schema for the content? Jenkins and Heliotis (1981) noted that "many children who are characterized as poor comprehenders earn this distinction because they lack the requisite background knowledge that authors assume they possess" (p. 37). The following passage was taken from *Look Who's Playing First Base* by Matt Christopher, a book written at the 2.7 reading level as calculated with the Dale-Chall readability formula.

> Art's first pitch missed the plate for ball one. His next missed, too. His third was over. The Maple Leaf then drove the two-one pitch for a single over short.
> A bunt advanced him to second base. Art fielded the ball and threw out the hitter. One out.

To comprehend this passage, and a number of other sections of the novel, the youngster would need a fairly complete understanding of baseball terminology and, probably, personal experience in playing the game.

A second, but related, problem in reading a new text is *schema selection.* This problem occurs when the youngster possesses ample background knowledge but does not use it to interact with the text. Pearson and Spiro (1982) found that sometimes children are unaware that they possess relevant schemata. They also found that some children focus on an inappropriate schema because they are misled by a nonsalient feature of the passage or because the text requires combinations of background knowledge. Pearson and Spiro observed that problems in schema selection are often associated with overreliance on bottom-up processing, or decoding of individual words.

One example of how children who are deaf can have difficulty with schema selection is illustrated by a chapter in the novel *Ellen Tebbits* by Beverly Cleary. Near the beginning of one of the chapters, Beverly Cleary writes, "To Ellen Tebbits and Austine Allen spring meant something much more important. It meant no more winter underwear." A few paragraphs later, Ellen, bragging about her ability to ride a horse, says to Austine, "Once I rode bareback." The rest of the chapter deals with Ellen's predicament when she and Austine have an opportunity to go bareback riding and her boasting is put to the test. The child who focuses early in the chapter on the phrases "no more winter underwear" and "bareback" may misinterpret the actual meaning of these phrases, overestimate their importance for understanding the rest of the chapter, and not even notice the central idea of the chapter.

A third problem is *schema maintenance* and *schema shift.* It has been observed that able readers continue to use schema as long as it is appropriate, and they are able to shift schema when the passage calls for it.

However, some youngsters have difficulty in flexibly maintaining and shift-ing schema as they interact with text. The ability to maintain and shift schema requires that the youngster be aware of what he or she knows, does not know, and what to do about it. This awareness of one's own knowledge and thinking involves metacognitive abilities, which will be discussed in greater depth later in this chapter.

Not only do readers use their schemata for text content, they use their schemata for text structure.

Textual Schema   *Textual schema* is the reader's mental organization of how typical text is structured. Most of the research regarding textual schema has focused on the structure of narrative text. Expository text schema will be discussed later in this section.

Story Schema   The reader's cognitive representation of narrative text is referred to as *story schema*. Because story schema provides the reader with an expectation of what form a typical story takes, the skilled reader uses this schema to notice important or relevant aspects of the material, to pay atten-tion to the ways story components are sequenced and fit together, and to reconstruct the story after it has been read (Mandler, 1978; Mavrogenes, 1983; McConaughy, 1982).

Story grammars have been developed to describe the structure of a particular kind of narrative text. They are meant to reflect both the exter-nal structure of stories and the internal cognitive structures within readers (Mandler, 1987; McConaughy, 1982). Four major story grammars are cur-rently discussed in the literature: Mandler and Johnson's (1977; Johnson & Mandler, 1980), Rumelhart's (1975, 1977), Stein and Glenn's (1979), and Thorndyke's (1977). These grammars were derived from oral folktale and fairy tale traditions in western cultures. With some variation in structural elements, all of these grammars include a *setting*, a series of *episodes*, and a *resolution*. In the *setting*, the central character is introduced, and location and time may be described. Within each episode is an *initiating event* that causes the central character to have a *reaction* and to formulate a goal. The central character *attempts* to achieve the goal or solve the problem. (An attempt is sometimes referred to as the *action*.) For each attempt there is either a successful or failed *outcome*, sometimes called a *consequence*. If there is more than one episode in the story, the consequence of each episode is the initiating event of the subsequent episode. Thus, the consequence acts as the consequence of the preceding episode and the initiating event of the next episode. *Resolution*, or *ending*, represents the final outcome or long-range consequence of the action. In Figure 3-1, the story structure of *The Three Bears* is represented.

The psychological reality of story grammar has been confirmed by a number of researchers. In studies where readers were presented with stories that were well formed and stories that varied in differing degrees from well-formed stories, recall was found to be directly related to how closely the stories conformed to ideal story structure (Mandler, 1978; Stein &

FIGURE 3-1

Story Structure of "The Three Bears"

	Setting	Once upon a time, there was a family of bears—a papa, mama, and a baby. The lived in the woods.
Episode 1	Initiating Event	Mama Bear made porridge for breakfast but it was too hot to eat.
	Reaction	The bears decided to go for a walk in the woods while the porridge cooled off.
	Action	Goldilocks walked up to the Bear's house. Since no one was home, she walked in.
	Consequence	Goldilocks saw three bowls of porridge.
Episode 2	Reaction	Since she was hungry, she decided to eat some porridge.
	Action	The porridge in the big bowl was too hot. The porridge in the middle size bowl was too cold. The porridge in the small bowl was just right and she ate it all up.
	Consequence	She saw three chairs.
Episode 3	Reaction	Since she was tired, she decided to sit down.
	Action	The big chair was too hard. The middle size chair was too soft. The small chair was just right. Suddenly, the chair broke.
	Consequence	Goldilocks walked upstairs.
Episode 4	Reaction	Since she was tired, she decided to lay down.
	Action	The big bed was too hard. The middle size bed was too soft. The small bed was just right and she fell asleep.
	Consequence	The bears came home. They saw that someone had eaten their porridge, sat in their chairs, and slept in their beds. Baby Bear's porridge was all eaten up, his chair was broken, and someone was in his bed.
	Ending	Goldilocks woke up. When she saw the bears, she ran out of the house and never came back again.

117

Nezworski, 1978). When asked to divide into parts stories that systematically varied in structure, adult readers demonstrated sensitivity to story structure constituents regardless of the content (Mandler, 1987).

Children have also been found to expect stories to have a predictable structure, with their schemata becoming more differentiated as they become older (Buss, Yussen, Mathews, Miller, & Rembold, 1983; Fitzgerald, Spiegel, & Webb, 1985; Golden, 1984; McClure, Mason, & Barnitz, 1979; McConaughy, 1980; Pappas & Brown, 1987; Whaley, 1981). When presented with stories that followed the rules of story grammar and stories that deviated from ideal story structure, even children in second grade have been observed to have better comprehension and recall of the well-formed stories (Brennan, Bridge, & Winograd, 1986; Feldman, 1985; Glenn, 1978; Hartson, 1984).

Yet some children seem to develop a sense of story structure sooner, or with less difficulty, than other children. Several researchers have found a positive relationship between reading ability and story schema, with more able readers demonstrating more highly developed story schemata (Fitzgerald, 1984; Krein & Zaharias, 1986; Rahman & Bisanz, 1986; Weaver & Dickinson, 1982; Wilkinson & Bain, 1984).

Schema for Expository Text   It is difficult to examine readers' schemata for expository text because there is no single structure for writing that, according to *A Dictionary of Reading and Related Terms* (Harris & Hodges, 1981), is used for the purpose of setting forth or explaining. Almost all expository writing includes a combination of structures.

Much of the research on expository text structure has focused on the five patterns identified by Meyer (Mulcahy & Samuels, 1987; Ohlhausen & Roller, 1988; Richgels, McGee, Lomax, & Sheard, 1987). Meyer (1975; Meyer & Freedle, 1984) found the following five basic expository text organizations, often referred to as *rhetorical predicates* in the literature. In each of these structures, information is organized hierarchically.

1.   *Collection*. A collection structure is information grouped by association and grouped by sequence, such as in a time sequence or a list. Richgels, McGee, Lomax, and Sheard (1987)* illustrated this structure with the following graphic organizer:

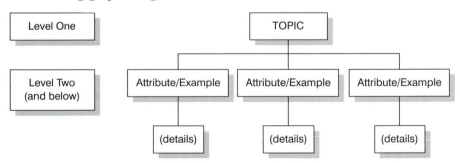

*Reprinted with permission of Donald J. Richgels and the International Reading Association.

2.   *Description.* A description structure is a specific type of grouping by association in which one element is subordinate to another. In a description, an attribute, specific, or setting is presented to support the topic.

3.   *Causation.* In a causation structure, elements are not only grouped by association and sequenced but they are causally related. Richgels and associates illustrated this structure with the following graphic organizer:

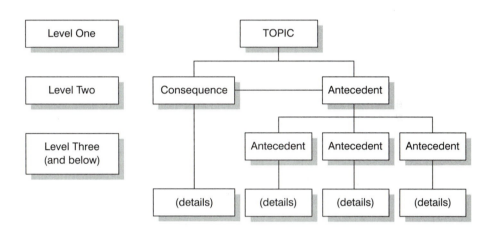

4.   *Problem/solution.* A problem/solution structure contains all the elements of a causation structure with the addition that at least one aspect of the solution matches the content and blocks a cause of the problem. Richgels and associates used the following graphic organizer to illustrate this structure:

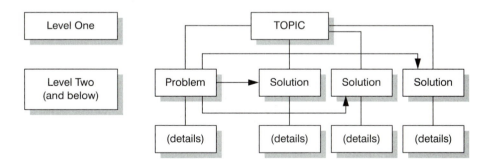

5.   *Comparison.* A comparison structure is organized on the basis of similarities and differences. The following graphic organizer was developed by Richgels and associates to illustrate this structure:

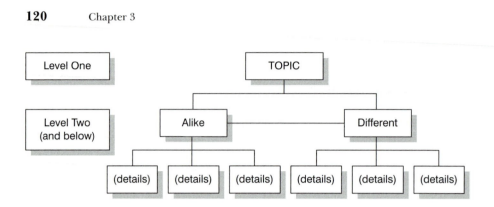

Currently, only limited research suggests that awareness of expository text structure increases with age and reading ability and that awareness of text structure is related to comprehension and recall of text information (Horowitz, 1985a, 1985b; Langer, 1985; McGee, 1982; Ohlhausen & Roller, 1988; Richgels, McGee, Lomax, & Sheard, 1987; Taylor & Samuels, 1983; Williams, Taylor, & deCani, 1984).

Surface Structure Schemata   *Surface structure* is a construct used in transformational-generative grammar to refer to the relationship among the syntactic and morphologic elements of a spoken, sign, or written sentence. Surface structure is contrasted with *deep structure,* which is the meaning of a sentence. Sentences can have different surface structures but the same deep structure. (For example, John threw the ball. The ball was thrown by John.) Sentences can also have the same surface structure but different deep structures. (For example, Mary asked John to fix the bike. Mary promised John to fix the bike.)

Content schema and textual schema are used by readers for deep structure processing, but to be able to get to the deep structure of a passage readers need to be able to first process the surface structure efficiently. Schemata for surface structure include *word recognition, text cohesion, sentence transformations,* and *figurative language.*

Word Recognition   Word recognition includes *lexical cues, graphophonic cues, structural cues,* and *context cues.* The goal of word recognition strategies is to identify a word as being in the reader's vocabulary and so activate a content schema for the word. *Lexical cues* are cues that signal an immediate recognition of the word as a whole. All of the other word recognition cues are used to enable the reader to figure out the identity of individual words. *Graphophonic cues* are used by readers to analyze a word with predictable letter-sound relationships. When readers use *structural cues,* they are analyzing a word through roots, prefixes, suffixes, and compounds. *Context cues* include syntactic and semantic cues. Syntactic cues are the help that the order of known words offers readers, and semantic cues are the help that the meaning of known words offers readers when they are trying to identify an unknown word in the same context. (Detailed descriptions of word identification skills are provided in many current reading methodology text-books such as Finn, 1990; Leu & Kinzer, 1991; Mason & Au, 1990; and Vacca, Vacca, & Gove, 1991.)

When readers have highly developed schemata for word recognition, they are able to quickly and successfully identify words in written discourse. The more attention readers need to give to word recognition the less attention they can give to processing text at a deep structure level (Beck, 1989; Holdaway, 1979; Wood, 1985).

Text Cohesion   *Cohesiveness in text* refers to the links, ties, order arrangements, or patterns that connect and integrate text elements and provide discourse with unity and clarity. The reader's subjective judgment regarding how well a text "hangs together" is referred to as coherence of text (Chapman, 1979; Harris & Hodges, 1981). When readers have well-developed schemata for text cohesiveness, they are able to identify anaphoric references (expressions, usually pronouns, that substitute for a preceding word or group of words), follow the sequence of action signalled by words such as *then* and *before*, understand the order of events through use of verb tenses, and recognize other cohesive ties in text. While content and textual schemata are primary factors in reading comprehension, ability to process cohesive ties does have an effect on comprehension (Chapman, 1979; McClure, Mason, & Barnitz, 1979).

Sentence transformations   Some linguistic structures are clearly more difficult for youngsters to comprehend than others. The surface structure of simple active declarative sentences, such as "Mary painted the picture," provide a direct signal to the deep structure. *Transformations* of this sentence complicate the readers' road to the deep structure, however, as indicated by even simple questions such as "What did Mary paint?" negatives such as "Mary didn't paint the picture," and passives such as "The picture was painted by Mary." Schemata for English grammatical constructions obviously have an influence on the reader's ability to process written text since confusion at the sentence level can create misunderstanding at the discourse level.

Figurative Language   The reader's ability to understand *figurative language* depends on content, textual, and surface structure schemata. When skilled readers encounter figurative language, their schemata for surface structure tells them that the expression makes no literal sense. They then must use their content and textual schemata to remind them that sometimes writers use nonliteral language such as similes, metaphors, hyperbole, irony, and other figures of speech. Finally, they must use context cues available in the surface structure of the text as well as their prior understanding of the passage as a whole to deduce the possible meaning of the figurative language.

Whole language approaches tend to deemphasize the child's development of surface structure schemata. And, indeed, most of the strategies discussed in Chapters 4 and 5 pertain to the development of the deaf child's content and textual schemata. The reason for this emphasis is to provide some balance to the traditional overemphasis by teachers of youngsters who are deaf on word identification and meaning at the individual sentence level. However, strategies to help develop the child's surface structure schemata should not be overlooked in our enthusiasm to build the child's background knowledge and knowledge of text structures.

Implications for Youngsters Who Are Deaf

It is commonly believed that the average high school graduate who is deaf reads at the fourth/fifth grade level. As educators, we need to examine this figure carefully. In Wolk and Allen's (1984) study of the reading comprehension of 1,664 hearing impaired students enrolled in special education programs, it was found that "the typical growth rate in reading comprehension is very moderate for the average hearing impaired student, and approximates one-third of a grade-equivalent change each year through the elementary and secondary school grades" (p. 174). The high school-aged group in the study reflected "a leveling off in reading-comprehension development at a point equivalent to the performance of the average fourth-grade hearing student" (p. 174). Wolk and Allen also found that severity of hearing loss was the most prominent characteristic directly influencing achievement growth, and that the presence of an additional behavioral or learning handicap significantly influenced reading comprehension performance. The authors noted, "Of some interest is that for hearing impaired students, the presence of a behavioral or learning problem may be as important to overall reading comprehension as is a profound degree of hearing loss" (p. 170).

Achievement of the average student tells us very little, though, about the potential of any single youngster. There is considerable evidence to suggest that many youngsters who are deaf achieve at levels commensurate with normally hearing youngsters, and that the reading process itself is not different for deaf children (Erickson, 1987; Ewoldt, 1978, 1987; Gaines, Mandler, & Bryant, 1981; Geers & Moog, 1989; Gormley & Franzen, 1978; Griffith & Ripich, 1988; Kyle, 1980; LaSasso & Davey, 1987; Peterson & French, 1988; Sarachan-Deily, 1985).

The reading performance of youngsters who are deaf often differs from the performance of youngsters who are hearing and sometimes, though not always, this difference represents a poorer ability to comprehend text. If the reading process itself is not different but performance is often different, all of us need to analyze the literacy learning environment in which we immerse students who are deaf. Before discussing strategies for accomplishing this, I would like to discuss emergent literacy.

EMERGENT LITERACY

Emergent literacy represents a relatively recent concept in understanding reading and writing development in young children. It replaces the concept of reading readiness. The emergent literacy view "is based on observations of very young children whose experiences with reading and writing are responded to and nurtured by attentive adults who are willing to support the children's earliest notions of what written language is and how people use it as readers and writers" (Finn, 1990, p. 59).

The traditional concept of reading readiness considered early childhood and kindergarten as a period of preparation for learning to read. Hall (1987) observed that this view of literacy development was based on the following assumptions:

❏ reading and writing are primarily visual-perceptual processes involving printed unit/sound relationships;

❏ children are not ready to learn to read and write until they are five or six years old;

❏ children have to be taught to be literate;

❏ the teaching of literacy must be systematic and sequential in operation;

❏ proficiency in the "basic" skills has to be acquired before one can act in a literate way;

❏ teaching the "basic" skills of literacy is a neutral value-free activity. (p. 2)

The scope of emergent literacy includes the kinds of literacy learning that take place prior to formal school instruction or prior to the time when children learn to read and write in what adults would interpret as conventional ways (Holdaway, 1979; Teale, 1987).

Teale (1987) considered the terminology *emergent literacy* to be extremely significant. *Literacy* emphasizes the developmental relationship between reading and writing. *Emergent* emphasizes the process and continuity of development, and suggests the importance of home and community over formal teaching.

Hall (1987) observed that the emergent literacy view of literacy development is based on the following assumptions, which look quite different from the reading readiness assumptions:

❏ Reading and writing are cognitive and social abilities involving a whole range of meaning-gaining strategies.

❏ Most children begin to read and write long before they arrive at school. They do not wait until they are "taught."

❏ Literacy emerges not in a systematic, sequential manner, but as a response to the printed language and social environment experienced by the child.

❏ Children control and manipulate their literacy learning in much the same way as they control and manipulate all other aspects of their learning about the world.

❏ Literacy is a social phenomenon and as such is influenced by cultural factors. Therefore the cultural group in which children grow up will be a significant influence on the emergence of literacy. (p. 8)

What Do Young Children Learn About Literacy?

Children learn that reading and writing have purposes, functions, and uses. They learn that print conveys a message and that people can communicate their ideas and feelings through reading and writing (Isom & Casteel, 1986; Mavrogenes, 1986; Teale, 1987).

Children develop attitudes toward literacy during their early years. They learn whether or not reading and writing are valued by the adults around them (Morrow, 1989; Teale, 1987).

Children learn the conventions of reading and writing. They learn that books are read from front to back, and print from left to right and top to bottom on a page (if they are reading English, that is). They also learn that print is followed word by word and, furthermore that print consists of letters, words, spaces, and punctuation. They learn that print is different from pictures (Dyson, 1984; Garton & Pratt, 1989; Hall, 1987; Mavrogenes, 1986; Teale, 1987).

Children become aware of some decoding strategies. They learn to distinguish between words and between letters, notice repetitions and patterns among words, identify letters, and make the connection between written words and spoken and sign words (Dyson, 1984; Garton & Pratt, 1989; Mason & Allen, 1986; Mavrogenes, 1986; Teale, 1987).

Children learn that the written language system has major differences from their oral or sign language system (Andrews & Mason, 1986; Bock & Brewer, 1985; Cox & Sulzby, 1982; Sulzby, 1982; Teale, 1987). Mason and Allen (1986) described these differences as physical, situational, functional, form, and structural.

1. The *physical differences* involve language in print versus language in voice or through-the-air. The authors use the example of speed. "Readers can vary their speed but listeners cannot. The same language sample, such as a paragraph from a speech, may take 6 minutes to write but as little as 1 minute to read aloud and half a minute to read silently" (p. 11).

2. *Situational differences* involve the face-to-face context of oral and sign language versus the decontextualized nature of reading. For example, speakers and signers can modify their information as they receive feedback from their communication partners.

3. *Functional differences* refer to the different purposes for which written language and spoken and sign language are used. For example, written

language can be used to record a body of information for many readers to use over time.

4. *Form differences* relate to physical differences but include the restrictions in written language for expressing meaning. For example, spoken language can use intonation, pitch, and loudness, and spoken and sign language can use stress and rhythm.

5. *Structural differences* refer to the more formal, precise, and explicit nature of written language when compared to spoken and sign language.

Young children also develop knowledge about the world that builds their content schema, and they develop a sense of story that builds their story schema (Applebee, 1978, 1980; Hall, 1987).

How Do Young Children Learn About Literacy?

Children use their environment to make sense of print. They pay close attention to restaurant signs, messages on tee shirts, advertisements in newspapers and magazines, labels on food products, and the many other kinds of environmental print they encounter. While researchers argue over the relationship between environmental print awareness and learning to read continuous text, it does appear that knowledge of environmental print plays a role in literacy development (Garton & Pratt, 1989; Mavrogenes, 1986; Teale, 1987). Current research suggests that "experience with environmental print is an intrinsic part of becoming a literate language user, but that such experiences operate in conjunction with many other oral and written language experiences" (Hall, 1987, p. 28).

Children also learn about literacy through storybook reading. Researchers have studied parent-child interactions and teacher-child interactions during storybook reading, and they have studied how children function independently with storybooks. It has been found that when parents and teachers read to children, they rarely read word-for-word. Instead, they encourage much conversation, and this conversation changes as the same story is reread over time (Hall, 1987; Mason & Allen, 1986; Pappas & Brown, 1987). As Teale (1987) noted, "The words of the author are surrounded by the language and social interaction of the adult reader and the child(ren). In this interaction the participants cooperatively seek to negotiate meaning. Viewing storybook reading as social interaction has revealed that reading books aloud to children is fundamentally an act of construction" (p. 60).

Children use their emerging understanding of literacy in their pretend readings of storybooks, their imaginative play, and in the stories they tell (Cox & Sulzby, 1982; Galda, 1984; Isenberg & Jacob, 1983; Pappas & Brown, 1987; Purcell-Gates, 1989; Roskos, 1988; Sachs, Goldman, & Chaille, 1984; Teale, 1987).

Why Do Young Children Want to Learn About Literacy?

From the moment they become aware of print, children seem strongly motivated to learn to read and write. Most cultures in the United States place a high value on literacy and children seem to figure that out quite quickly. Children are surrounded by print. They see adults reading and writing, and they clearly like to emulate adult behavior. When adults read them a story, ask what they want for dinner while looking at a menu, or tell them about a birthday party after opening the mail, children are implicitly told that literacy is part of social interaction. They observe a purpose and need for reading and writing each time they see a parent cutting out a food coupon, reading the directions on a package to assemble a new toy, following a recipe to prepare a special dessert, looking through the TV listing to decide on a television program, and all of the other myriad activities involving literacy. And they see that reading and writing are important when they see adults reading a book, newspaper, or magazine and writing a letter or a shopping list.

LITERATURE-BASED CURRICULUM

In the last several years considerable debate has surrounded the role of literature in literacy development (Goodman, Y., 1989; Sawyer, 1987). A review of the research shows that no articles or books have been written by educators who are opposed to literature in reading programs. (There are not even anecdotal references to such educators.) The lines of this debate have not been drawn between the pros and cons of actually using literature to teach reading. Instead, the heat from this debate seems to emanate from differing definitions of literature and differing views on how literature should be packaged for instruction. In the interests of fairness, I would like to start this discussion with "basal reading series" since basals have dominated reading instruction for the past 40 years or more. Equal time will be given to "literature in trade books."

Basal Readers

A *basal reader* is "a text in a basal reading program or series," and a basal reading program or series is "a comprehensive integrated set of books, workbooks, teacher's manuals, and other materials for developmental reading instruction", according to *A Dictionary of Reading and Related Terms* (Harris & Hodges, 1981, p. 30). Basal reading series were traditionally characterized by controlled vocabulary, progressive difficulty, and detailed teaching instructions. However, basal reading series have changed in response to recent research in literacy development. Some of the differences between older and newer basals and current research and viewpoints regarding the value of basals in reading instruction will be discussed in the following paragraphs.

It was difficult to find advocates of basal reading series in the published literature. On the one hand, this seemed a strange finding since surveys have shown that basal readers are used in 80% to 90% of classrooms (The Commission on Reading, 1989; LaSasso, 1987). On the other hand, it was a clear signal that basals are not politically popular, or to use the current lingo, it does not seem to be politically correct to publicly advocate the use of basal reading series.

Stahl and Miller (1989) quantitatively synthesized the data from instructional studies that compared the effects of a whole language or language experience program to a basal reading program. Their results indicated that overall these programs produced approximately equal effects, that whole language/language experience programs were more effective in kindergarten or prior to formal reading instruction, and that more recent studies and studies that met more rigorous criteria for inclusion showed stronger effects for basal reading programs. In critiques of Stahl and Miller's study, Schickedanz (1990) and McGee and Lomax (1990) noted that language experience approaches should not be equated with whole language approaches and that more relevant comparisons would be between older language experience approaches and basal reader programs, and newer whole language approaches and basal reader programs.

Holland and Hall (1989) compared the reading achievement of first-grade students who had been taught with a basal reading program with first graders taught with whole language approaches and found no statistically significant differences in reading achievement test scores between the two groups of students.

McCallum (1988) pointed out that basal reading series have always changed over time as editors have tried to translate research findings and theory into materials and activities that take into consideration the realities of time, energy, and expertise faced by classroom teachers. For example, most basals now use literature selections rather than stories written expressly for basal readers at particular readability levels. By incorporating current insights regarding literacy development into text selections and instructional suggestions for teachers, McCallum believed that basals can serve as an important source for preservice and inservice teacher training.

One of the major criticisms leveled against basals has been the contrived nature of text selections. To create texts in an easy to progressively more difficult sequence, authors traditionally developed stories and passages in which sentence length and complexity were monitored, vocabulary was controlled, and content selection was limited. In numerous studies it has been found that contrived texts are actually more difficult for youngsters to read, regardless of whether the youngsters are deaf or hearing (Bouffler, 1984; Davison & Kantor, 1982; Ewoldt, 1984; Gourley, 1978; Hare, Rabinowitz, & Schieble, 1989; Israelite & Helfrich, 1988). Israelite and Helfrich concluded that "hearing impaired students should be reading well-written stories created by skilled children's authors, instead of basal materials developed to meet a predetermined set of rules for syntax, sentence length, or vocabulary" (p. 271).

A number of other criticisms have also been brought against basals. The following ones were taken from the report on the state of American reading instruction produced by The Commission on Reading of the National Council of Teachers of English (1989):

❏ Basal reading systems leave very little room for other kinds of reading activities in the schools where they have been adopted.

❏ Basal reading series typically reflect and promote the misconception that reading is necessarily learned from smaller to larger parts.

❏ The sequencing of skills in a basal reading series exists not because this is how children learn to read but simply because of the logistics of developing a series of lessons that can be taught sequentially, day after day, week after week, year after year.

❏ Students are typically tested for ability to master the bits and pieces of reading, such as phonics and other word-identification skills, and even comprehension skills. However, there is no evidence that mastering such skills in isolation guarantees the ability to comprehend connected text, or that students who cannot give evidence of such skills in isolation are necessarily unable to comprehend connected text.

❏ So much time is typically taken up by "instructional" activities (including activities with workbooks and skill sheets) that only a very slight amount of time is spent in actual reading—despite the overwhelming evidence that extensive reading and writing are crucial to the development of literacy.

❏ Basal reading series typically reflect and promote the widespread misconception that the ability to verbalize an answer, orally or in writing, is evidence of understanding and learning.

❏ Basal reading series typically tell teachers exactly what they should do and say while teaching a lesson, thus depriving teachers of the responsibility and authority to make informed professional judgments. (pp. 88–89)

Harste (1989a) has promoted the view that basals cannot be improved because intrinsically they encourage limited thinking by teachers. It is his observation that "teachers come to think that step-by-step instructional procedures followed in a basal lesson constitute what it means to teach reading comprehension. Children come to think of questions and what they do on worksheets as what reading comprehension is. Basals as texts legitimate particular contexts of language and thought in classrooms" (p. 270).

At this point, the reader may be wondering why teachers use basals. Shannon (1982) found that teachers rely on commercial reading materials for four reasons: they do not feel deeply involved with reading instruction, they believe these materials can be used successfully to teach reading, they believe the materials embody scientific truth, and they think their school administrations require them to use the materials. While teachers reported that their major reason for using published materials was to fulfill administrators' expectations, Shannon found that administrators thought teachers were using these materials because of belief in their effectiveness.

Trade Books

A *trade book* is "a book published for sale to the general public" (p. 333) and literature is defined as "writings of high quality and significance because of a successful integration of style, organization, language, theme, etc." (p. 184) according to *A Dictionary of Reading and Related Terms* (Harris & Hodges, 1981).

When educators discuss literature-based programs for teaching reading, they usually mean that trade books, as well as other materials published for a wide audience such as newspapers and magazines, should be used for instruction. The difference between trade books and basal readers can be illustrated by imagining both kinds of books in a classroom library. Which books would youngsters spend time reading if they were given a choice?

Educators who advocate using literature in reading programs believe that there is a great difference between reading stories or excerpts from books and reading whole books. Huck (1987) called it getting children hooked on books. "Instead of reading 'bits and pieces' of a story, they have a chance to become engrossed in an entire book" (p. 376). Smith and Bowers (1989) made the point that "it takes more than ten pages for a student to understand and really fall in love with a book" (p. 345).

Proponents believe that literature embodies other values as well. Literature can stretch imagination, educate about cultures, foster reasoning, provide language models, encourage thinking, help children understand emotions and gain compassion, and nurture the desire to read (Cullinan, 1987; Fuhler, 1990; Hickman & Cullinan, 1989; Huck, 1987; Morrow, 1989; Pillar, 1979; Sage, 1987; Tunnell & Jacobs, 1989; VanDongen & Westby, 1986). Huck (1982) expressed her belief in the significance of literature when she wrote, "I am not so naive to think literature will save the world, but I do believe it is one of the things that makes this world worth saving" (p. 316).

A literature-based reading program requires the teacher to make decisions regarding pedagogy since instructional planning resides with the teacher and not the author of the basal reader. Hiebert and Colt (1989) identified three patterns of reading instruction that incorporate a blend of instructional format and literature selection:

❏ Pattern 1. teacher-selected literature in teacher-led groups

❏ Pattern 2. teacher- and student-selected literature in teacher- and student-led small groups

❏ Pattern 3. student-selected literature read independently

Hiebert and Colt advocated the use of all three patterns within the same classroom. Smith and Bowers (1989) identified these same patterns but noted two other decisions that teachers need to make. The first decision is whether to integrate literature into content subject instruction, and the second decision is whether to use literature to replace or to supplement basal readers.

Huck (1987) presented five components she believed to be crucial to the success of a literature-based approach:

1. a read-aloud program for youngsters at all grade levels
2. daily opportunity to read self-selected books
3. in-depth discussion groups
4. the use of literature across the curriculum
5. time for children to respond in various ways to books

Whole Language Materials

Spiegel (1989) wrote that the phrase "whole language materials" is almost an oxymoron, or contradiction in terms, because "whole language, at least in theory, is not materials driven nor materials dependent" (p. 168). Nevertheless, teachers are responsible for choosing materials for instruction and the decisions can be particularly time-consuming and difficult when trying to implement a literature-based reading program. Furthermore, teachers must be able to select materials that highlight and celebrate cultural diversity.

One scenario is for teachers to embrace one of the new basal reading series, reading packages, or theme collections that promise a whole language and literature-based approach. A second scenario is for teachers to seek out trade books themselves. Both scenarios require that the teacher carefully evaluate the materials, decide how appropriate they are for individual students who are deaf, and develop instructional strategies incorporating the materials. Implied within both scenarios is that teachers will make these decisions based on their own conceptualizations of the kinds of literacy experiences they want to provide the deaf children in their classrooms.

Readability

One of the side issues in literature-based reading programs is readability. When teachers choose their own books, they have to be able to determine if the texts will be comprehensible to the youngsters.

A number of factors, within texts and within readers, contribute to readability. Content, structure, cohesiveness, format, typography, literary form and style, vocabulary difficulty, sentence complexity, idea or proposition density, level of abstractness, and organization are *within-text* factors. *Within readers*, motivation, ability, interest, purpose for the reading, cultural background, knowledge of vocabulary, extent of background knowledge and experience with the topic, and knowledge of text structure contribute to the ease with which the text will be comprehended (Dreyer, 1984; Harris & Hodges, 1981; Irwin & Davis, 1980; Israelite, 1988; Koenke, 1987; Lange, 1982; Marshall, 1979; Zakaluk & Samuels, 1988).

The most frequently used tool for determining readability is a readability formula. Most formulas rely on two factors, average sentence length and vocabulary difficulty. Clearly, these two factors do not exhaust all of the possible variables that influence text readability. When used as probability statements or estimates, though, formulas can provide predictive information regarding how easily a text will be understood by the average reader (Dreyer, 1984; Fry, 1989; Koenke, 1987). But they will not predict precisely whether a given reader will interact successfully with a particular text (Lange, 1982).

The use of readability formulas is actively being discouraged by a number of educators. I think there are two reasons for this phenomenon. The first is that whole language advocates find it anathema to use only two characteristics of a text for evaluating the potential interactions between reader and text. The problem with this criticism is that readability formulas are not meant to be the only measure of text comprehensibility. The use of formulas should be augmented with other methods for estimating the readability of text. As Lange (1982) wrote, "In the final analysis, it is not the use of readability formulas that presents problems, but the use of the formulas either as the only evaluation of a text or as the starting point for adapting a text to 'fit' a particular reading level" (p.861).

Lange's last point leads to the second criticism of readability formulas, that readability formulas have been used to create texts written at specific difficulty levels. The problem with this criticism is that readability formulas were never meant to be writeability formulas. Fry, developer of the Fry Readability Graph, argued that "readability formulas are not and never were intended to be writer's guides. . .The most common misuse of formulas is for writers to take the two simple inputs of most formulas and manipulate them irrationally" (1989, p. 293).

The use of readability formulas is relatively simple and straightforward, and microcomputer technology can make the process relatively quick (Anderson, 1983; Burmeister, 1976; Klare, 1988; Koenke, 1987; Kretschmer, J., 1984; Layton, 1980; Rush, 1985). However, formulas cannot be used without other methods of determining readability, although it might be very tempting to rely solely on computer software, with its aura of scientific validity. Some of the other readability approaches suggested in the literature are useful for determining readability.

One suggestion is for teachers to read the target texts themselves, using their own knowledge and understanding of their students to compare against the demands of the text (Dreyer, 1984; Israelite, 1988; Rush, 1985). A second suggestion is to give a selection of the text to the youngsters for a trial reading (Rush, 1985). A third suggestion is to use a cloze procedure, in which the youngsters are given a reproduced portion of the text from which words have been systematically deleted (Rush, 1985). In the second and third suggestions, the teacher needs to predetermine a criterion level of comprehension that the students can demonstrate through answering questions, retelling the passage, or filling in syntactically and semantically appropriate words in the cloze passage.

A fourth suggestion is to use a checklist for evaluating the comprehensibility of text. Teachers could create their own checklists using within-reader and within-text characteristics discussed previously in this section, or use one published in the literature, such as the Irwin and Davis readability checklist (1980). In Figure 3–2, I have presented my own readability checklist.

The true test of readability ultimately resides within the interaction of reader and text. I agree with Israelite's suggestion regarding the evaluation of readability by teachers of children who are deaf that "teachers reserve evaluation until they have observed their students interacting with texts, for in the final analysis, the most informed judgments are those of the readers, themselves" (1988, p.17).

METACOGNITION AND LITERACY

Metacognition refers to thinking about thinking, reflecting on one's own cognitive processes, or monitoring one's own thinking (Babbs & Moe, 1983; Guthrie, 1982). When applied to the reading process, *metacognition* (sometimes labeled metacomprehension in the context of reading) includes readers' awareness and control over their own comprehension (Raphael, Myers, Tirre, Fritz, & Freebody, 1981).

A. Brown (1980) identified four elements of metacognition. The first element is *knowing when you know* (and knowing when you don't know). For readers, it means knowing when they understand and knowing when they do not. The second element is *knowing what you know*. In schema theory, knowing what you know means being able to activate relevant schemata during reading. The third element is *knowing what you need to know*. For readers, it means being able to benefit from knowing the purposes for reading. The fourth factor is *knowing the utility of active intervention*. In reading, this element involves the ability to invoke strategies to improve comprehension.

It is our goal as teachers to help youngsters who are deaf to become conscious of their own reading and writing processes and to use their self-awareness for monitoring and directing their own learning. Metacognition lies within the core of an autonomous and empowered learner. In the next two chapters, I will discuss instructional strategies in reading and writing that can enable children who are deaf to reach this goal.

FIGURE 3–2
Readability Checklists

(Scale is from 1 to 5, with 1 as "low," 3 as "adequate," and 5 as "high.")

Book Title _____

Author   _____

	1	2	3	4	5

Readability Factors Within Texts
Word frequency
Concept density
Level of abstraction
Organization
Cohesiveness
Clarity in presentation of ideas
Format/Design/Typography (e.g., print size, length of line of print, length of paragraph, punctuation, typeface, color)
Use of illustrations
Sentence complexity
Vocabulary difficulty
Literary form and style
Textual structure

Readability Factors Within Readers
Interest
Motivation
Extent of background knowledge
Vocabulary knowledge
Knowledge of text structure
Purpose for the reading

DEVELOPMENT OF WRITING

Two decades ago this section would not have been titled "development of writing." It would perhaps have been called "stages of writing" and the models of writing would have been discussed, models that conceptualized composing as proceeding in linearly sequenced and discrete stages, such as prewriting to writing to rewriting. Or, perhaps, it would have been called "types of writing" in which modes of discourse that conceptualized composing as mastering aspects of narration, description, exposition, and argumentation would have been discussed. Traditional writing paradigms resulted in teaching strategies designed to provide youngsters instruction in skills and rules, practice in mastering techniques, and evaluation based on how error-free finished products were (Hull, 1989; Laine & Schultz, 1985; Shah, 1986). The emphasis on teachers' comments, corrections, and grades on children's completed compositions led researchers to label this view of writing instruction as a writing-as-product approach. "Writing was a skill that one either possessed or did not, a process students experienced through native genius or discovered through trial and error" (Hull, 1989, p. 106).

In the early 1970s, researchers began to ask different questions about writing. Instead of only asking questions about the teaching, evaluation, and development of writing skills they started to ask questions about what individuals think about when they write. Findings from this body of research caused a shift in the ways that writing, writers, and teaching writing were understood.

Current writing-as-process approaches conceptualize writing as a problem-solving process. Prewriting-writing-rewriting are no longer seen as linear and discrete stages. When writers engage in prewriting, their planning, rehearsing, and organizing are interrelated with their writing and revising. Movement between rehearsing, writing, rereading, and revising is ongoing and dynamic. Writers are in a continuous discovery state.

We used to think that writers had only one problem to solve: how can I communicate my ideas? In other words, what words and what grammatical constructions should I use? We now know that writers have many problems to solve. Who is my audience? What style do I want to use? Have I expressed my intent? Will the reader understand my meaning? And so on. The questions are internally generated and help writers to monitor their own progress. Through self-questioning during rehearsing, writing, and revising writers come to understand and clarify their ideas. In a writing-as-process paradigm, editing is viewed as a final step in the composing process. In this view, editing is not equated with revision but rather is a part of revision, when the writer makes adjustments in spelling, punctuation, and other surface mechanics (Britton, Burgess, Martin, McLeod, & Rosen, 1975; Calkins, 1986; Emig, 1971; Graves, 1975, 1983).

Hull (1989) captured the essence of current thought in writing when she wrote that "literacy researchers are learning of late to broaden their notions of writing as a complex cognitive process, of students as possessing immature or incomplete or perhaps flawed representations of that process, of research as the description of process, and of pedagogy as providing instruction on the process as well as occasions to experience it" (p. 113).

Writing Process

In the discussion of language development, syntax, semantics, and use were examined separately to emphasize that these language processes work interdependently within the individual. Literacy development was examined in the same way by pulling apart spoken language, sign language, writing, and reading while recognizing their interrelationships. In order to examine the writing process, each aspect will also be discussed separately. But for the writer, whether emergent or experienced, highly skilled or novice, the process is recursive. It seems as if each researcher has developed his or her own set of terminology to describe the subprocesses. The following terminology will be used here: planning, writing, and revising.

Planning

Planning includes generating ideas for topic and content, organizing, and setting goals (Humes, 1983). Planning for some writers involves prewriting, such as in the form of outlines, notes, or even a rough draft. Planning can also include rehearsal activities such as drawing and conversing with others. And planning often means quiet thinking (Calkins, 1986; Dyson, 1983, 1986; Humes, 1983; Newkirk, 1987). Planning takes place before, during, and after writing.

Writing

Writing has been called drafting, translating, and articulating as well as many other terms. It has been observed that skilled writers recognize that what they put on paper (or computer) is tentative, whether it is a word, sentence, paragraph, or complete piece (Birnbaum, 1982; Flower & Hayes, 1980).

Revising

Revising includes rereading (or reviewing) and rewriting. Revising can mean rereading a word, thinking about several other choices, using a dictionary or thesaurus, crossing it out, trying a new one in its place, rereading it, and so on. Revising can mean rereading a phrase or sentence and then trying out several structures. Revising can mean going back to a paragraph several pages ago, rereading it, and moving it several pages ahead. Revising can mean feeling satisfied with the meaning and style, but going back over the last few sentences to change punctuation or check spelling.

The research on the writing process has focused largely on instructional implications of the theory. In Chapters 4 and 5, I will describe teaching approaches that reflect understanding and respect for the role of the writing process in children's writing development.

Emergent Writing

Children write long before they begin to use conventional print symbols. Their writing development is linked to their spoken and sign language development and to their reading development.

Harste, Woodward, and Burke (1984) identified eight concepts that served to organize the patterns they found in the writing of children between the ages of 3 and 6: (a) organization, (b) intentionality, (c) generativeness, (d) risk-taking, (e) social action, (f) context, (g) text, and (h) demonstrations.

Organization

The first concept is *organization*. Children as young as 3 years old have been found to distinguish between scribbles and drawing and to invest their scribbles with written language meaning (Dyson, 1986). Organizational patterns have also been observed in young children's attention to syntactic, semantic, and pragmatic features in their own early writing (Harste, Woodward, & Burke, 1984; Hoffman & McCully, 1984).

Children's attempts at using graphophonic cues also reflect their efforts at figuring out the organizational principles of writing. Harste, Woodward, and Burke (1984) found that young children use three spelling strategies: the phonemic (spelling the way it sounds), the graphemic (spelling the way it looks), and the morphemic (spelling the way it means). Gentry (1982) found that children move through five stages of spelling development:

❑ precommunicative—using symbols from the alphabet to represent words,

❑ semiphonetic—using letters to represent sounds in words but only providing a partial mapping of all the sounds in a word,

❑ phonetic—sometimes called "invented spelling," the child is using letters to map all the sounds in a word. "Though some of the inventive speller's letter choices do not conform to conventional English spelling for some sounds, the choices are systematic and perceptually correct" (Hoffman & McCully, 1984, p. 195),

❑ transitional—moving from reliance on sounds to represent words to using visual and morphologic features,

❑ correct spelling—using traditional orthography.

Intentionality

According to Harste, Woodward, and Burke (1984), the second concept is *intentionality*. From the time children begin to use scribbles, they appear to invest their written symbols with meaning. In other words, they intend for their scribbles to be viewed as writing.

Generativeness

The third concept is *generativeness*. Young children have been found to arrange and rearrange their written language to create varieties of meanings and forms, and to serve changing needs within the child both to think about meaning and to communicate meaning. Generativeness in language means the ability to create an infinite variety of meanings from a finite set of words and a finite set of rules for combining these words. Generativeness in emergent writing means that the child is able to take a finite set of written symbols and create an infinite variety of meanings.

Risk-Taking

The fourth concept is *risk-taking*. By the time children are 4 years old, they seem more aware of the constraints of "real literacy" and less willing to try something new in their written language. By 5 and 6, they often prefer to produce text with which they feel safe. However, Harste, Woodward, and Burke called this attitude a "learned vulnerability, not something inherent in the literacy process" (p. 140).

Social Action

The fifth concept is *social action*. Harste, Woodward, and Burke observed that children as young as 3 years of age recognized that written language, along with other forms of language, is social as well as personal in nature. "Not only do writers assume there are readers and speakers assume there are listeners, but interaction with real or supposed social others involving all of the expressions of language is an integral part of any instance of the language and language learning process" (p. 145).

Context

The sixth concept is *context*. The young children studied by Harste, Woodward, and Burke demonstrated sensitivity to the importance of the linguistic, situational, and cultural context of their written language. For example, they typically used more "formal" language registers in their written language than in their spoken language.

Text

The seventh concept is *text*. Early in their writing development, children were found to seek unity in their written language and to recognize that the text in their heads, what is called text potential, is not identical to the text they create.

Demonstrations

The eighth concept is *demonstrations*. Harste, Woodward, and Burke found that young children are keen observers of the literacy behaviors of others. The children's writings often contained features they had observed in environmental print, storybooks, the creations of other children, and the writing of parents and teachers.

The research in emergent writing has shown that children begin to explore writing long before they enter school. When we look at the young child engaged in imaginative play, drawing, writing, reading, communicating with others, talking and signing to him or herself, we are witnessing the child's ability to represent reality in thought. As teachers, we need to recognize our students' cognitive potential and language abilities, whether they are preschoolers or high schoolers.

Writing Development Through the School Years

We do not have a very neat and clear picture of how writing develops during the school years against which we can compare the writing of youngsters who are deaf. What the literature provides is a theory about the writing process and implications for instruction. Unlike the literature in language acquisition, no models of writing acquisition are available that could be used to analyze the writing of children who are deaf. The reader might very well ask, "Is that all? Can't you tell me when I can expect my students to use traditional spelling? When will their paragraphs look like paragraphs? When will their stories be one paragraph long? two paragraphs? ten? When will they stop using illustrations? When will their stories conform to story structure? When will 'The End' no longer signal the end? When will they be able to write reports, diaries, letters, essays, thank-you notes, directions, recipes, and all of the other kinds of writing?"

The answer is, at least for now, it depends on the child. And it depends on the learning environment. Do children who are deaf learn to write differently than children who are hearing? Do they have greater difficulties? Is the process harder? Is it less fun? No. At least, it doesn't have to be. The literature is replete with studies and observations of deaf youngsters who are meeting their literacy potentials in writing and in reading (Bensinger, Santomen, & Volpe, 1987; Ciocci & Morrell-Schumann, 1987; Conway, 1985; Ewoldt, 1978, 1985; Manson, 1982; Nower, 1985; Olson, 1987; Staton, 1985; Truax, 1985).

The next two chapters will discuss strategies and activities that have been used successfully with children who are deaf to enable them to develop as writers and readers. Chapter 6 will discuss techniques for monitoring their progress.

RELATIONSHIPS BETWEEN READING
AND WRITING DEVELOPMENT

Whole language principles are based, in part, on the assumption that learning to speak, sign, read, and write are interrelated processes. The precise characteristics of these interrelationships, however, have only recently been explored. This section will examine specifically what is currently known about the relationships between reading and writing.

Reading and writing both involve the construction of meaning through text (Schewe & Froese, 1987; Squire, 1984). Tierney and Pearson (1983) took this view even further by demonstrating how the composing process in writing can be used to understand the reading process. They found that both writers and readers engage in *planning* (goal-setting and knowledge mobilization), *drafting* (refinement of meaning as readers and writers deal with print), *aligning* (assuming of stances and roles in relation to the author or audience), *revising* (interpreting, changing hypotheses, analyzing, modifying purposes), and *monitoring* (conversing with oneself to decide how well one's goals have been met).

Fitzgerald (1989) found that revision specifically draws on similar thought processes during reading and writing because readers and writers are both actively involved in comparing the text (the actual text for readers and the evolving text for writers) to their goals and expectations. When readers and writers experience consonance, they continue reading and writing. When writers experience dissonance, they revise their text. When readers experience dissonance, they revise their understanding, goals, beliefs, or expectations.

Another parallel between reading and writing observed by some researchers is that achievement levels in reading and writing seem to be related. In other words, better readers tend to be better writers, although this pattern does not hold true for all children (Shanahan, 1980; Stotsky, 1983; Tierney & Leys, 1986). It has been suggested by some investigators that reading and writing are reciprocal processes that are mutually reinforcing. Others claim that reading influences writing development, while yet others believe writing influences reading development (however the movement of influence does not work in reverse according to these two viewpoints). Smith (1983) argued that everyone who becomes a competent writer "must read like a writer in order to learn how to write like a writer. There is no other way in which the intricate complexity of a writer's knowledge can be acquired" (p. 562).

In their study of three theoretical models of the reading-writing relationship, Shanahan and Lomax (1986) found that second and fifth grade children used both their reading knowledge in writing and their writing knowledge in reading, and that in general the children used more reading information in writing than vice versa. However, they noted that the children in their study may not have had much opportunity to write and that in an instructional program that emphasized writing, writing knowledge might exert more influence on reading than they found.

Dobson (1989) studied the emergent literacy of kindergarten and first-grade children and found that they transferred strategies learned in writing to reading, and reading to writing. He concluded that "reading and writing are mutually supportive and connected at each step to learners' knowledge of the system of written language and how it works" (p. 100). Mason, Peterman, Powell, and Kerr (1989) found support for the conclusion that at early reading levels, writing activity affects reading while at higher reading levels, reading affects writing.

By focusing on the parallels between reading and writing, it is tempting to ignore the differences. Yet as a number of authors have pointed out, while reading development and writing development are closely related, they are individual processes and important differences exist between them (Langer & Applebee, 1986; Noyce & Christie, 1989). Rosenblatt (1989) observed that the "transaction that starts with a text produced by someone else is not the same as a transaction that starts with the individual facing a blank page" (p. 171). She viewed cross-fertilization as possible but not automatic without instruction that encouraged youngsters to gain metalinguistic insights into their own reading and writing processes.

FINAL COMMENTS

Literacy development involves reading development and writing development. The relationship between the development of face-to-face language and the development of literacy in children who are deaf is not completely clear, but we do know a great deal more today than we did even a decade ago. Most significantly, we know that deaf children have the cognitive ability to become proficient readers and expressive writers, and that we do not have to wait for some arbitrary level of language development prior to initiating reading and writing instruction. Indeed, we know that literacy and language are interrelated and that learning environments which encourage the development of literacy also encourage the development of face-to-face language, and vice versa. We also know that children do not wait for us to teach them to read and write; they start to understand and use written symbols long before they come to school.

This chapter discussed what is currently known about the reading process and the writing process in children who are deaf. The next chapter will contain models, methods, and strategies for encouraging and enhancing the development of reading and writing in deaf children.

SUGGESTED READINGS

Garton, A., & Pratt, C. (1989). *Learning to Be Literate: The Development of Spoken and Written Language*. Oxford, England: Basil Blackwell.

Harste, J., Woodward, V.A., & Burke, C.L. (1984). *Language Stories and Literacy Lessons*. Portsmouth, NH: Heinemann.

Hickman, J., & Cullinan, B.E. (1989). *Children's Literature in the Classroom: Weaving Charlotte's Web*. Needham Heights, MA: Christopher-Gordon.

Mason, J.M. (1989). *Reading and Writing Connections*. Boston: Allyn and Bacon.

Morrow, L.M. (1989). *Literacy Development in the Early Years: Helping Children Read and Write*. Englewood Cliffs, NJ: Prentice-Hall.

Approaches to Promote Reading and Writing Development

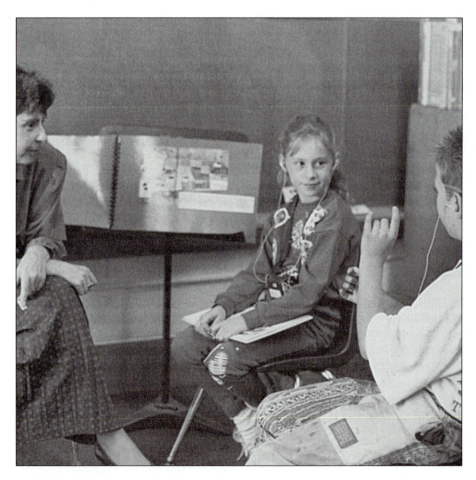

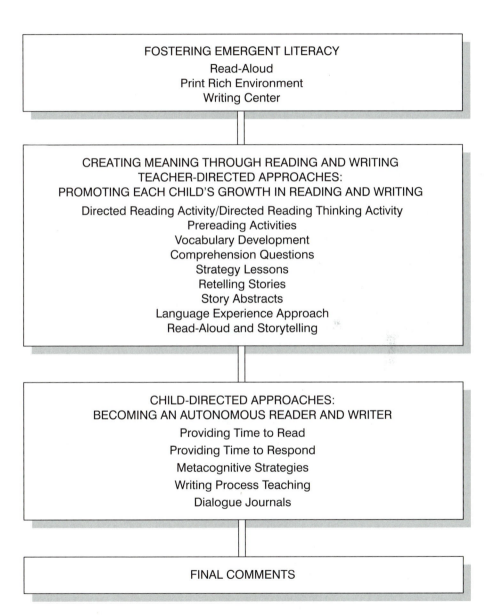

FOSTERING EMERGENT LITERACY
Read-Aloud
Print Rich Environment
Writing Center

CREATING MEANING THROUGH READING AND WRITING
TEACHER-DIRECTED APPROACHES:
PROMOTING EACH CHILD'S GROWTH IN READING AND WRITING
Directed Reading Activity/Directed Reading Thinking Activity
Prereading Activities
Vocabulary Development
Comprehension Questions
Strategy Lessons
Retelling Stories
Story Abstracts
Language Experience Approach
Read-Aloud and Storytelling

CHILD-DIRECTED APPROACHES:
BECOMING AN AUTONOMOUS READER AND WRITER
Providing Time to Read
Providing Time to Respond
Metacognitive Strategies
Writing Process Teaching
Dialogue Journals

FINAL COMMENTS

Most teachers own crates of files or index boxes full of teaching ideas gathered from education journals and magazines, workshops, books, and other teachers. The goal of this chapter is not to randomly add to this array of ideas. The goal is to offer suggestions for teaching activities that can form the core of a literacy program for children who are deaf. Whenever such information is available in the published literature, I have included these descriptions of actual classroom applications or cited the research on the strategy as it was used with children who are deaf.

Chapter 3 provided a theoretical framework of literacy development. This chapter will link theory with practice. I encourage readers to critically scrutinize these ideas and to ask at least three questions about each suggestion. Is this strategy grounded on sound theoretical principles? Has this strategy ever been used successfully with children similar to the ones you teach? Will you be willing to work through the problems if this strategy doesn't work smoothly at first?

FOSTERING EMERGENT LITERACY

Several components of an early childhood curriculum seem to be central for supporting children's explorations into reading and writing. Parents and teachers have always known that these particular activities are valuable to young children. The last several years, however, have given us empirical evidence that when young children are provided daily opportunities to interact with print, they develop complex notions of reading and writing well before they are engaged in formal instruction.

Read-Aloud

If parents and teachers of deaf children were only able to consistently carry out one activity every day, I would strongly suggest that it be read-aloud. As Trelease (1989) pointed out, "A large part of the educational research and practice of the last twenty years confirms conclusively that the best way to raise a reader is to read to that child—in the home and in the classroom" (p. xiv).

Read-aloud helps to develop children's story schema, background knowledge, and awareness of written language conventions. Read-aloud provides opportunities for meaningful conversations between teachers and children, and parents and children. Children who are read to regularly are likely to develop an interest in reading and love of stories (Morrow & Weinstein, 1982; Wells, 1982).

Teachers of children who are deaf are sometimes reluctant to read-aloud because they believe their students' language development levels are not advanced enough to enable them to understand the stories being read. This concern is not very different from that of parents of hearing infants and toddlers. Trelease (1989) responded to the question, "How old must the child be before you start reading to him?" by asking one of his own:

> "When did you start talking to your child? Did you wait until he was six months old?" "We started talking to him the day he was born," parents respond proudly. "And what language did your child speak the day he was born? English? Japanese? Italian?" They're about to say English when a puzzled look comes over their faces as they realize the child didn't speak any language yet (pp. 19–20).

If we view reading and read-aloud as a milieu for creating readers then we can begin read-aloud with children who are deaf long before they can understand every word and concept in the stories we read. We all can envision a classroom in which children are conversed with and read to because that is precisely the language-rich environment they need.

Some research has been conducted on the "how-to's" of read-aloud. One of the best sources on the subject is Trelease's *The New Read-Aloud Handbook* (1989), although a number of authors have written about read-aloud. It has been suggested that teachers and parents make read-aloud part of a routine and carefully consider the children's attention spans. For most young children who are deaf, 5 minutes of watching or listening is a *long* time. It has also been suggested that well-written, enjoyable stories with a variety of themes be chosen. Teachers and parents are also encouraged to converse with children about the stories being read, before and after reading them (Butler, 1980; Rasinski & Fredericks, 1990). And reading the same story again and again over time is a time-honored and now research-proven activity (Martinez & Roser, 1985; Yaden, 1988).

Prescribing a set of behaviors for read-aloud is probably not necessary. Long before researchers decided that it was a great idea, parents read aloud to their children. Some evidence suggests that teachers and parents already know how to read to children effectively. Altwerger, Diehl-Faxon, and Dockstader-Anderson (1985) found that mothers match their read-aloud to the experiential, linguistic, and literacy background of their children by adapting, extending, clarifying, and sometimes disregarding the print. The researchers observed that "the mother begins to relinquish her role as text constructor for her child, and moves to a closer reading of the print as she perceives the child better able to bear the responsibility alone" (p. 483).

One of the few studies on read-aloud with hearing impaired children was conducted by Rogers (1989). The 5- to 9-year-old children in this study were read to four nights each week in their dormitory rooms at bedtime, with several parents continuing the read-aloud during weekends and vacations. Rogers reported positive results in the children's language development, ability to converse about stories, and comprehension.

Shared Book Experience

Read-aloud traditionally has taken two forms. The school form has been *one teacher-group of children*. The home form is *one parent-one child*. By combining features of school and home, two new forms of read-aloud are currently being suggested to augment the traditional school form.

The first form, *one-to-one* story reading in school between the teacher and one child, can provide the child with an enriching experience. However, demands on the teacher's time may make this an impractical suggestion in many classrooms of children who are deaf. The research to support this activity has been accomplished with a team of research assistants individually assigned to one child each (Morrow, 1987, 1988).

The second form is story reading with *big books*. This form is modeled on lap reading between parent and child in which the open book is viewed by both parent and child simultaneously, with the parent sometimes tracking the actual words with his or her finger. By using enlarged texts called big books (or using the regular book with a group of no more than three children sitting close enough to the teacher to see the print), the teacher can provide a lap reading experience to a group of children (Brown, Cromer, & Weinberg, 1986; Combs, 1987; Holdaway, 1979, 1982; Slaughter, 1983; Strickland & Morrow, 1990; Trachtenburg & Ferruggia, 1989). For the teacher who is signing, the book can be placed on an easel or one of the children can hold the book.

In the early 1980s, a number of suggestions were offered to teachers for making their own big books, such as cutting out the pictures and handwriting the text on large sheets of paper or using overhead transparencies for each page. Big books are currently available commercially and many of them are accompanied by regular-sized copies for classroom libraries.

Print Rich Environment

A classroom environment that implicitly communicates the message that *literacy is valued here* can exert a powerful influence on early literacy development. Strickland and Morrow (1989) have observed that "purposefully arranging the physical setting to develop literacy can wield an active and pervasive influence on the activities and attitudes of teachers as well as on those of the children in their classrooms" (p. 178).

One way to create a print rich environment is through the use of *environmental print*. Labeling objects in the classroom, creating charts of classroom routines and rules, and using print in bulletin boards are just a few ways that teachers can meaningfully display print in the classroom.

A *library center* is another essential part of a print rich classroom environment. It has been suggested that the library center be comfortable, obvious, and inviting. It should afford privacy and display books attractively.

If possible, the library center should contain variety in terms of reading levels, topics, and genre. And children should be given time to use the library center (Morrow & Weinstein, 1982; Strickland & Morrow, 1988).

An excellent resource on the topic of print rich environment is Loughlin and Martin's *Supporting Literacy: Developing Effective Learning Environments* (1987). In this text, the authors provide numerous suggestions for arranging the physical environment of classrooms to stimulate literacy behaviors.

Writing Center

Writing centers are a new idea in preschool and kindergarten classrooms. In a writing center, the teacher creates a special table where children can sit and select from paper in an array of sizes and colors, pens, pencils, felt-tipped markers, and crayons. Most important, the writing center is a place where children can choose what to do with these materials. It has been observed that most young children start out doing a great deal of drawing at these centers but gradually and spontaneously combine scribbling and then writing with their drawing (Crowell, Kawakami, & Wong, 1986; Heald-Taylor, 1984; Noyce & Christie, 1989; Strickland & Morrow, 1988).

Ewoldt (1987) found significant growth in the writing of 3- to 7-year-old deaf children who were given opportunities to engage in self-selected reading and writing over a three-year period. Manson (1982), a teacher in the Ewoldt study, observed that "one of the advantages that became apparent as the project continued was that freedom of expression in drawing and/or writing allowed proficiencies to emerge individually while simultaneously exposing the students to additional print concepts as they emerged for classmates" (p. 36).

CREATING MEANING THROUGH
READING AND WRITING

The core activities discussed in this section are important in helping to build the deaf child's content, textual, and surface structure schemata for reading and writing. While some of the activities are clearly more appropriate for younger children, and some only appropriate for older youngsters, most teachers could incorporate the majority of these activities into their reading and writing instruction with deaf youngsters from grades 1 through 12.

The following sections, teacher-directed approaches and child-directed approaches, highlight the differences between approaches in which the teacher actively guides the children and approaches in which the teacher paves the way for the children.

TEACHER-DIRECTED APPROACHES: PROMOTING EACH CHILD'S GROWTH IN READING AND WRITING

Directed Reading Activity/Directed Reading Thinking Activity

The Directed Reading Activity (DRA) was first suggested by Betts (1946). It was adapted as the basic lesson format by most basal reading series in preference to the older and questionable round-robin format. With some changes and adjustments over the past 40 years, the DRA is still widely recommended as a format for daily reading instruction. The DRA includes the following steps:

1. *Concept development.* This step is sometimes called prereading activities, preparation, and background building (Finn, 1990; Lapp, Flood, and Gleckman, 1982; Noyce & Christie, 1989; Pieronek, 1979; Spiegel, 1981). In this step, the teacher is trying to activate and build the deaf child's content schema so that new information in the text will connect to the child's prior information. This step also includes the presentation and teaching of new vocabulary. Strategies for building background knowledge are discussed in the section on Prereading Activities, and strategies for building vocabulary are discussed in the section on Vocabulary Development.

2. *Sight vocabulary.* In this step, the teacher introduces words for the youngsters to learn to recognize immediately as a whole. Sight vocabulary involves learning to recognize in print words one already knows in speech or sign. Building a child's sight vocabulary with 6 to 8 words daily that the child immediately encounters in text is considered to be a particularly critical activity for youngsters who are deaf since other word identification strategies, such as phonic analysis, may not prove to be particularly useful.

3. *Guided reading.* In this step, the teacher divides the story or chapter into segments for silent reading. For young children who are deaf a segment might be one sentence or one paragraph. For older children a segment is usually one or two pages, and sometimes several pages. If the youngsters can read the whole story or chapter with no guidance from the teacher, the DRA is probably not the most appropriate strategy to be using. For each segment, the teacher sets a purpose, asks the children to read the segment silently, encourages the children to discuss the purpose-setting question and several other comprehension questions, and asks each child to orally or in sign reread relevant sentences or paragraphs to clarify answers.

    a. *Purpose setting.* In this part of the guided reading step, the teacher sets a purpose, either through a question (such as "What will happen to Jennifer when she meets the old woman?") or through a statement (such as "Find out why the old woman has been hiding").

   b.   *Silent reading*. At this time, the children are asked to silently read the segment. Some children will subvocalize or sign to themselves. Silent reading and reading aloud, in voice or sign, serve different purposes. For most children, comprehension is best achieved through silent reading (Holmes, 1985; Taylor & Connor, 1982). Indeed, since adult fluent readers rarely read aloud, it should make us wonder why silent reading in school should seem so strange. Furthermore, in classrooms of severely or profoundly deaf children it is not possible to both read and watch at the same time, so we find children reading aloud to an audience of one, the teacher, or perhaps worse, children reading very little because most of their time is spent watching the reader. There is a place for purposeful oral or sign rereading of a passage, which will be discussed shortly.

   c.   *Questions*. When the children have completed reading the segment silently, their attention is drawn back to the purpose previously set by the teacher. The teacher then asks several additional questions. The children's answers often lead to purposeful oral or sign rereading.

   d.   *Purposeful oral or sign rereading*. When the child has answered a question correctly or incorrectly, the teacher can ask, "What part of the story made you think of that answer. Please read it to all of us." Thus, the rereading has a purpose. For the child, the purpose is to share more information about an answer. For the teacher, the purpose can be to identify problems related to the child's silent reading, to help the child develop fluency, or to encourage the child's voice or sign expression.

   The questions and purposeful rereading in voice or sign can provide the teacher with diagnostic information regarding the children's reading abilities. This information can then be used to design strategy lessons that can be taught as minilessons during the DRA or at another time during the day. Strategy lessons will be discussed in greater depth later in this chapter.

   4.   *Discussion*. When the cycle of purpose setting, silent reading, questions, and purposeful rereading is complete, global questions are asked to stimulate discussion about the central story line and to engage the children in higher-order thinking.

   5.   *Skills development*. Traditionally, skill-building activities have involved worksheets on sight vocabulary, word meaning, phonic analysis, structural analysis, and other skills considered to be essential for fluent reading. One purpose is for the student to practice a skill that was needed in the story or segment of the story that he or she just finished reading with the teacher. The other purpose is to provide seatwork for one group of children while the teacher works with another group.

6. *Enrichment.* In this step, the teacher creates opportunities for the children to extend their comprehension through activities such as field trips, dramatizations, art projects, writing, and other reading.

The Directed Reading Thinking Activity (DRTA) was developed by Stauffer (1969). The difference between the DRA and DRTA is that in a DRTA, the teacher helps students to set their own purposes for reading by encouraging them to make predictions. After silent reading the teacher uses questions to direct the youngsters back to their predictions for confirmation, modification, and creation of new predictions for the upcoming passage.

Two types of questions are typically asked in a DRTA. The first are questions requiring speculation and prediction such as "What do you think?" "Why do you think so?" and "Can you prove it?" The second are questions requiring support for conclusions such as "What makes you think that?" "Why?" and "How do you know that?" (Haggard, 1988; Widomski, 1983). Some evidence suggests that the DRTA results in better comprehension and recall of stories than the DRA (Marshall, 1984). The kinds of questions asked in a DRTA encourage higher-order thinking in children who are deaf.

Prereading Activities

Chapter 3 discussed the clear connection between background knowledge and reading comprehension. The goals of prereading activities are to activate and build background knowledge and to establish motivation for reading the text. Which kind of activity the teacher chooses and the amount of time allotted to the prereading activity depend largely on the extent to which the students are already familiar with the topic.

The 10-Minute Prereading Discussion

In a traditional Directed Reading Activity or Directed Reading Thinking Activity, prereading involves two steps. First, the students are engaged in a brief discussion about the story topic through questions such as "Do you have a pet at home?" for a story about a puppy who misses its brothers and sisters after being adopted. Second, the youngsters are directed to look at the title and picture on the first page and asked what they think the story will be about.

Some researchers have suggested that teachers should ask questions designed to evoke deep-level thinking about the story topic. Hansen (1981) developed an activity in which the teacher selects three important ideas from a story and introduces them one at a time by first, asking a question that relates the child's possible previous experience to an event in the story and second, asking the children to predict something similar that might happen in the story they will read.

Purpose-setting questions can also be used to activate the reader's pertinent knowledge of a topic, although these questions cannot build knowledge the reader does not have. Purpose-setting questions that focus on the major elements of a passage have been found to be considerably more effective than questions dealing with story details (Blanton, Wood, & Moorman, 1990; Hawes & Schell, 1987; Rowe & Rayford, 1987).

The 10-minute prereading discussion is probably the easiest and most efficient way to activate background knowledge with students who are deaf. However, it is simply too brief for building new knowledge.

Reconciled Reading Lesson

Reutzel (1985a) noticed that some of the best ideas for prereading activities were those suggested for enrichment in the teacher's manuals of basal reading series. He proposed that an enrichment activity should be the first step instead of the last step in a DRA or DRTA. In a reconciled reading lesson, activities such as performing a play, writing a recipe, and viewing a film are conducted before rather than after reading the story. Furthermore, the youngsters are engaged in a full discussion of the story prior to reading.

In their study of 45 children in grades 1 through 5, Prince and Mancus (1987) found strong support for the finding that reconciled reading lessons improved story comprehension. Because of the amount of time needed for a reconciled reading lesson, it would seem to be most appropriately used when the youngsters are getting ready to read material, such as a novel, which will take at least two weeks to complete.

Previews

A *preview* is a summary of text material that is read in advance of the full text. Most of the research on previews has specifically related to previews of expository text, which will be discussed in Chapter 5. However, there is some support for the use of previews with narrative text. Graves, Cooke, and Laberge (1983) found that previews significantly improved the comprehension and recall of the seventh and eighth graders in their study, and that the students reported they liked the previews and found them useful. It should be noted that the previews used in this study did not take the form of brief, introductory statements. Rather they were designed to seriously engage the students in the upcoming passages and to tell the students a great deal about the stories. Previews began with a series of short questions and statements that were followed first by a story synopsis, then by an identification of each character, and finally by a definition of several difficult words.

Previews would seem to be a particularly valuable strategy for deaf children preparing to read material in which they may be unfamiliar with the text structure. For example, one teacher developed a preview for *The Diary of Anne Frank* which one of the deaf students in her high school resource room was getting ready to read in his mainstream classroom. He had not previously read a book written as a diary and, furthermore, was not completely familiar with the historical context of the book. In the preview, the teacher included information about the author, the other key individuals in the book, and background information on the period during which Anne Frank kept her diary. This preview enabled the youngster to participate more fully in the class discussions and to gain greater appreciation of the book.

Semantic Mapping in Prereading

Semantic mapping is "a categorical structuring of information in graphic form" (Heimlich & Pittelman, 1986, p. 1). Semantic mapping has most commonly been used for vocabulary development, prereading, postreading, and as a study skill technique. As a prereading activity, the teacher writes a central story concept on the board and circles it. Lines are drawn to radiate from the circle. These lines are sometimes called web strands. From each line a new circle is drawn within which the teacher writes a question about the story. The youngsters are encouraged to make predictions that are written, circled, and connected by lines to the questions (Freedman & Reynolds, 1980; Sinatra, Stahl-Gemake, & Berg, 1984; Spiegel, 1981).

Semantic mapping is a relatively quick way to activate interest in an upcoming story and to encourage thinking that goes beyond the literal level. Teachers using this strategy with children who are deaf have noted that not only do the predictions help the children to become interactive readers but the semantic map itself becomes a focal point throughout the reading for seeing how the story components fit together.

ReQuest

In the ReQuest procedure (Manzo, 1969; Spiegel, 1981), the students read the title and first sentence of a story, and look at the picture. They then ask the teacher anything they want to know about the title, sentence, and picture. When the teacher finishes answering all of their questions, the procedure is repeated for the second sentence. If the students run out of questions to ask, the teacher can suggest questions. Teacher questions not only add to the students' understanding of the upcoming passage but they also serve as a model for good questions. After all the questions are answered, the teacher asks the students what they think will happen in the passage. At that point, the youngsters read the passage silently.

Larking (1984) found that after two months of using this Reciprocal Questioning procedure, the seventh-grade students in his study asked significantly more inferential and evaluative questions, and their reading comprehension scores improved significantly. Larking further found a positive relationship between reading comprehension scores and the number of higher-order questions the youngsters asked.

For youngsters who are deaf, an added benefit of the ReQuest procedure is that it encourages language development in the area of asking questions, including all types of *wh-* questions and *yes/no* questions.

Experiential Activity

Several of the previously discussed activities are based on the assumption that children who are deaf are able to learn new information during prereading instruction that they can apply toward understanding story content when the information is presented didactically. However, many young children need to have personal experience about a topic in order to build their knowledge. For example, with only a brief prereading discussion about the rules of lacrosse, older youngsters might be able to understand a story in which this game plays a crucial role. But younger children might need to engage in mock-playing lacrosse.

It is an education maxim that learning proceeds from the concrete to the abstract. This maxim relates to prereading activities in that prior experience has been found to exert a more powerful effect on comprehension than prereading instruction, particularly with younger individuals (Roberts, 1988). For some story topics, experiential activities can be the most effective way to build background knowledge.

Needless to say, experiential activities can be very time-consuming, and teachers need to be careful in balancing actual reading time with other activities during the reading instruction period. Some teachers of deaf students have solved this problem by carrying out experiential activities during other class times. This works particularly well for teachers who are "theming." They can involve the children in experiential activities during art, science, social studies, or other content periods because the same topic is being explored in all these subject areas.

Writing Before Reading

It has been suggested that writing before reading can activate the child's content and textual schemata as well as reinforce the connection between reading and writing. Several kinds of writing activities have been found to be particularly worthwhile.

In a *Personal Involvement* writing activity, the youngsters are given a scenario and asked to write a story as if they are a character in the scenario. The teacher bases the scenario on major concepts in the actual story the youngsters will read and designs the scenario to encourage the youngsters to become personally involved in the story's plot and characters (Noyce & Christie, 1989). For example, Marino, Gould, and Haas (1985) gave the following writing assignment to a group of fourth graders:

> Pretend you are a young person in 1845. You are a pioneer heading for the Oregon country. You and your family have stopped to make camp for the night on the Snake River when you meet a group of young orphans. The oldest is a 13-year-old boy who tells you of his determination to carry on with his father's plan to take the family to Oregon. John, you learn, is a very brave and clever boy who has just saved his sister from drowning. Write a letter home to your grandparents describing this boy and the story he has told you. (p. 204)

After writing their stories, the youngsters were given the actual story to read and tested on their recall one day later. They demonstrated significantly better recall than a control group of youngsters who had been asked to write a prereading story on a non-text-related topic.

Similar to Personal Involvement is an activity called *Plausible Stories* developed by Blanchard (1988). In this activity, the teacher creates a word list that reflects the content of an upcoming story. The youngsters are asked to write a story using the word list as a guide. The youngsters then share their stories as a group, explain their predictions for the upcoming story, and discuss how they used the words from the list in their own stories.

Another writing before reading activity is called *Story Impressions*. Story impressions are story fragments written as clue words linked in the same order as the actual events occur in the story. The youngsters create a written story guess which is supposed to represent their hypothesis regarding the structure and content of the story they will read. Denner, McGinley, and Brown (1989) gave the following Story Impressions to a group of second graders:

> Ground hog
>
> Frightened by dog
>
> Popped into hole
>
> Asleep
>
> Flood
>
> High rock—safety
>
> Puppy dog
>
> Fright
>
> Stayed together
>
> Not enemies
>
> One year later
>
> Big fierce dog
>
> Wagged tail
>
> Old friends (p. 323)

The children who engaged in the story impressions activity prior to reading the actual story demonstrated better comprehension than a control group of children who only read the story.

Brainwriting is a writing before reading activity suggested by Noyce and Christie (1989). In a Brainwriting activity, the teacher gives small groups of students a topic such as "What is popularity?" The students individually write as many ideas as possible and then exchange lists and add ideas to the lists of others. In each small group, the students select and combine ideas to create a final list which the group leader reads to the class. After reading the story, the students discuss how their ideas compared to the ideas in the actual story.

"Writing before reading" activities are particularly appealing to teachers of youngsters who are deaf because first, the children have direct experience with linking writing and reading, and second, much of the time involved in the activity can be accomplished outside of the reading period, such as during language, thus leaving time for actual reading during the reading period.

Vocabulary Development

A direct relationship has been found between vocabulary knowledge and reading comprehension. However, the relationship between vocabulary instruction and reading comprehension is tenuous (M. Graves, 1986; Mezynski, 1983; Roser & Juel, 1982; Ruddell, 1986; Stahl & Fairbanks, 1986). The implication seems to be that while vocabulary knowledge is critical to reading comprehension, we do not always teach new vocabulary in ways that enable children to develop or use deep-level word concepts.

One of the problems faced in discussing vocabulary development is defining what is meant by "new" words. M. Graves (1986) identified six word-learning tasks to distinguish between levels of the child's current word knowledge. One task is learning to read known words (referred to as sight vocabulary in a previous section). The other tasks are learning new meanings for known words, clarifying and enriching the meanings of known words, learning new labels for known concepts, learning words that represent new and difficult concepts, and moving words from the youngster's receptive vocabulary to productive vocabulary.

The most common approaches to vocabulary instruction have involved *definitions, context,* or a *combination* of the two (Herman & Dole, 1988; Kolich, 1988; Nagy, 1988; Stahl, 1985). Stahl (1985) defined definitional knowledge as "the knowledge of the relations (synonymic, superordinate, subordinate, etc.) between a word and other known words, as in a dictionary definition" (p. 17). In the definition approach to teaching vocabulary, students typically learn definitions and synonyms.

Stahl defined contextual knowledge as "knowledge of a core concept and how that concept is realized in different contexts" (p. 17). In the context approach, students figure out the meanings of new words through context clues within individual sentences or longer passages.

A combination approach involves providing a definition after the word has been read in context or providing a context after a definition has been obtained.

Herman and Dole (1988) noted that these common approaches can be inadequate for developing underlying concepts related to a word. To help youngsters understand a new concept and its relation to similar concepts, they suggested a *conceptual approach*. In a conceptual approach, the new word is not only defined but characteristics of its definition are compared to characteristics of concepts already familiar to the children.

Three qualities of effective vocabulary instruction have been identified: *integration*, *repetition*, and *meaningful use* (Graves & Prenn, 1986; McKeown, Beck, Omanson, & Pople, 1985; Nagy, 1988; Roser & Juel, 1982; Stahl, 1986; Stahl & Fairbanks, 1986; Thelen, 1986). Integration involves relating new words to the child's background knowledge. Repetition involves providing the child more than one encounter with the meanings and uses of new words. Meaningful use involves developing rich conceptual frameworks for new words and providing opportunities for the youngster to encounter new words in real text.

Definition-Based Approaches

Definition-based approaches commonly take two forms. In one form, the youngsters are asked to look up the definitions of a list of words in the dictionary, copy them, and write a sentence for each word. In the other form, the teacher briefly discusses the meaning of the new words in an upcoming reading selection. Often, these two approaches are followed by worksheets in which words and definitions are manipulated through crossword puzzles, columns to be matched by drawing a line from the word to its definition, or with cloze sentences. Studies have shown that definition-based approaches can be effective when ample time is spent in teacher-student discussion about the new vocabulary (Duffelmeyer, 1985; Eeds & Cockrum, 1985; Vaughan, Castle, Gilbert, & Love, 1982).

For youngsters who are deaf, opportunities to discuss word meanings provide a milieu for language development not only in the area of vocabulary but also in the areas of conversation and pragmatics. However, looking up lists and lists of words in a dictionary, writing their definitions, and creating isolated sentences for each word is usually tedious for the child and is not likely to result in significant word learning. Furthermore, dictionary definitions are often written in complicated sentence structures that children who are deaf have difficulty understanding, and the definitions themselves often include words that are unfamiliar to the children.

Context-Based Approaches

A number of issues surround the power of context-based approaches for teaching vocabulary. One issue is the connection between direct instruction and context-based learning. It has been found that direct instruction, whether through a definition-based approach or concept-based approach, is more effective when combined with context. In other words, youngsters ultimately need to encounter a word in context to develop a full sense of its meaning (Gipe, 1980; Gipe & Arnold, 1979). This issue may help explain why youngsters who are deaf often have difficulty remembering the meaning of words they have been taught. Teaching the meaning is important but not sufficient.

A second issue is the probability that new words can be learned through context. Obviously, when context is explicit, it is more likely that youngsters will be able to derive the meaning of a new word. Nevertheless, even when context is not particularly supportive, it has been found that youngsters will acquire some aspects of a word's meaning but often not complete enough to write a definition or choose a synonym. With further exposures to the word in various contexts, more complete understanding of the word's meaning usually takes place (Jenkins, Stein, & Wysocki, 1984; Moore, 1987; Nagy, Herman, & Anderson, 1985; Schatz & Baldwin, 1986). This issue serves to remind us that one or two encounters with a word is simply not enough to build full understanding.

Based on their own study of eighth graders' ability to develop word knowledge from context as well as their review of the literature, Nagy, Herman, and Anderson (1985) concluded that "incidental learning from context accounts for a substantial proportion of the vocabulary growth that occurs during the school years" (p. 233).

A third issue is what I call the reality issue. In reality, the teacher cannot teach all of the new words the students will encounter in every reading selection. By necessity, deaf students will need to figure out the meanings of many words through context. As Nagy (1988) pointed out, "Most growth in vocabulary knowledge must necessarily come through reading. There is no way that vocabulary instruction alone can provide students with enough experiences with enough words to produce both the depth and breadth of vocabulary knowledge that they need to attain" (p. 32). Nagy suggested that teachers find a balance between explicit vocabulary instruction and incidental learning through context. He offered four criteria in choosing words for explicit instruction:

1. Conceptually difficult words that are not part of the youngster's common experiences.
2. Words with related meanings or that all relate to a single topic.
3. Words that are important to understanding the passage or are important to the language in general.
4. Words the teacher wants the students to incorporate into their writing, speaking, or signing vocabularies.

It has been suggested that youngsters be taught strategies for using context. Ryder (1986) described an instructional approach that took into consideration that learning vocabulary through context is an ability that develops over time. In stage one, the teacher shows the youngsters how pictures can be used as clues to unknown words within individual sentences. In stage two, the teacher presents sentences that offer increasingly less direct support for the unknown word's meaning. In stage three, the teacher demonstrates the kinds of clues available within whole paragraphs.

Ultimately, the deaf child's ability to learn new meanings from context depends on the amount of experience the child has with actual reading. As Nagy (1988) pointed out, "The single most important thing a teacher can do to promote vocabulary growth is to increase students' volume of reading" (p. 38).

Concept-Based Approaches

Concept-based approaches are grounded on the assumption that new knowledge is gained from finding new relationships in old knowledge and from relating new information to old knowledge.

Semantic Mapping for Vocabulary Development   In semantic mapping for vocabulary development, the teacher starts by writing a word that represents a key concept. The youngsters are asked to think of words that relate to the key word. These words are grouped around the key word in categories, either pre-set by the teacher or created by the youngsters. The teacher then suggests new words and encourages a discussion about where these words might fit into the map (Heimlich & Pittelman, 1986; Johnson & Pearson, 1984; Johnson, Pittelman, & Heimlich, 1986). Figures 4–1 and 4–2 represent two different vocabulary semantic maps developed in classrooms of children who are deaf.

FIGURE 4–1
Semantic Map for Vocabulary Development: Dogs

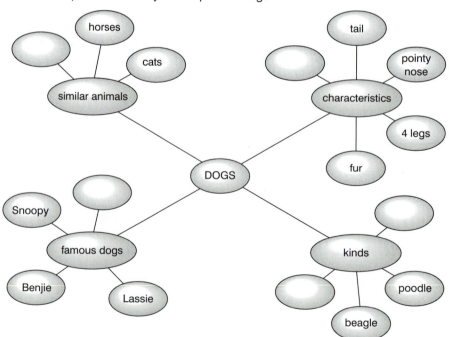

FIGURE 4–2

Semantic Map for Vocabulary Development

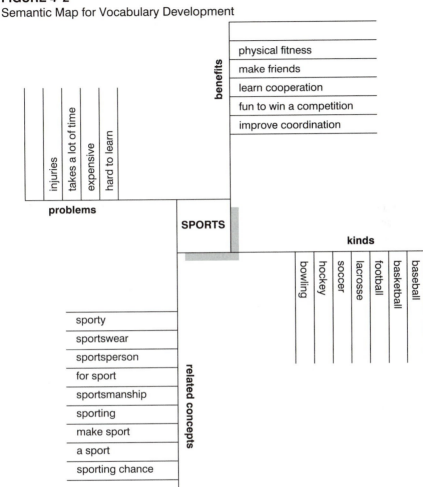

Two aspects of semantic mapping seem to account for much of its power as a teaching strategy. The first aspect is that the map provides a visual display of the relationships between concepts in a key word. The second aspect is that it involves intense discussion which in turn encourages active thinking. As Stahl and Vancil (1986) noted, "It is this active thinking that leads to effective vocabulary learning" (p. 66).

In one variation of the semantic map approach, definitions are combined with mapping. In this approach, called a *word map*, the map becomes a visual display of the definition. The word is placed in the center of the map and three questions form the three categories surrounding the word: What is it? What is it like? What are some examples? (Schwartz & Raphael, 1985).

Semantic Feature Analysis   In a *semantic feature analysis,* the teacher chooses a word or phrase that represents a major topic or category about which the students will read. In a column, the teacher lists some words related to the topic. In a row, the teacher lists some features shared by some of the words already listed in the column. At the intersection of row and column, the teacher asks the students to put a plus (+) if the word possesses the feature and a minus (-) if the word does not possess the feature (or a Likert-type scale from 0 to 5 can be used). The students are also asked to add words to the column and features to the row. Student discussion is as critical to the semantic feature analysis as it is to the semantic mapping strategy, particularly discussion that focuses on the students' reasoning (Anders & Bos, 1986; Johnson & Pearson, 1984). An example of a semantic feature analysis is provided in Figure 4–3. This semantic feature analysis was developed by an upper elementary reading group. One of the students in the group was deaf. The group had been reading a story where the characters were playing in a school orchestra. The semantic feature analysis helped the children to get a clearer idea of musical instruments, which the teacher felt was an important concept in the story.

In semantic mapping, the discussion is generally quite congenial because all ideas can be accommodated in the map. But in semantic feature analysis the youngsters have to come to a consensus, so the discussion tends to involve pragmatic skills such as persuading, disagreeing, expressing opinions, and suggesting.

Concept Attainment Model   When using the *concept attainment model,* the teacher begins by presenting examples and nonexamples of a key word. The teacher then encourages the youngsters to identify critical or relevant attributes of the concept, in other words the attributes or characteristics

FIGURE 4–3
Semantic Feature Analysis: Musical Instruments

	strings	blow into	hit	pluck	press
harp	+	–	–	+	–
violin	+	–	–	+	+
piano	+	–	–	–	+
clarinet	–	+	–	–	+
drum	–	–	+	–	–
flute	–	+	–	–	+
tamborine	–	–	+	–	–

important to the meaning of the word. The youngsters are encouraged to separate the relevant attributes from the irrelevant attributes. The teacher can then ask the youngsters for subordinate terms (examples of the concept), superordinate terms (more general concepts), and coordinate terms (concepts that share some of the same attributes as the targeted concept). Or the teacher can ask for further examples and nonexamples of the key word (McNeil, 1987; Wixson, 1986).

The concept attainment model is unique in that it encourages the child who is deaf to think about how aspects of a word's meaning relate to other concepts. One teacher who used this model periodically with a group of middle school students reported to me that while the model wasn't appropriate for all vocabulary instruction, it provided a nice divergence from his typical vocabulary lessons. He also found that the comparing and contrasting encouraged by the model carried over into other discussions of concepts in reading as well as other subject areas.

Comprehension Questions

Comprehension questions can be used to assess children's comprehension or they can be used to extend comprehension. Assessment will be discussed in Chapter 6. In this section, we will examine the kinds of questions that help children who are deaf to understand text more deeply and which provide models of self-questions.

Levels of Questions

Comprehension taxonomies have been widely used by teachers for constructing varying types of comprehension questions. The most frequently used taxonomy is Bloom's classification of the intellectual objectives of education into six lower to higher levels: knowledge-comprehension-application-analysis-synthesis- evaluation (Bloom, Engelhart, Furst, Hill, & Krathwohl, 1956). Another popular taxonomy is Barrett's (1976), which was specifically designed to distinguish among the cognitive and affective dimensions of reading comprehension through four major levels: literal-inferential-evaluation-appreciation. Both taxonomies are further divided into multiple subcategories that teachers can use in creating comprehension questions.

Tatham (1978) cautioned that taxonomies should be viewed as classification systems and not as developmental frameworks of comprehension skills. "These taxonomies are nothing more than efficient systems for organizing types of reading behavior under clearly defined labels. The labels can be very useful when teachers want categories in which to place comprehension questions from instructional materials in order to analyze the types of thinking these questions promote" (p. 193).

In 1978, Pearson and Johnson proposed what they referred to as a simple taxonomy of questions that was designed "to capture the relationship between information presented in a text and information that has to come from a reader's store of prior knowledge" (p. 157). Their taxonomy included three types of questions: textually explicit, textually implicit, and scriptally implicit. *Textually explicit questions* have answers that are obvious in the text. *Textually implicit questions* have answers in the text but the answers are not obvious. To answer a textually implicit question, the reader must use inference. *Scriptally implicit questions* have answers that come from the reader's prior knowledge, the answers are not in the text, but the question is related to the text. "It is similar to textually implicit comprehension in that an inference is involved; however, it is different in that the data base for the inference is in the reader's head, not on the page" (p. 162).

Regardless of the taxonomy used, teachers are strongly encouraged to ask some questions that promote higher-order thinking along with the questions they ask that require recall of factual information (Daines, 1986; Hansen & Pearson, 1983; Jones, 1982). It seems self-evident that the difficulties experienced by many youngsters who are deaf in thinking critically, creatively, and abstractly are due in large part to their lack of experience in this kind of thinking. When children have not been asked questions that encourage higher-order thinking, it is very hard for them at first to think at levels beyond the literal. Instead of giving up and assuming that deaf children cannot answer inferential, evaluative, and other higher-level questions, these are precisely the kinds of questions they need to be asked. But teachers need to realize that promoting higher-order thinking takes time.

Comprehension questions can enhance another dimension of thinking, that of thinking about text structure.

Questions That Highlight Text Structure

It may be possible to teach children to identify the parts of a story, but there is no strong evidence that learning to analyze the grammar of stories and other text will improve children's reading comprehension (Dreher & Singer, 1980; Johnson & Bliesmer, 1983; Schmitt & O'Brien, 1986; Sebesta, Calder, & Cleland, 1982). If this finding seems familiar, it is because more than a decade ago educators learned that being able to analyze sentences into their grammatical components was not found to be related to the children's spoken, reading, or writing abilities.

Research into text structure does, however, have implications for instruction. Instead of teaching children the labels for text components, it has been suggested that teachers use questions to bring significant text components and the causal relationships between components to the children's attention. Through questions that highlight the information which reflects the basic structure of narrative or expository text, the teacher in essence can "show" children what it means to understand written discourse. Ultimately, such questions over time can help children to internalize the structure of text into their textual schemata (Carnine & Kinder, 1985; Indrisano, 1979; Mavrogenes, 1983; McConaughy, 1980; Sadow, 1982).

Teachers can create questions that emphasize text structure by first analyzing the structure of the text themselves and then creating questions based on key components. Figure 4–4 shows questions that were developed for *The Three Bears*. (The reader might want to look back at the story structure of *The Three Bears* presented in Figure 3–1).

Text structure questions can serve two objectives. They not only can guide children who are deaf in recognizing the underlying structure of typical narrative and expository text but they can also be developed to encourage different levels of thinking.

Think Time

One characteristic of comprehension questions that many of us tend to forget is that wonderful questions will not enhance comprehension if children are not given time to think about their answers. It has been observed that teachers give children an average of one second to answer a question. After one second, teachers ordinarily repeat or rephrase the question, answer it themselves, call on another student, or ask another question (Gambrell, 1983; Rowe, 1974; Tobin, 1986).

What happens when teachers wait three seconds, five seconds, or longer before soliciting an answer? In Tobin's (1986) study of students in grades 6 and 7, he found that waiting between 3 and 5 seconds resulted in significantly fewer failures of students to respond, greater length of student responses, and better comprehension. In a review of studies involving wait time, Tobin (1987) found that a wait time of between 3 and 5 seconds seemed to be optimal for improving the quality of teacher and student discourse and for affecting higher cognitive level achievement. In Gambrell's

FIGURE 4–4

Comprehension Questions Based On Story Structure

		The Three Bears
Setting	1.	Where did the three bears live?
Initiating Event/ Reaction	2.	Why did the three bears go for a walk?
Action	3.	Who showed up at the Bear's house?
Consequence	4.	What did Goldilocks do when she entered the house?
Reaction/Action	5.	What happened when Goldilocks tasted the porridge, sat in the chairs, and walked upstairs?
Consequence	6.	What happened when the three bears came home?
Ending	7.	What did Goldilocks do when she woke up?

review of the literature (1980), she found evidence that wait time of 5 seconds or more resulted in student responses that were longer, more appropriate, and demonstrated higher-order thinking. She also found that when teachers increased their wait time, they tended to ask more varied questions and to stimulate greater student involvement.

In reviewing her own series of studies on wait time in elementary and high school classrooms along with a review of the studies conducted by other researchers, Rowe (1986) found that wait time influenced students and teachers in a number of ways. When the interval between the end of a teacher question and the start of a student response was 3 to 5 seconds as compared to only 1 second:

1. the length of student response increased 300% to 700%
2. students were much more likely to use evidence and logical argument to support their inferences
3. students engaged more often in speculative thinking
4. students asked considerably more questions
5. students paid more attention to each other
6. "I don't know" responses decreased dramatically
7. off-task behavior decreased
8. greater percentages of students participated particularly from groups rated as poor performers
9. student confidence increased
10. test performance improved on cognitively more complex test items
11. classroom discourse more closely resembled discussion than question-answer routines
12. teachers asked fewer questions and those they asked tended to invite clarification and elaboration
13. teacher expectation for student performance rose, particularly with students for whom they had previously held low expectations

Wait time is particularly pertinent to deaf children who are in mainstream classes and receiving information from the teacher through an interpreter. Because interpreting is not simultaneous with the teacher's utterances, unless the teacher waits between asking a question and soliciting answers, the child who is deaf may have no opportunity to answer and certainly no opportunity to think.

Strategy Lessons

The concept of strategy lessons is important because children who are deaf should spend more time actually reading than being taught how to read.

Strategy lessons involve children in brief, clear, and concise discussions of specific aspects of the reading process (Weaver, 1988). Holdaway (1979) described the difference between skills teaching and strategy teaching as involving "the presence or absence of self-direction on the part of the learner. In skills teaching the teacher tells the learner what to do and then 'corrects' or 'marks' the response. In strategy teaching the teacher induces the learner to behave in an appropriate way and encourages the learner to confirm or correct his [or her] own responses—the teacher does not usurp the control which is crucial to mastering a strategy" (p. 136).

Strategy lessons are 5- to 10-minute lessons that can take place before, during, or after reading. Before reading, strategy lessons might focus on letter-sound relationships in the sight words being taught to the children. They might center on the names of characters or figurative language used in the story. The teacher might use before-reading strategy lessons to discuss genre, text structure, or the author's use of voice. During reading, the teacher might engage the students in a strategy lesson to analyze a confusing sentence, figure out anaphoric references between sentences, or structurally analyze an unknown word into its root and affixes. After reading, strategy lessons might be used to learn how to summarize the text, figure out the meanings of unknown words from context, or reconstruct the sequence of action.

Goodman and his associates (Goodman, 1986; Goodman, Smith, Meredith, & Goodman, 1987) suggested that strategy lessons be used with groups of students who demonstrate a common need. They used the example of students who tended to substitute *what* for *that*, *when* for *then*, *where* for *there*, and vice versa but did not confuse *th* with *wh* in other words. Instead of creating drill and practice exercises for these words, they recommended that the teacher find or write meaningful passages in which only one of these words is suitable at a time. Thus the passages themselves would lead the students to self-correct.

Collins (1988) described a reading strategy lesson for teaching the use of context to develop meaning. Using the board or overhead projector, the teacher reveals the first sentence of the text, the students predict the meaning of the unknown concept, and these predictions are written on the board. The second sentence is then revealed, the students eliminate predictions that are no longer appropriate, and they add new predictions. When the procedure is completed for all sentences in the text, the students discuss their thinking processes during the activity.

Atwell (1987) used minilessons to precede reading workshop each day in her junior high school English classes. Some of her minilessons dealt with procedures and routines of reading workshop such as guidelines for using reading time, keeping a reading journal, choosing books to read, and using the classroom library. Some minilessons focused on evaluation and included the grading system and evaluation conferences. Literature was the topic of several minilessons on genres, authors, and elements of literary works. Her minilessons on skills focused on strategies that would enable the youngsters to be more efficient and fluent readers. She also included minilessons on study techniques, conventions of standardized tests, and the decisions that readers sometimes make to reread good books and abandon unrewarding books.

Strategy lessons serve three important goals. They enable the teacher to focus on specific reading skills on an as-needed basis, when the skill is relevant to the deaf child's current reading needs. Strategy lessons also explicitly let the child know that individual skills are important because they are applicable to the reading process and not because they are an end in themselves. Furthermore, strategy lessons implicitly communicate the message that the most important part of the reading class period is reading, since the strategy lessons involve considerably less time than actual reading of text material.

Retelling Stories

Retelling stories after reading provides children who are deaf with the chance to make sense of the text as a whole. In the past, retellings have been used predominantly to assess reading comprehension (Gambrell, Pfeiffer, & Wilson, 1985). However, viewing retellings as reconstructions and using them to monitor comprehension may be considerably less valuable than viewing retellings as constructions and using them as a strategy to enhance comprehension.

It has been found that retelling significantly improves reading comprehension and recall (Gambrell, Pfeiffer, & Wilson, 1985; Koskinen, Gambrell, Kapinus, & Heathington, 1988). Gambrell and her associates observed that "practice in verbal rehearsal of what has been read results in significant learning with respect to the comprehension and recall of discourse, and that what has been learned, as a result of practice in retelling, transfers to the reading of subsequent text (Gambrell, Pfeiffer, & Wilson, 1985, p. 220).

Practice in retelling has been found to improve both the richness of children's retellings as well as their reading comprehension (Kapinus, Gambrell, & Koskinen, 1987; Morrow, 1985a, 1985b). In other words, experienced retellers demonstrate better comprehension than novice retellers. Kapinus and her associates (1987) related the following vignette which they believed provided some insight into why retelling enhances reading comprehension:

> The fourth grader said, "Through the whole story I thought about what
> I was going to say. When you said, 'Think,' I thought about it some more.
> I always thought I didn't have to pay attention to stories, but now I have
> to so that I can retell it." (p. 140)

Story retelling has also been found to help develop children's story schema (French, 1988; Morrow, 1985a, 1985b, 1986). French (1988) observed that hearing impaired elementary students who retold stories as a group activity were able to learn from each other which components of a story carried the most meaning.

Several guidelines have been suggested for using retellings in the classroom. Y. Goodman (1982) encouraged teachers to use unaided retellings followed by open-ended questions that serve to prompt the child. Koskinen, Gambrell, Kapinus, and Heathington (1988) advised teachers to model retelling for students with no retelling experience, guide students' practice of retelling through prompts, and provide students with opportunities for repeated practice with partners. They further suggested that students be given guidance in how to provide positive feedback when someone else is retelling a story. French (1988) reported that in the language arts program at the Kendall Demonstration Elementary School, retelling with hearing impaired students was conducted as a group activity which the teacher recorded on the board, chart paper, or overhead transparency.

Story Abstracts

The purpose of story abstracts is similar to the purpose for retelling stories. The process of creating story abstracts helps the child who is deaf to think about the central story line, important characters, and significant details in the text they have completed reading.

Story Maps

Story maps are a type of semantic map. In a story map, the key elements of a story and the relationships between elements are displayed graphically. Story maps are typically used after children have finished reading a story, chapter, or book. The story map is created as a group activity through in-depth discussion (Davis & McPherson, 1989; Idol, 1987; Reutzel, 1985b; Widomski, 1983).

The most common type of story map is the main idea-sequential detail map. Reutzel (1985b) presented the following steps for constructing this type of map:

1. Construct, in sequence, a summary list of the main idea, major events, and major characters in the story.
2. Locate the main idea in the center of the map.
3. Draw enough ties projecting out symmetrically from the center circle to accommodate the major events/characters on the summary list.
4. Enter the major concepts or events in circles attached to these ties, including them in sequence clockwise around the center circle.
5. Enter subevents and subconcepts in clockwise sequence around the circles containing major events or concepts in the story map. (pp. 400–401)

Other types of story maps are character comparison maps, inferential story maps, cause-effect relationships, comparison/contrast maps, and drawing conclusions story maps (Davis & McPherson, 1989; Reutzel, 1985b). Story maps can be used by youngsters after reading to write a summary of the story, write a book report, or as a conceptual model to create an original composition (Olson, 1984; Pehrsson & Denner, 1988; Sinatra, Stahl-Gemake, & Morgan, 1986).

It seems logical that children who are familiar with semantic mapping for activities such as vocabulary development would find story mapping a relatively easy strategy to learn and indeed, teachers of children who are deaf have informally reported that this is true. They have observed that once the children understand and practice semantic mapping, they are enthused to use it for organizing their ideas about stories or novels they have read.

Story Frames

Story frames are summaries with information left out for the youngsters to fill in. Some authors view them as story level cloze (Cairney, 1987; Cudd & Roberts, 1987). Story frames are usually based on story structure components but they have also been used to guide children in analyzing characters, setting, and other aspects of the text. The teacher can include a great deal of information in the frame and expect just a small amount of writing from the children, or the teacher can provide minimum guidance in the frame and expect the children to write quite a lot. Figure 4–5 illustrates a story frame developed for *The Three Bears*.

When using semantic maps or story frames, there is a tendency for all ideas to be seen as equally important. It is, therefore, important for teachers to use these activities in ways that help children clearly differentiate between central story ideas or central story problems and supporting details (Au & Scheu, 1989; Moldofsky, 1983).

Language Experience Approach

The *language experience approach*, frequently referred to as the LEA, is a reading instruction method in which youngsters dictate ideas or experiences to the teacher, the teacher records their dictation into the form of an experience story, and the story becomes the youngster's reading material. It is used as an adjunct strategy for beginning reading instruction or remedial instruction.

Through the language experience approach, children become aware of the relationship between spoken or sign language and written language, and they experience success in reading and understanding text precisely because they created the text. The language experience approach also capitalizes on children's motivation to discuss and read about their own personal experiences (Ewoldt & Hammermeister, 1986; Hammermeister & Israelite, 1983; Karnowski, 1989; Reimer, 1983).

FIGURE 4–5

Story Frame for *The Three Bears*

Title ___The Three Bears___

This story takes place ___in the house of the three bears.___
___They live in the woods___   .

In this story, the problem starts when ___Mama bear makes___
___porridge but it is too hot to eat. So the Bears___
___go for a walk in the forest___   .

After that, ___Goldilocks visits the house___

_____ .

Next, ___She eats some porridge. The porridge in the___
___big bowl is too hot. The porridge in the middle size___
___bowl is too cold. The porridge in the small bowl___
___is just right and she eats it all up___   .

Then, ___She sits down. The big chair is too hard.___
___The middle size chair is too soft. The small___
___chair is just right but it breaks___   .

After that, ___she goes upstairs. She lays down on___
___the big bed but it is too hard. The middle___
___size bed is too soft. The small bed is just___
___right and she falls asleep___   .

Finally, ___the bears come home. They see that___
___Someone ate their porridge, sat in their___
___chairs, and slept in their beds___   .

The problem is solved when ___they see Goldilocks___

_____ .

The problem ends when ___Goldilocks wakes up, sees___
___the bears, and runs out of the house___   .

The language experience approach also has some drawbacks. It can leave children with the impression that the relationship between spoken or sign language and written language is a direct one and that writing is a one-step process in which one's first thoughts are recorded into a final draft. Furthermore, most experience stories follow no common narrative or expository text structure. As Heller (1988) noted, "Group dictated stories that are recorded verbatim often lack the continuity that distinguishes a story from lists of sentences" (p. 130).

Experience stories can be individually dictated or group-dictated. The steps usually include the following:

1. The teacher introduces a stimulus. It can be an object, animal, field trip, movie or videotape, art project, celebration, or anything else that is likely to stimulate a discussion.

2. The children dictate their thoughts or impressions about the experience. The teacher writes the children's words on a large sheet of paper, overhead transparency, or the chalkboard.

3. The children read the story aloud, in voice or sign, while the teacher points to each word. Known words can be underlined and later written on word cards for each child's word bank.

4. The children copy the experience story or the teacher makes a copy for each child's notebook, which the children can illustrate.

5. The children use the experience story and word bank over time. For example, stories are usually reread periodically to the teacher, peers, and parents. Also, words are continuously added to the word bank (Ewoldt & Hammermeister, 1986; Johnson & Roberson, 1988; Jones & Nessel, 1985; Mallon & Berglund, 1984; Reimer, 1983).

One of the challenges in using the language experience approach arises when the deaf child's dictated story differs noticeably from standard written English. If the teacher writes the story as dictated, the text may be a poor model of written English. If the teacher modifies the story, the implicit message is that the child's language is inferior or flawed. Also, one of the benefits of the language experience approach may be lost if the child has difficulty with patterns that do not match his or her own expressive language. Two suggestions have been offered to solve this problem.

Gillet and Gentry (1983) proposed that teachers create at least two written stories for every language experience activity. The first should be a transcription of the child's language exactly as dictated. The second story should be the same story translated into standard written English. The second story is introduced as another story about the same topic, and both stories are then used in the conventional language experience activities.

LaSasso (1983) suggested that teachers create one well-written story that captures the important elements of the child's dictated story. The child can be told that the written story is the child's story as he or she "might see it in a magazine or newspaper if someone else had heard it and written about it" (p. 153).

Another challenge in using the language experience approach is making it clear that the first draft and the final draft of a story are not the same. Karnowski (1989) advised teachers to write "sloppy copy" at the top of the experience chart and then engage the children in discussion that encouraged on-going revision of the dictated story. The same process-oriented approach to creating a language experience story can also solve another problem of language experience activities which is that the "stories" the children produce tend to be strings of sentences with no cohesion and no text structure. Heller (1988) recommended that teachers ask questions designed to promote thinking of the text as a whole and to encourage the children to actively monitor their dictation. Both Karnowski and Heller suggested that dictated stories be read, reread, and rewritten by the children and teacher before a final draft is created.

The language experience approach is most typically thought of as appropriate for young deaf children. However, teachers of adolescent and adult deaf students often use language experience as a strategy to help these students gain confidence in themselves as readers. LEA seems to be particularly valuable in helping those students who have been unsuccessful with traditional reading approaches to realize that they can be successful readers. Once these students have developed some confidence with experience stories, other types of reading materials can be introduced.

Read-Aloud and Storytelling

I want to discuss again the topic of read-aloud to reiterate my belief that read-aloud should be a core activity for youngsters of *all* ages and to emphasize again the value I place on this activity for school-aged children who are deaf.

Teachers usually read aloud, in voice or sign, between 5 and 15 minutes daily from a novel slightly beyond the instructional reading levels of most of the youngsters in the class. It has been suggested that teachers choose books they like themselves and that reflect a variety of interests and genres. They should preread any books they plan to read aloud, set aside time every day for reading aloud, allow time for discussion, tell the youngsters something about the author, and end the day's reading at the conclusion of a chapter or at a suspenseful moment (Butler, 1980; Lindberg, 1988; Trelease, 1989).

Storytelling is an ancient art and a tradition in deaf culture, but only recently have educators begun to realize the power of storytelling in literacy development. It has been observed that storytelling can promote reading comprehension, writing development, listening or receptive sign skills, and spoken or expressive sign skills. Children who observe storytelling are often highly motivated to read the same story, to write the story or a similar story, to write their reactions in a journal, and to pay attention to stories in their reading that would be appropriate ones for their own storytelling.

As observers of the storyteller, they learn to give helpful feedback, to critically evaluate the storyteller's expressive skills, and to observe and listen carefully. As the storyteller, they learn to use meaningful expression, to notice and use audience feedback, and to develop poise. Storytelling also provides youngsters with opportunities to develop awareness of the structure of stories through listening, watching, and telling folktales, mysteries, biographies, and other types of stories (Farnsworth, 1981; Nelson, 1989; Peck, 1989; Roney, 1989).

CHILD-DIRECTED APPROACHES: BECOMING AN AUTONOMOUS READER AND WRITER

Child-directed approaches are based on the notion that children who are deaf need to engage in reading and writing experiences that empower them to make many, if not most, of the decisions regarding when, what, how, where, and why to read and write. It used to be thought that children learned to read at the early grade levels and read to learn at the later grade levels. We now know that learning to read and reading to learn occur simultaneously and continue virtually throughout our lifetimes. Just as we can no longer separate learning to read from reading to learn, I do not believe we should separate teacher-directed approaches from child-directed approaches. Both approaches should be incorporated into every classroom at every grade level, recognizing that some are more and less appropriate for different levels. However, I also believe that ultimately it is the child-directed approaches that will provide the child who is deaf with the skills and motivation to be a life-long reader and writer.

Providing Time to Read

It is a long-held belief that time spent in silent reading is vitally important to children's reading development. In their study of fifth- and sixth-grade children's reading growth over a four month period, Taylor, Frye, and Maruyama (1990) found a significant relationship between time spent reading in the classroom and reading achievement. Their results provided empirical support for "the conventional wisdom that it is valuable for students to actually read during reading class" (p. 359). Yet when researchers have examined how much time youngsters actually spend engaged in silent reading, it has been found that the average is 8 minutes daily for students at the elementary level (Thurlow, Graden, Ysseldyke, & Algozzine, 1984; Ysseldyke & Algozzine, 1983).

Sustained Silent Reading

For two decades, teachers have been urged to provide children time to read through regularly scheduled periods of *sustained silent reading*. Sustained silent reading has earned many acronyms over the years including DEAR (Drop Everything And Read), HIP (High Intensity Practice), SQUIRT (Sustained Quiet Uninterrupted Reading Time), and the original acronym, USSR (Uninterrupted Sustained Silent Reading).

Sustained silent reading has been found to positively affect reading achievement and improve attitudes toward reading among youngsters from first grade through high school (Cline & Kretke, 1980; Collins, 1980; Dry & Earle, 1988; Hicks, 1983; Holt & O'Tuel, 1989; Kaisen, 1987; Leechford & Manarino, 1982; Levine, 1984; Minton, 1980; Moore, Jones, & Miller, 1980; Sadoski, 1980; Summers & McClelland, 1982; Wiesendanger & Bader, 1989; Wiesendanger & Birlem, 1984). Yet, to be successful, the research has shown that a sustained silent reading program should follow these guidelines:

1. Everyone in the room should read during the entire sustained silent reading time including every child, the teacher, aide, volunteer, and whoever else is in the classroom.
2. Each child should have a self-selected book that he or she is able to read independently. Many children will need guidance in choosing appropriate books, and younger children may need to have several books next to them.
3. The time period should be appropriate for the developmental levels of the children. It is advisable to begin the program at 5 minutes per day and gradually increase to no more than 30- to 40-minute periods.
4. The children should be given frequent opportunities to choose new books from the classroom and school libraries.
5. Sustained silent reading periods should be designed to reflect careful scheduling, adherence to time limits, and protection from outside interruptions.

The major question I have observed teachers of deaf students to struggle with is whether to allow the children to read materials other than books during silent reading time. There is no right answer to this question that can be found in the literature. The most successful sustained silent reading experiences I have seen are those in which the teacher helps each child make the decision regarding what kind of material the child should be reading. In classrooms where reading is a valued activity, children generally choose to read material in which they can become engrossed. For some deaf children, and for some periods of time during the school year, materials such as comic books and magazines may serve that purpose for them.

Reading Workshop

Reading workshop is built on the belief that three basic principles underlie a supportive literacy program—time, ownership, and response. In reading workshop, only the first 5 to 10 minutes of class time are spent in direct teacher instruction (i.e., strategy lessons or minilessons). The greatest proportion of the reading instruction period is devoted to independent reading. Atwell (1987) developed the following rules for reading workshop with her classes of middle school students:

1. Students must read for the entire period.
2. They cannot do homework or read any material for another course. Reading workshop is not a study hall.
3. They must read a book (no magazines or newspapers where text competes with pictures), preferably one that tells a story (e.g., novels, histories and biographies rather than books of lists or facts where readers can't sustain attention, build up speed and fluency, or grow to love good stories).
4. They must have a book in their possession when the bell rings; this is the main responsibility involved in coming prepared to this class. (Students who need help finding a book or who finish a book during the workshop are obvious exceptions.)
5. They may not talk to or disturb others.
6. They may sit or recline wherever they'd like as long as feet don't go up on furniture and rule #5 is maintained. (A piece of paper taped over the window in the classroom helps cut down on the number of passers-by who require explanations about students lying around with their noses in books.)
7. There are no lavatory or water fountain sign-outs to disturb me or other readers. In an emergency, they may simply slip out and slip back in as quietly as possible.
8. A student who's absent can make up time and receive points by reading at home, during study hall (with a note from a parent or study hall teacher), or after school. (pp. 159–160)

In Atwell's reading workshop program, students receive points each day for following these guidelines or lose points for not following them, and these points eventually represent one-third of the student's grade for the term.

In reading workshop, ownership is as important as time. Ownership means that the youngsters are free to choose the books they will read. Advocates of this approach to reading instruction believe that when youngsters are given choice, everyone in a classroom gets hooked on literature (Atwell, 1987; Hansen, 1987).

The third basic principle in reading workshop is response. Providing children opportunities to respond to literature is not only important to reading workshop but to other reading approaches as well, and so response to literature will be discussed as a separate topic in the next section.

Providing Time to Respond

It is generally agreed that opportunity to respond is a key element to all learning. For young readers, it may be essential. As Atwell (1987) wrote, "I think opportunities to respond, to engage in literary talk with the teacher, are crucial. It is not enough for schools simply to make time and space for independent reading. For too many kids, sustained silent reading programs are little more than a nice break in the day's routine. With nothing happening before or after the reading, the context in which readers read doesn't support or extend their interests" (p.164).

For most children, however, the classroom provides limited opportunities to converse about literature. For example, Gambrell (1987) studied the purpose and proportion of student responses during reading lessons and found that in grades 1 through 3, the children's language was predominantly in response to teacher-initiated, known-answer questions. Furthermore, their responses were primarily at the one-word level and rarely exceeded one sentence in length. Gambrell observed that "students do not talk to accomplish personal goals, such as telling about what they thought was the most exciting or interesting part of the story. Their talk about stories is not self-generated. Instead, it is always dictated by teacher request for specific responses" (p. 197). Gambrell also observed that teachers were reluctant to engage students in open-ended discussions because of time constraints and the inability of many students to listen or watch attentively during extended turn-taking.

Reading Conferences

Reading conferences are one way to provide children who are deaf with opportunities to respond to literature and can be devised to avoid the pitfalls of large-group discussions. In large-group discussions, each child has relatively little opportunity to contribute ideas because of having to share time with six or eight other students. Also, teachers generally find that encouraging children who are deaf to track the movement of a discussion, from child to child, is a tremendous challenge.

Teacher-Student Conferences and Peer Conferences   *One-to-one conferences* between teachers and students can be scheduled for as little as 5 minutes and as long as 15 minutes. These conferences can be used to teach children how to respond to literature through supporting their ideas about what they are reading, through questions with no "known" answers, and through real conversations about mutually interesting stories and characters

(Hansen, 1987; D. Smith, 1987; Strickland, Dillon, Funkhouser, Glick, & Rogers, 1989).

Once the children know the kinds of open-ended questions that should be asked during conferences and they have learned how to be an interested listener/partner, peer conferences can be used to proportionally increase the amount of opportunity for students to engage in literature discussion.

Literature Response Groups: Reader's Chair   During reader's chair, one student shares what he or she has read or is currently reading with a group of fellow students and then "chairs" the subsequent discussion. I use the term *reader's chair* because the functions of this type of literature response group is quite similar to author's chair in writing workshop, which will be described later in this chapter.

In their study of four elementary classrooms (one first/second grade, one second grade, one gifted/talented third grade, and one sixth grade), Strickland and her associates (1989) found that student-led literature discussion groups were a valuable resource for learning language, learning through language, and learning about language. They observed that "one of the most significant features of these discussion groups is that it puts the student in the role of expert or resource. The presenter makes the decisions about what is important to reveal about the book and what is to be read aloud. Not only do students have a greater sense of control over the talk, they have more opportunities to talk in an interactional pattern that is likely to criss-cross among the group members rather than remain dyadic" (p. 199).

Literature Response Groups: Book Club   During book club, youngsters who are reading the same book come together periodically to discuss what they are reading. I use the term *book club* because the purpose and function of this type of literature response group is similar to book clubs for adults. In an adult book club, a small group of enthusiastic readers decides on a book they are all interested in reading and then get together for an animated discussion after the members have had time to read the book.

Discussion can play an important role in enhancing student understanding, but discussion that extends comprehension needs to be distinguished from teacher-student dialogue used to evaluate comprehension. Alvermann, Dillon, and O'Brien (1987) use the term recitation to describe the traditional question-answer-evaluate dialogue between teachers and students. In contrast to recitation, they believe discussion is characterized by three criteria: "discussants should put forth multiple points of view and stand ready to change their minds about the matter under discussion; students should interact with one another as well as with the teacher; and the interaction should exceed the typical two- or three-word phrase units common to recitation lessons" (p. 7).

Book clubs can be informal in nature or they can be formalized into reading groups that are led by the teacher or individual students on a rotating basis. Bear and Invernizzi (1984) developed a strategy for student-directed reading groups in which a pair of students planned and carried out Directed Reading Thinking Activities with a small group of peers. They used their strategy with students in grades 4 through high school and concluded that the conversational "interaction in student-directed groups facilitates the development of cognitive strategies necessary for independent reading outside of class" (p. 249).

Reading Response Journals

In addition to reading conferences, *reading response journals* can provide youngsters who are deaf with a meaningful way to respond actively to the literature they are reading. Harste, Short, and Burke (1988) called this kind of journal a *literature log*. They considered it to be one type of learning log. In a learning log, children are asked to write about their reaction to something new they learned that day or their response to how they went about learning it. In a literature log, children are asked to write their responses and reactions to what they are reading.

The reading response journals used by Atwell (1987) with her middle school students took the form of letters between herself and the students. These dialogue journals provided the youngsters not only with opportunity to respond but to engage in a written conversation with the teacher about the piece of literature being read. After using these journals with her students for two years, Atwell reported that "in our correspondence we've gone far beyond plot synopses and traditional teacher's manual issues such as genre, theme, and character to give accounts of our processes as readers, to speculate on author's processes as writers, to suggest revisions in what we've read, to see connections between a published author's work and our own writing, to see connections between books and our own lives, and to engage in some serious, and not so serious, literary gossip" (p. 165).

Drama

Drama can provide youngsters who are deaf with an experiential mode for responding to literature. It is believed that drama can have a positive influence on reading comprehension, student motivation to read, and oral and sign language development (Bidwell, 1990; Wagner, 1988).

In preschool and kindergarten, it has been suggested that children be provided with structured and free-play opportunities to recreate stories that are read aloud to them (Christie, 1990; Galda, 1982). Pellegrini and Galda (1982) compared the effects of dramatic play, discussion, and drawing as story reconstruction activities used to follow up read-aloud to 108 kindergarten, first- and second-grade children. They found that dramatic play was the most effective facilitator of comprehension.

At the elementary and middle school levels, it has been suggested that youngsters be provided with opportunities to create dramatic presentations of novels, parts of novels, or stories. Performances can be improvisational or the students can write a script based on the actual story, which is a technique sometimes referred to as Readers Theatre (Bidwell, 1990; Harste,

Short, & Burke, 1988; Shanklin & Rhodes, 1989). In her investigation comparing drama with discussion, Gray (1986) found that the sixth-grade students in her study who participated in creative dramatic presentation demonstrated better ability to answer inferential questions than the matched group of students who took part in a story discussion with the teacher.

Drama is a strategy that has been used for many years by teachers of children who are deaf. It can take a relatively brief amount of time if the presentation is impromptu, or it can become a class project that takes several weeks if the presentation is performed for parents and other youngsters in the school.

Providing Time to Respond: A Final Word

I would like to conclude this section by saying that there are myriad ways for teachers to provide youngsters who are deaf with time to respond to literature. I have not discussed art activities, games, bulletin boards, and many of the other techniques educators have developed. One particularly good source of ideas is Harste, Short, and Burke's book, *Creating Classroom for Authors* (1988).

Metacognitive Strategies

Metacognitive strategies are used to help children become aware of, monitor, regulate, and evaluate their own cognitive processes. Metacognitive instruction is designed to take teaching strategies and turn them into learning strategies that youngsters can use independently. Review of the research indicates that instruction in metacognitive skills can have a powerful effect on comprehension (Haller, Child, & Walberg, 1988; Harp, 1988; Johnston, 1985; Palincsar & Brown, 1989). As Johnston (1988) noted, "Teachers need to be concerned about improving children's comprehension ability rather than just their comprehension" (p. 645).

Applying Background Knowledge

Chapter 3 discussed the importance of background knowledge to reading comprehension. Background knowledge is organized cognitively into memory structures called content schemata and includes the individual's general world knowledge, particular information, and personal experiences about a topic. Traditional instruction is aimed at activating and building background knowledge. Metacognitive instruction is aimed at helping children who are deaf to apply their background knowledge toward understanding what they are reading.

When the research on the relationship between background knowledge and comprehension is examined, several issues emerge. One issue is that prior experience tends to be more salient than prereading instruction

(Roberts, 1988). In other words, children seem more able to apply their prior experiences toward understanding what they read than they are able to apply information learned during classroom instruction. A second issue is that when prior knowledge and text information are contradictory, comprehension suffers because children tend to rely more heavily on their prior knowledge, particularly young and less able readers (Lipson, 1982, 1984). A third issue is that good readers tend to use their background knowledge spontaneously but that poor readers do not apply their prior knowledge toward comprehending what they read (Holmes, 1983).

In a study conducted with 24 students in grades 5 through 8 from three state schools for the deaf, a colleague and I found that activating the children's background knowledge through the use of thematic organizers was not sufficient for improving their comprehension of narrative text. It seemed apparent to us that the organizers did not give the students enough direction in how to apply their background knowledge toward understanding the text material (Schirmer & Winter, 1991).

The implication of these issues is that activating and building background knowledge is necessary but not sufficient. Children who are deaf need to be given strategies that encourage them both to apply their existing knowledge and to test their information in light of the ideas presented in the text. The following strategies can help them accomplish this.

Thematically Related Material   One strategy is to have the youngsters read *thematically related material*. Crafton (1983) conducted a study in which she asked one group of 11th graders to read two magazine articles on the same topic, and one group to read two magazine articles on unrelated topics. In their retellings, the group that read articles on the same topic focused on larger segments of text, generated more inferences, applied more background information to text-based information, and demonstrated more personal involvement in the reading. Reading thematically related material fits in very well to an interdisciplinary curriculum such as the models described in Chapter 2.

Metacognitive Modeling   A second strategy is *metacognitive modeling*. In this strategy, the teacher acts as a role model for the kinds of thinking being encouraged within the youngsters. One example of this strategy is Heller's (1986) "What I know" technique. In this technique, the students are given a sheet of paper with three columns—What I Already Knew, What I Now Know, and What I Don't Know. Over the course of reading the narrative or expository text, the sheet is completed individually by the students as well as by the teacher who uses his or her sheet as an example of the thinking processes involved in monitoring one's own comprehension.

Question-Answer Relationships   A third strategy is the *Question-Answer Relationship* (QAR) program developed by Raphael (Raphael, 1982, 1984, 1986; Raphael & McKinney, 1983; Raphael & Pearson, 1985; Raphael & Wonnacott, 1985). The QAR program was based on the Pearson and

Johnson (1978) question taxonomy discussed previously in this chapter. Pearson and Johnson categorized questions as textually explicit, textually implicit, and scriptally implicit. Textually explicit questions have obvious answers written directly in the text. Textually implicit questions have answers in the text but the answers are not so obvious. Scriptally implicit questions require the reader to use his or her own background knowledge.

In her most recent revision of the QAR program, Raphael (1986) divided question-answer relationships into two primary categories: (a) In the Book and (b) In My Head. The *In the Book* category includes two types of QARs. The first is called *Right There* and is the appropriate strategy to use when the answer can be found explicitly stated within a single sentence of the text. The second is called *Think and Search* or *Putting It Together* and is the appropriate strategy to use when the answer can be found in the text but requires the reader to synthesize information from different parts of the text.

The *In My Head* category also includes two types of QARs. The first is called *Author and You* and is the appropriate strategy when the reader needs to combine background knowledge with text information. The second is called *On My Own* and is the appropriate strategy when the answer cannot be found in the story and could even be answered if the story was not read. On My Own questions require the reader to rely completely on background knowledge.

Similar to the recommended sequence of instruction in many of the metacognitive strategies, instruction in the QAR program begins with direct teaching, teacher guidance, and teacher modeling. Over time, the children are given increasing occasions to use the strategy independently.

Making Predictions

It is believed that good readers are constantly predicting, testing their hypotheses to confirm or disconfirm them, and integrating information by separating important ideas from less important ideas and interpreting the important ideas (A. Brown, 1980; K. Goodman, 1986; McNeil, 1987). Hansen (1981) found that teaching children to use their prior knowledge to predict upcoming story events improved their comprehension.

The key to prediction as a metacognitive strategy is the child's testing and revising of hypotheses. Kimmel and MacGinitie (1985) observed that children often have difficulty revising hypotheses, particularly when they are reading expository text written in an inductive style. In an inductive style, the author provides several contrasting ideas or examples that lead up to a main point. Kimmel and MacGinitie suggested that one way to help children who are inflexible readers revise their hypotheses is to use a guided reading approach in which the teacher provides direct instruction and guided practice.

Garrison and Hoskisson (1989) recommended a strategy that emphasizes teaching children to look for evidence that refutes hypotheses rather than evidence that confirms hypotheses. They believed that this strategy helps children to realize that predictions are rarely proven to be completely true and that different interpretations can be equally valid.

Also, many of the strategies presented in the section on Prereading Activities involve children who are deaf in making predictions before and during reading.

Self-Questioning

Self-questioning is a strategy that has emerged from three bodies of research—active processing, metacognitive theory, and schema theory (Wong, 1985). According to the active processing perspective, self-questioning is critical to the reader being able to actively engage in comprehending because the act of generating questions creates an interaction between the reader and the text. According to metacognitive theory, self-questioning is crucial to the reader's ability to focus on important information and to monitor his or her own comprehension. In schema theory, self-questioning grows out of the connection between background knowledge and the learning of new information. According to schema theory, self-questioning is seen as a fundamental strategy for the reader to use in activating relevant background knowledge.

In her review of the literature, Wong (1985) found that self-questioning is effective in enhancing comprehension when children are given explicit instruction in how to generate questions and they are given ample time to think during reading.

One strategy for teaching children to self-question is for the teacher to ask a question that encourages a question in response rather than an answer. Singer (1978) used the example of a teacher directing children to examine a picture at the beginning of a story and asking, "What would you like to know about the picture?" instead of "What is going to happen?" (p. 905). Another strategy is for the teacher to model the kinds of questions that the children could be asking themselves. Nolte and Singer (1985) proposed combining these two strategies so that self-questions are phased in and teacher-directed questions are phased out through a transition of teacher questions requiring student questions as responses.

Mangano, Palmer, and Goetz (1982) noted that youngsters need to be taught that the questions one asks oneself before reading are different than questions asked during and after reading, and the questions asked about narrative text are different from the questions asked about expository text. For example, they listed the following questions as ones children should ask themselves during the reading of expository text:

1. Was the hypothesis that I made prior to reading correct?
2. What was the main idea of this section?
3. What facts support this main idea?

4. How does this section relate to what I have read thus far?

5. What are some questions related to this material that the teacher may ask me on a test? What are the answers to these questions?

6. From what I read thus far, and the ideas generated by reading the next subtitle, what do I think this next section will be about? (p. 368)

Encouraging children who are deaf to generate their own questions requires that the teacher spend a substantial amount of time in modeling appropriate questions. Also, the teacher needs to support the children's continued efforts in developing their own questions because many deaf children have considerable difficulty with the syntactic structures of English question forms.

Reciprocal Teaching

Reciprocal teaching is a strategy developed by Palincsar and Brown (1986, 1988) for enhancing reading comprehension through dialogue that encourages collaborative problem solving between teachers and students. In reciprocal teaching, four activities form the basis of the dialogue: (a) *summarizing* involves identifying the main idea, (b) *question generating* involves creating appropriate questions about the passage, (c) *clarifying* involves monitoring comprehension and using repair strategies when comprehension has broken down, and (d) *predicting* involves making and testing hypotheses. Palincsar and Brown reported that these four activities were chosen because successful readers routinely employed them; they represent activities that readers engage in before, during, and after reading; and students are forced to monitor their understanding by focusing on information presented in the text itself.

Palincsar (1986) described a typical reciprocal teaching lesson as beginning with a review of the four activities. The students are then encouraged to make predictions, after which they read the passage. The "teacher," who can be the classroom teacher or one of the students, asks questions and the students respond. The teacher summarizes and asks for modifications to the summary, or the teacher asks for a summary. The summary leads to a discussion of any clarifications that are needed by any of the students. In the last part of the daily dialogue, the students make predictions for the next passage and a new teacher is chosen.

The transition from teacher-directed to student-directed reciprocal teaching lessons occurs gradually. "During the initial days of instruction, the adult teacher is principally responsible for initiating and sustaining the dialogue. He or she models and provides instruction regarding the four strategies. However, with each day of instruction, the teacher attempts to transfer increased responsibility to the students while providing feedback and coaching them through the dialogue" (Palincsar, 1986, p. 119).

In his review of the research, Moore (1988) found reciprocal teaching to be an effective strategy with students identified as disabled readers, particularly with students who had comprehension difficulties. Andrews (1988) found that using the reciprocal teaching procedure for teaching prereading skills to kindergarten and first-grade students with severe-to-profound and profound hearing losses resulted in significant gains in their letter, word, and story knowledge.

Mental Imagery

Mental imagery is generally thought of as the formation of visual or spatial representations in one's mind, although all sensory modalities can be represented in imagery. It has been suggested that mental imagery can serve two metacognitive functions. The first is that mental imagery can be a means for activating background knowledge prior to reading (Gambrell, 1982; Johnson, 1987; Long, Winograd, & Bridge, 1989). The second is that mental imagery can serve a comprehension monitoring function (Gambrell & Bales, 1986; Sadoski, 1983, 1985).

Because sign language is a visual-spatial language, it might be argued that mental imagery could be a particularly powerful strategy for many deaf youngsters to use in comprehending text. In the only study of imagery with this population that I was able to find, Fusaro and Slike (1979) found that imagery influenced the ease with which 9- to 12-year-old hearing impaired children learned to identify words.

A number of strategies have been suggested for encouraging youngsters to use mental imagery during reading. Johnson (1987) recommended that teachers use visual aids, role playing, and drawing to foster mental imagery. Fredericks (1986) suggested that teachers engage children in mental imagery activities apart from reading that require the children to create images of something or someone being described or which they have just seen. He stressed that teachers should encourage children's elaboration of their mental images through discussion and open-ended questions. Gambrell and Bales (1987) proposed that teachers use think-alouds, a procedure in which the teacher stops periodically to talk about his or her own mental imagery while reading a passage aloud or in sign.

Self-Talk

Instruction in metacognitive strategies is ultimately successful when youngsters who are deaf engage in self-talk before, during, and after reading. The Reading/Language in Secondary Schools Subcommittee of the International Reading Association (1989) wrote that effective learners talk to themselves, they have an inner voice that guides and monitors their cognitive activities.

This view of the role of an inner voice is an extension of Vygotsky's concept of inner speech, which was discussed in Chapter 1. Vygotsky viewed inner speech as speech turned into inward thought. Some researchers believe that inner speech is used by individuals to consciously clarify and guide their thoughts. Many reading researchers believe that this same inner voice is used by good readers to clarify and guide their thoughts during reading. It seems logical that inner speech does not have to be in voice but that for some individuals who are deaf, inner speech is in sign.

Based on his study of the comprehension monitoring strategies used by second-, fourth-, sixth-, and eighth-grade readers and adult readers, Winser (1988) proposed that young readers and poor readers would benefit from instruction that helps them to gain conscious control of reading strategies. He found that good readers use the following alternative strategies when comprehension difficulties arise and that they are able to consciously choose the appropriate strategy:

1. Read on—moving further on into the text.
2. Sound out—referring to phonemes/graphemes.
3. Inference—using prior knowledge.
4. Reread—repeating the reading.
5. Resume task—continuing to read.
6. Suspend judgment—being prepared to wait for more information.
7. Aware—indicating knowledge of comprehension problem. (p. 259)

In the previous section, I discussed strategies that encourage the child who is deaf to develop the ability and interest in becoming an autonomous reader. In the next section, strategies that motivate the deaf child to become an autonomous writer will be discussed.

Writing Process Teaching

Writing process teaching is based on the conviction that children will write when they are in a classroom environment that nurtures their inner desire to express themselves in words. As Graves (1983) wrote, "Children want to write. They want to write the first day they attend school. This is no accident. Before they went to school they marked up walls, pavement, newspapers with crayons, chalk, pens or pencils. . .anything that makes a mark. The child's marks say, 'I am'" (p. 3).

In writing process teaching, a nurturing environment is one that provides each child with choice, time, and a real audience for his or her writing. In Calkins's (1986) view, "When we invite children to choose their form, voice, and audience as well as their subject, we give them ownership and responsibility for their writing. This transforms writing from an assigned task into a personal project" (p. 6).

Writing process teaching is often called writing workshop or writer's workshop. *Writing workshop* is a teaching model that evolved from the research on process writing that was conducted in the early- and mid-1970s. In writing workshop, the process of prewriting-writing-rewriting that was observed in skilled writers was applied as planning-writing-revising stages in the teaching model. These stages are not seen as linear or discrete in the writing workshop model since the research on the writing process showed that skilled writers move back and forth between these operations. However, the concept of stages gives the teacher a framework for the kinds of activities the child engages in at each step in the writing process.

Planning, writing, and revising can be conceptualized as the heart of the model. Food and oxygen to the heart come in the form of conferencing and minilessons.

Stages in the Writing Process

Planning   Planning can include choosing a topic, identifying a purpose, considering the audience, and choosing the form for the writing (Tompkins, 1990). Choosing a topic can be particularly difficult for some children. Graves (1983) noted that "children who are fed topics, story starters, lead sentences, even opening paragraphs as a steady diet for three or four years, rightfully panic when topics have to come from them" (p. 21).

It has been suggested that each child should keep a writing folder or author's folder. One page in this folder can be a list of topic ideas that the child is encouraged to generate from personal experiences and interests, from topics he or she has read about, and from other students' ideas. The list of topics is meant to be a growing and changing list.

Planning also includes rehearsal activities. For some children, drawing serves an important rehearsal function. For others, discussion is vital. Sometimes a young author needs to gather information through an experience or through reading. Calkins (1986) observed that during rehearsal, writers "experience a growing readiness to put themselves on the line" (p. 17).

Writing   Writing is the stage of getting one's ideas on paper (or the computer screen). Calkins (1986) preferred the term *drafting* to writing because drafting more clearly demonstrates the tentativeness of the writer's early efforts.

The author's folder continues to be valuable to youngsters during the writing stage. By having an author's folder in which to keep writing-in-progress, the child has choice over whether to keep working on one piece of writing or to switch to another piece which may be at a different point toward completion.

It is at the writing stage that children's concerns over spelling need to be addressed. If children believe that every word in a draft must be correctly spelled using standard orthography, they may be unwilling to do any writing at all. A number of educators have recommended that children should be encouraged to use letters or written symbols that make sense to them (Calkins, 1986; Graves, 1983; Harste, Short, & Burke, 1988). It is assumed that using invented spelling allows the child's writing to flow more freely. When Clarke (1988) studied the effects of invented versus traditional spelling on the writing of first graders, she found that children who used invented spelling wrote longer texts at the beginning of the study and showed greater increase in text length after five months.

However, not all children are comfortable with invented spelling. Wood (1989) proposed that teachers present children with invented spelling strategies such as drawing, scribbling, using strings of letters, and phonetic spelling, and model how these strategies can be used to write and read back what has been written. When children ask for correct spelling, Wood suggested that teachers remind the children of the strategies they can use by themselves.

Revising   Revising has been defined as seeing again, a re-vision (Calkins, 1986; Tompkins, 1990). Calkins believed that writers ask the same basic questions of themselves over and over again:

- ❏ What have I said so far? What am I trying to say?
- ❏ How do I like it? What's good here that I can build on? What's not so good that I can fix?
- ❏ How does it sound? How does it look?
- ❏ How else could I have done this?
- ❏ What will my reader think as he or she reads this? What questions will they ask? What will they notice? Feel? Think?
- ❏ What am I going to do next? (p. 19)

Movement between planning, writing, and revision can happen at the word level, sentence level, paragraph level, and text level. At one point the writer may change a single word a dozen times and at another point write several paragraphs without stopping to reread and revise. Editing is usually thought of as a final clean-up for the written conventions of spelling, capitalization, grammatical structure, and writing style yet many writers cannot move forward if a word is spelled incorrectly, the punctuation confuses the meaning, a sentence seems awkward, or the copy is messy.

Teachers typically report that youngsters do not like to revise and are reluctant to do much more than peripheral revision. In her review of the literature on revision, Fitzgerald (1987) found that researchers had made the identical observation. It appeared that without extensive support from teachers or peers, beginning writers do little independent revision and that even older and more experienced writers tend to make editing revisions only. Yet the research also supports the positive effects of revision on the writer's thought processes and on the quality of the final written composition.

Fitzgerald (1988) found some support in the literature for three kinds of instructional strategies that encouraged children to revise their writing. The first is *naturalistic classroom support*. In this strategy, natural opportunities to think about and experiment with revision are provided. Naturalistic classroom support is provided whenever children are given lots of time to write and lots of time to talk with others about their writing. The second strategy is *direct instruction in the problem solving process of revision*. In this strategy, the teacher demonstrates the revision process, provides guided practice, and gives the youngsters written suggestions about revision. The third strategy is *procedural facilitation of revision*. In this strategy, the teacher provides the youngsters with a set of evaluative statements that they can use to assess their writing and guide their revisions. Some examples are, "People won't see why this is important," "This is good," "I'm getting away from the main point," "I'd better give an example," "I'd better change the wording" (p. 128). Teachers can develop evaluative statements that are appropriate for individual children.

Many teachers include revision checklists or editing/proofreading lists inside the author's folder. Ultimately, the author's folder contains a rich history of the child's writing: topic ideas, drafts, completed pieces, self-evaluations and teacher evaluations, and writing suggestions.

Publishing   Not every piece that children write leads to publishing, but the opportunity to publish provides youngsters with the sense that they are writing for a real audience. Graves (1983) contended that "publishing serves as a specific anchor for the future during the composing. Even more important, when the child is composing a new piece, publishing is a hardcover record of past accomplishments" (p. 54).

Many schools have taken on publishing as a school-wide project that has included the purchasing of book-binding equipment, the involvement of parent volunteers, and the establishment of a school publishing house. Regardless of how simple or elaborate the publishing process is, most children seem to enjoy seeing some of their work placed and catalogued into a well-used classroom or school library. As Hubbard (1985) noted, "If the goals of an effective writing program include helping writers go beyond themselves, taking pride in their work and their classroom community, then publishing books should be an integral part of that program" (p. 662).

Conferencing

When asked the question, "Why conference?" Graves (1983) responded with three answers: when the child converses, the teacher learns, the child learns, and the teacher can help. As I stated earlier, conferencing is the oxygen to the writing workshop's heart.

Calkins (1986) observed that conferences fell into five categories: content, design, process, evaluation, and editing. In *content conferences*, the focus is on the subject of the writing, and the conference partner asks questions that help the writer to figure out what he or she knows about the topic, needs to learn about it, and what he or she wants to convey to the reader. In *design conferences*, the focus is on the form of the writing and the conference partner asks questions that help the writer make decisions about mode, style, amount of detail, focus, and balance.

Process conferences focus on the writing process and the conference partner asks questions that help the writer to reflect on the strategies that he or she is using which work well and those which are not working well. *Evaluation conferences* focus on evaluating the writing and the conference partner asks questions that encourage the writer to be a critical reader of his or her own writing. In *editing conferences*, the focus is on mechanics, and the conference partner draws the writer's attention to correct usage of spelling, punctuation, capitalization, and sentence structure.

There are not only different categories of conferences but different forms of conferences as well. One-to-one conferences can be between the teacher and one student or between two peers. When they are between peers, the teacher has to make sure that the youngsters are taught how to interact with one another in conferences, often the topic of several mini-lessons.

Group conferences can be conducted for the purpose of seeking advice or for sharing. Harste, Short, and Burke (1988) make this distinction with the terms Author's Circle and Author's Chair. In *Author's Circle*, the author reads his or her piece to the group and gives the group direction regarding the kind of feedback being solicited. "Author's Circle is under the direction of whichever author is presenting a piece. The presenting author shares the piece of writing, tells what he or she particularly likes about it, asks if it is clear, and identifies sections that are weak and that require the group's suggestions for improvement" (p. 69). In *Author's Chair*, the child reads to the group a composition that he or she likes just the way it is.

Atwell (1987) found that group conferences provided positive closure to the day's writing workshop for all the youngsters in a class. She called these conferences *Group Share* and found that over the course of a year, youngsters used Group Share to audition something new, share a technique, try out an alternative approach, solicit perspectives on a piece, and follow up on information presented in minilessons.

Minilessons

Minilessons are 5- to 10-minute lessons that are often used to open writing workshop class periods. As I stated earlier, minilessons supply the food, or nourishment, to the writing workshop. Minilessons offer a whole-group forum for the teacher to provide direct instruction in a skill or concept with which the youngsters have been grappling in their writing. Atwell (1986) organized minilessons around eight major categories, though she emphasized that there are many other possible categories:

❏ *Early Writing*—showing children the functions and characteristics of print, as in a minilesson on road signs.

❏ *Topic Choice*—providing the children with suggestions for finding topics.

❏ *The Launch*—presenting the youngsters with an introduction to writing workshop.

❏ *Conferences*—providing the children with ways that help them to be good conference partners.

❏ *Classroom Procedures*—presenting the rules, responsibilities, and routines involved in writing workshop.

❏ *Rehearsal and Revision Strategies*—providing specific ideas that the youngsters can use in planning and revising their compositions.

❏ *Qualities of Good Writing*—discussing components of good writing that are particularly relevant to the age, developmental level, and interest of the children.

❏ *Literature*—reading good literature.

Atwell (1987) described minilessons as a sharing of personal knowledge of writing. Yet she cautioned teachers against viewing the content of minilessons as information that each student should master. "I don't expect every one of my students is going to take to heart every word of the minilesson and put it immediately into effect" (p. 78). Rather, she suggested that teachers view minilesson content as options for the youngsters, options which they might not otherwise have considered but which may not be useful or appropriate for them at the moment.

Writing Process Teaching with Youngsters Who Are Deaf

The writing process approach has been used successfully with deaf youngsters from preschool through high school (Bensinger, Santomen, & Volpe, 1987; Ciocci & Morrell-Schumann, 1987; Conway, 1985; Livingston, 1989; Truax, 1985). But children are not transformed into independent writers overnight and many teachers, particularly those who are used to a conventional skills approach to teaching writing, find the transition can be painstakingly slow and frustrating.

Conway (1985) reflected the impressions of many of his colleagues who have tried the writing process approach with students who are deaf when he concluded, "This type of teaching is not easy. The teacher must be willing to abandon long-held notions of what a teacher's role should be. There are no manuals with step-by-step procedures to help the teacher become adept at observing the child and recognizing when to move forward or step back. Even with the conceptual growth the children demonstrated almost daily, at times the teachers needed reassuring that they were indeed doing their job. However, as they witnessed the gains made by the children in the first year, their enthusiasm and expectations grew" (pp. 124–125).

Dialogue Journals

In a dialogue journal, the child and the teacher carry on a private, written conversation. The conversation can last a month, a term, or a year. Staton (1988) considered dialogue journal writing to be a unique kind of classroom writing. "Unlike much school-assigned writing, which is often only for purposes of evaluation, dialogue journals are functional, interactive, mostly about self-generated topics, and deeply embedded in the continuing life of the classroom" (p. 198).

The special characteristics of dialogue journal writing offer benefits that other kinds of writing cannot. I will discuss four of these benefits which I consider to be especially important to children who are deaf, though many other benefits have been reported in the literature.

One benefit is the conversational voice used in this type of writing. As Shuy (1987) pointed out, "Children already know how to talk, so conversational writing does what education has always claimed to do but, in reality, seldom manages to do—it starts with what the learner already knows and then tries to build on this knowledge" (p. 892).

Another benefit to dialogue journal writing is that it provides children a forum for using language to accomplish goals. In other words, this kind of writing is functional. Conway and his associates (1988) reported that the hearing impaired youngsters they observed expressed a variety of language functions in their dialogue journals including explaining, persuading, requesting help, reporting, apologizing, asking questions, and expressing feelings. Bode (1989) found that the function used most frequently by the first-grade students in her study of dialogue journal writing was complaining, and the second most frequently used function was asking questions that challenged the teacher. Bode believed that the use of these functions made it obvious how empowering dialogue journal writing can be for the child.

A third benefit to dialogue journal writing is that it enables the teacher to facilitate the deaf child's language development through mutual collaboration and support. As the teacher questions, expands, and restates in response to the child's written comments, the teacher is in essence providing a scaffold of language learning for the child (Conway et al., 1988; Staton, 1988).

A further benefit to dialogue journal writing is that it provides youngsters with an immediate and obvious connection between reading and writing. The written conversation is perpetuated when the child reads the teacher's comments and responds in writing, and the child knows that the teacher must read the child's comments in order to respond in writing. Thus, dialogue journal writing is a teaching-learning activity that reflects a whole language philosophy (Bode, 1989; Staton, 1985).

Several guidelines have been suggested for maximizing the positive outcomes of dialogue journal writing. In terms of materials, bound composition books are generally recommended. In terms of time, most educators urge classroom teachers to set aside a specific time daily for reading and writing in the journals, with 5 to 10 minutes being appropriate for younger children or children new to the activity and 20 minutes for older children (Gambrell, 1985; Strackbein & Tillman, 1987). Bode (1989) noted, however, that children can be given the choice of responding immediately to the teacher's comments or keeping the journal with them throughout the school day and writing in it whenever they chose.

In terms of responding, the teacher is strongly encouraged to keep in mind that writing in the child's journal is like writing a letter to the child. In letters between pen pals, for example, one pen pal does not correct the spelling or punctuation of the other pen pal. And one pen pal does not give the other pen pal instructions and directions. Instead, pen pals generally share experiences and insights, react to each other's written thoughts, ask for clarification or more information, and respond to one another's questions. And pen pals respect the confidentiality of their communication.

When Peyton and Seyoum (1989) investigated the effects of teachers' responses on the quality of student dialogue journal writing, they found that the most successful teacher in their study responded to student topics considerably more often than she initiated topics, she almost always contributed information or opinions on the topic, and she relied much less heavily on questions than the less successful teachers. Peyton and Seyoum believed that this teacher was effective because she was "a co-participant in the writing. She did not remain aloof to review, comment on, and question what the students expressed, but entered into the interaction herself, as a writer with each student" (p. 329).

FINAL COMMENTS

The teaching strategies presented in this chapter for promoting reading and writing development in children who are deaf are classified under three headings: strategies designed to foster emergent literacy, teacher-directed approaches, and child-directed approaches. The section on fostering emergent literacy is clearly aimed at the teacher who works with children and parents in early intervention, preschool, and kindergarten programs. The sections on teacher-directed and child-directed approaches are aimed at teachers of deaf children from grades 1 through 12.

The distinction between teacher-directed and child-directed approaches is meant to reflect a differential application of whole language principles. The teacher-directed approaches presented in this chapter embody the following whole language principles: all forms of expressive and receptive language work together; and focus is on meaning of spoken, sign, and written language in authentic context. The child-directed approaches presented in this chapter embody these two principles and also embody the following three principles: classrooms are communities of learners in which language and literacy are acquired through use; children are empowered when they are given choice and ownership; and processes should be emphasized, not products. In the next chapter, the strategies presented will embody the sixth whole language principle: literacy development and content should form an integrated curriculum.

SUGGESTED READINGS

Atwell, N. (1987). *In the Middle: Writing, Reading, and Learning with Adolescents*. Portsmouth, NH: Heinemann.

Calkins, L.M. (1986). *The Art of Teaching Writing*. Portsmouth, NH: Heinemann.

Loughlin, C.E., & Martin, M.D. (1987). *Supporting Literacy: Developing Effective Learning Environments*. New York: Teachers College, Columbia University.

Noyce, R.M., & Christie, J.F. (1989). *Integrating Reading and Writing Instruction in Grades K–8*. Boston: Allyn and Bacon.

Trelease, J. (1989). *The New Read-Aloud Handbook*. New York: Penguin.

5

Learning Through Reading and Writing in the Content Areas

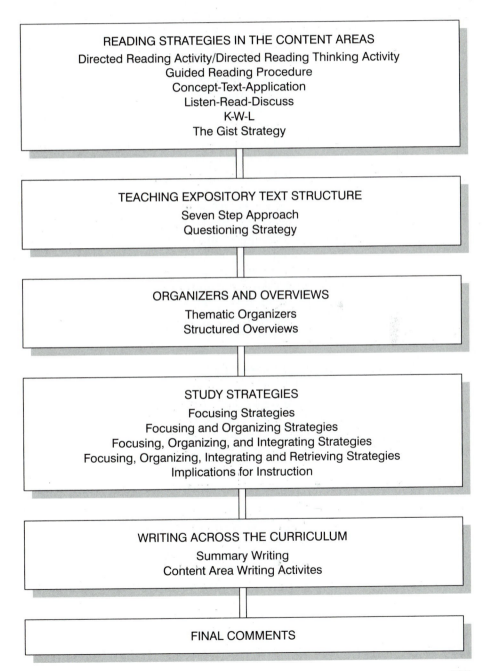

READING STRATEGIES IN THE CONTENT AREAS
Directed Reading Activity/Directed Reading Thinking Activity
Guided Reading Procedure
Concept-Text-Application
Listen-Read-Discuss
K-W-L
The Gist Strategy

TEACHING EXPOSITORY TEXT STRUCTURE
Seven Step Approach
Questioning Strategy

ORGANIZERS AND OVERVIEWS
Thematic Organizers
Structured Overviews

STUDY STRATEGIES
Focusing Strategies
Focusing and Organizing Strategies
Focusing, Organizing, and Integrating Strategies
Focusing, Organizing, Integrating and Retrieving Strategies
Implications for Instruction

WRITING ACROSS THE CURRICULUM
Summary Writing
Content Area Writing Activites

FINAL COMMENTS

Much of what has been written about reading and writing in the content areas has centered on the secondary level. Perhaps this is because at the primary and elementary levels the curriculum tends to be more integrated, reading and writing play a particularly important role in the curriculum, and teachers of deaf children are more likely to view themselves as responsible for teaching all areas of the curriculum. Yet, clearly, teachers at all levels are confronted with the challenge of helping their students who are deaf to read subject area material and to gain skill in the style of expository writing.

In this section, I will present strategies for helping deaf children to read and write in the content areas. I will not be presenting current theories of content area teaching. Content area material, specifically textbooks, present particular difficulties for youngsters who are deaf. Indeed, they present so much difficulty that many teachers use textbooks for reference only or rewrite portions for their students to read. Both of these strategies may be appropriate at times, but neither strategy enables the child who is deaf to become an independent reader of expository material, which they will need for success in college and in the workplace, as well as to be informed citizens throughout their lives.

Teachers of subject areas are always struggling with a double agenda; they are responsible for teaching the content curriculum of science, social studies, math, health, and other courses, but they are also responsible for teaching the skills that will give their students access to the body of written information on these subjects, written information that is as likely to be in the form of newspaper and magazine articles as in the form of textbooks, biographies, self-help books, and reference materials.

READING STRATEGIES IN THE CONTENT AREAS

The literature is replete with instructional strategies designed to facilitate the reading of expository text. Many of the strategies are similar to one another with slight modifications, and others represent original ideas. Almost all of them have acronyms such as DRA, DRTA, GRP, CTA, LRD, and KWL.

Directed Reading Activity (DRA)/
Directed Reading Thinking Activity (DRTA)

One strategy that seems to work as effectively with expository text as it does with narrative text is the DRA or DRTA (Alvermann & Swafford, 1989; Haggard, 1985; Montague & Tanner, 1987) which were discussed in detail in Chapter 4. When used with subject area text, the steps in this approach can enable students to read the material with good comprehension. However, it requires that the teacher make a commitment of classroom time toward the actual reading of the text.

Most teachers of deaf children who use this approach include the first three steps (concept development, sight vocabulary, and directed reading) and eliminate the last two steps (skills development and enrichment). The concept development step tends to be used for presenting new terminology the student will encounter in the text. Instead of skills development and enrichment, teachers typically use the time that would be spent on those steps for presenting information on the topic that has not been covered by the text, for helping the students see relationships in the material that the text has not drawn, and for engaging the youngsters in activities, such as experiments, which help make the information more tangible.

Guided Reading Procedure (GRP)

In the *Guided Reading Procedure,* the assumption is made that the students are able to read the text independently but need guidance in comprehending it fully. The steps include the following: (a) a purpose is set and the students read the text, being told to remember all they can, (b) as a group, the students tell everything they can remember and the teacher records it on the board in no particular order, (c) the students are instructed to go back to the text to check on inconsistencies apparent from the differing information recorded on the board, (d) the students organize the information in the form of an outline, semantic map, or diagram. The remainder of the steps in the procedure are intended to be used for testing the students' recall of the information (Manzo, 1975).

Ankney and McClurg (1981) conducted a study in which they used the Guided Reading Procedure with fifth and sixth graders reading science and social studies textbooks and found that it took up a considerable amount of class time, it was appropriate with highly factual material, it was motivating to the students, and it was best used with passages of 500 words or 1 $1/_2$ pages of text at a time.

Because this strategy is built on the assumption that the students can read the text independently, it is not appropriate for many deaf students whose textbooks are written well above their reading levels. However, this strategy can be combined with the use of organizers and overviews, which will be discussed later in this chapter. This combination of strategies can enable many youngsters to read material that may otherwise appear to be too difficult for them.

Concept-Text-Application (CTA)

As developed by Wong and Au (1985), the *Concept-Text-Application* approach is quite similar to the DRTA. In the first phase, *concept,* the teacher assesses the students' background knowledge and introduces those concepts and vocabulary that are new to the students. In the second phase, *text,* the teacher sets a purpose, the students read the section silently, and the teacher asks literal level questions. When the entire section is completed, the teacher engages the students in a discussion during which the information is organized into some type of visual structure. In the third phase, *application*, the teacher encourages the students to evaluate the material and to think divergently about the information.

The Concept-Text-Application approach requires both a fair amount of teacher planning time and class time. The visual structure may be a particularly worthwhile part of the strategy for deaf youngsters who may otherwise miss some of the information contributed during the class discussion.

Listen-Read-Discuss (L-R-D)

Listen-Read-Discuss was developed by Manzo and Casale (1985) as a basic lesson design from which content area teachers could create personal elaborations. In the L-R-D approach, the teacher begins by presenting information from a portion of the text in the teacher's preferred style, such as lecture. The students are then directed to read the specific pages of the text covered in the lecture. The last step is discussion. An example of a teacher elaboration is for the students to be told that they need to locate some important details in the text that were omitted from the lecture.

Listen-Read-Discuss is actually just a reversal of the typical lecture approach used by many high school teachers and college/university instructors. Instead of lecturing on material the students have already read, in the L-R-D approach the students read the material after the lecture. Thus, the material in the text and the terminology used is already familiar to the students and so they are more likely to be able to read the text independently.

K-W-L

The *K-W-L approach* developed by Ogle (1986) emphasizes the reader's prior knowledge. The first step in this approach is Step K, which Ogle defines as accessing *what I know*. In the first part of this step, the teacher writes the topic on the board and the students brainstorm what they know about it. In the second part of this step, the students are encouraged to develop categories for the ideas they brainstormed. The second step is Step W—determining *what I want to learn*. In this step, the students are encouraged to create questions and are asked to write down the ones that interest them the most. The final step is Step L—recalling *what I did learn* as a result of reading. In this step, the students write or discuss what they have learned with specific attention to their original questions.

Teachers applying this approach with deaf students often use Step W to offer questions of their own that they know are likely to draw the children's attention to the most important information in the text. What is particularly attractive about using the K-W-L approach with students who are deaf is that it encourages them to become actively engaged in thinking about the relevance of the material before and after reading.

The Gist Strategy

In the *Gist Strategy* developed by Schuder, Clewell, and Jackson (1989), the teacher uses seven prompts to model and coach students in understanding the text material they are reading. The term *gist* is used to make it clear that the goal of this strategy is for the youngsters to get an overall sense of the text. When used with youngsters who are deaf, it can encourage them to make, test, and revise hypotheses during reading.

The steps follow the Directed Reading Thinking Activity with the exception that the teacher's guided questions are in the form of prompts that are meant to focus the students' thinking on making and proving their predictions. The first two prompts are used before the reading: (a) "What do you think this material is going to be about?" "What makes you think so?" and (b) "What do you think. . .(the text) is going to tell you about. . .(the predicted topic)?" "What makes you think so?"

The next three prompts occur during the reading: (c) "Did you find evidence that supports your prediction?" "What was it?" (d) "Did you find evidence that does not support your prediction?" "What was it?" and (e) "Do you want to change your prediction at this point?" "If not, why not?" "If you do, how do you want to change it?"

The last two prompts are used after the reading: (f) "Do you want to make any changes in your statement of what this is about?" "If yes, what changes do you want to make?" "Why do you want to make those changes?" and (g) "What did you learn that you did not know before reading?" (p. 230).

Teachers who have used the Gist Strategy with deaf students typically report that it is appropriate with particular kinds of expository material such as biographies, persuasive essays, and newspaper and magazine articles. In these materials, the sequence and pace in which ideas are presented and the amount of discussion about ideas allow for the kind of prediction-confirmation/disconfirmation-revise prediction that the strategy requires of the reader. The Gist Strategy works less well with other types of expository material, such as textbook chapters, which tend to be characterized by rapid presentation of new concepts.

TEACHING EXPOSITORY TEXT STRUCTURE

Researchers have found that instruction in expository text structure has a positive effect on recall and comprehension (Armbruster, Anderson, & Ostertag, 1987; Roller & Schreiner, 1985; Slater, 1985; Taylor & Beach, 1984). This seems a logical finding given the difficulty many youngsters have in identifying the important information in their textbooks, their personal lack of experience with expository text when compared to the amount of experience they have with narrative text, and the mix of structures used in most expository materials.

The following two strategies represent contrasting approaches to teaching expository text structure. One promotes deductive learning and the other inductive learning. Both can be used successfully with youngsters who are deaf and so the choice of strategies depends on the students' preferred learning styles.

Seven-Step Approach

In the seven-step approach (my name for it because the authors did not give it one), the teacher uses well-structured textbook passages and graphic organizers to teach youngsters expository text structure (McGee & Richgels, 1985; Richgels, McGee, & Slaton, 1989).

Step 1. The teacher locates an actual passage from the students' textbook that is a few paragraphs long, is well organized, clearly demonstrates one text structure (collection, description, causation, problem/solution, or compare/contrast), and contains clue words. A clue word gives the reader information about relationships between ideas. For example, the words *first*, *second*, and *next* are clues that the structure is based on collection. The words *therefore* and *because* are clues to a causation structure. *However* and *but* are clue words to a compare/contrast structure.

Step 2. The teacher creates a graphic organizer, which is a kind of outline with superordinate ideas at the top connected to subordinate ideas at lower and lower levels. Related ideas are connected with lines. Steps 1 and 2 are completed by the teacher in advance.

Step 3. The teacher explains the notion of text structure.

Step 4. The teacher explains the graphic organizer.

Step 5. The students write their own passage based on the graphic organizer.

Step 6. They read the actual text passage and compare it to their own compositions. The teacher then identifies the type of text structure they have just read and lists clue words that typically signal this type of structure. Steps 1 through 6 are repeated over time for each of the five expository text structures. At that point, step seven is added.

Step 7. The students read longer passages containing more than one structure and are encouraged to look at overall text structure.

Questioning Strategy

The questioning strategy developed by Muth (1987) is based on the assumption that teacher questions can focus students' attention on important relationships between ideas in expository text. In her view, good questions foster both internal connections (how text ideas relate to one another) and external connections (how text ideas relate to the reader's background knowledge). In the questioning strategy, teachers are encouraged to develop questions that build both internal and external connections while at the same time are aimed at the particular text structure the students are reading.

For the compare/contrast text structure, Muth (1987, p. 256) gave the following as examples of good questions in a passage about two breeds of horses. "What is the author comparing and contrasting?" and "What are the advantages of the Quarter horse for pleasure riding?" are two questions designed to build internal connections. "Which of the two horses would you pick and why?" is a question meant to build external connections.

For a passage on rust written in a causation structure, Muth (p. 257) used the example, "What is the cause-effect process that the author is describing?" as a question that helps build internal connections, and "When do you think things might rust in your house?" as the kind of question designed to build external connections.

ORGANIZERS AND OVERVIEWS

Organizers and overviews consist of written information presented to the student prior to reading the actual text. In general, the information contained in an organizer or overview is intended to activate the reader's background knowledge and highlight key concepts in the material to be read. In this section, I will use the term *thematic organizer* to refer to organizers or overviews written in a narrative form and *structured overviews* to refer to organizers or overviews written in graphic form.

The effectiveness of organizers and overviews with youngsters who are deaf is contingent on how independent the youngsters are in reading them and in thinking about how to apply the information. Thus teachers need to spend time explaining the kinds of information contained in organizers and overviews, and providing their students with direction in how to use this information while they are reading the actual text.

Thematic Organizers

Thematic Organizers and Advance Organizers are terms that are used almost interchangeably in the literature. The earliest reference to this strategy is the Advance Organizer, which was developed by Ausubel (1960). An *advance organizer* is written material that is (a) presented in advance of the actual text and (b) designed to provide the reader with concepts that are more general, abstract, and inclusive than the actual text. Lenz, Alley, and Schumaker (1987) found the following elements to characterize most advance organizers described in the literature:

1. Information about the benefits of the advance organizer;
2. Information that identifies the topics and/or subtopics to be covered in the lesson;
3. The physical acts the learner and/or instructor must perform to accomplish the task;
4. Background information related to the learning;
5. The concepts to be learned;
6. Examples or clarification of the to-be-learned concepts;
7. The organization or sequence in which the new information will be presented;
8. Motivational information;
9. New or relevant vocabulary; and
10. Information regarding outcomes of the material to be learned. (p. 54)

Alvarez (1983) modified the advance organizer strategy so that the organizer was written at the student's reading ability level and it included information specifically related to the topic. He called this kind of organizer a *thematic organizer*. According to Risko and Alvarez (1983), the following elements characterize a thematic organizer:

1. Each organizer has three paragraphs that define the implied thematic concept of the passage and relate this concept to prior knowledge and/or experiences of the reader.
2. The concept is defined by presenting its various attributes and non-attributes.
3. Examples of how the concept relates to real-life experiences and the ideas in the text are given to further illustrate the meaning of the concept.
4. Following the three paragraphs are a set of statements written on the interpretive level. The students are instructed to indicate whether they agree with these statements during and/or after their reading. (p. 85)

While early research on organizers produced equivocal results, recent research suggests that organizers are particularly beneficial when students have weak background knowledge, they are taught to use the techniques, and the concepts in the text are abstract or poorly defined (Lenz, Alley, & Schumaker, 1987; Risko & Alvarez, 1986; Townsend & Clarihew, 1989).

Structured Overviews

Structured overviews have been called graphic organizers, graphic overviews, and conceptual maps, but the original term comes from Barron and Earle (Barron, 1969; Earle, 1969; Earle & Barron, 1973). A *structured overview* is a graphic representation of key concepts from the text presented in a hierarchical structure that shows the relationships among superordinate, coordinate, and subordinate concepts. The flow of the structured overview is not meant to reflect the sequence of ideas presented in the text. An example is presented in Figure 5–1.

Brown (1981) recommended that the following steps be used in preparing a structured overview:

1. Read the text assignment analytically to identify and write down major concepts.
2. Add to the list any terms relative to the concepts that the students might already know.
3. Arrange them in a schema to represent hierarchical and parallel relationships among terms. (p. 200)

The research on structured overviews has a relatively lengthy history that may be surprising given that results have been largely disappointing. Moore and Readence conducted a meta-analysis of graphic organizer research in 1984 and found that graphic organizers produce a positive but small effect on learning from text. Investigations since 1984 have produced conflicting results with some researchers finding little effect for structured overviews (DeWitz, Carr, & Patberg, 1987; Simmons, Griffin, & Kameenui, 1988), some finding positive effect when structured overviews were used along with other strategies such as self-questioning or a study strategy (Billingsley & Wildman, 1988; Darch, Carnine, & Kameenui, 1986), and some finding positive effect when organizers were used both before and after reading text (Alvermann & Boothby, 1986).

Researchers have continued to investigate structured overviews because they are intuitively appealing given their appearance as a kind of visual schema on which new information can be visibly attached to prior knowledge. Although I could find no research on the effects of structured overviews with youngsters who are deaf, Flatley and Gittinger (1990) recommended the use of structured overviews for teaching concepts and vocabulary in the humanities and social sciences to deaf students.

STUDY STRATEGIES

Strategies to help youngsters who are deaf read and comprehend content area text material were discussed previously in this chapter. Most content area teachers want their students not only to comprehend the material but

FIGURE 5-1
Structured Overview: Genre

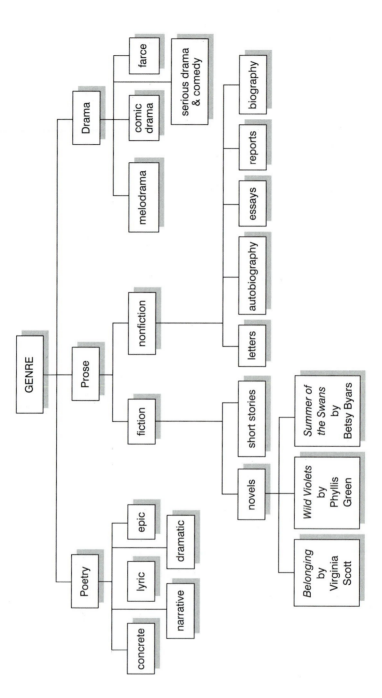

to remember it and be able to recall it on a test. While comprehension is an essential first step, comprehension alone is not sufficient to enable youngsters to study and learn from their texts. As Caverly and Orlando (1991) noted, being able to learn from text involves "learning how to learn when reading" (p. 86).

Study strategies are designed to help youngsters focus their attention on the important information in text material, organize this information in a way that makes sense, integrate it with other previously known information so that it can be retained, and retrieve it when needed. Each strategy tends to focus on one or a few of these goals. In order for youngsters to accomplish all four, they need to be able to use combinations of strategies. Furthermore, they need to be able to choose the most appropriate strategies based on the demands of the material and nature of the expected learning outcome.

The effectiveness of any given strategy depends on four factors—the student, the material, the student's degree of knowledge about the strategy and skill in using it, and the appropriateness of the strategy. After reviewing the research on study strategies, Caverly and Orlando (1991) concluded that the question "is not whether study strategies are successful, but rather where, when, and under what conditions they are successful" (p. 88).

Students who are deaf need to know an assortment of strategies and have the skill to apply them appropriately. The strategies presented in this section are the major ones discussed in the literature. I have organized them into four categories, categories that represent the learning goals of study strategies.

Focusing Strategies

Focusing strategies are study strategies designed to help youngsters focus their attention on the important information in the text. The most common focusing strategy is *underlining/highlighting*. As a matter of fact, underlining/highlighting is reported to be the most popular study strategy used by students (Blanchard, 1985; McAndrew, 1983).

Underlining/highlighting takes less time than virtually any other study strategy. This may be the reason it is used spontaneously by so many students. Although it is an efficient strategy, it is effective only under two conditions. The first is that the students take the time to review the underlined/highlighted material. The second is that they limit the amount of material they underline/highlight to higher level general statements. The research on underlining/highlighting also indicates that it is less effective for students below the fifth grade and for students at lower reading levels (Caverly & Orlando, 1991; McAndrew, 1983; Rickards, 1980).

Based on his review of the research on study skills instruction, Blanchard (1985) developed the following recommendations for teachers:

❑ Explain to students that they need to acquire a repertoire of study strategies and learn when to apply what strategy for best retention.

❑ Explain to students that their attitudes, beliefs, and opinions about a study assignment, as well as the text content, affect what they underline and remember.

❑ Help students understand that any knowledge they might have about the contents of a future test will affect what they underline and remember. In addition, tell them that prior knowledge about the type of questions that will be used in a test affects underlining and recall.

❑ Explain to students that prior knowledge about text content or familiarity with the text's structure or characteristics as well as the author's writing style affects what they underline and remember.

❑ Tell students that the more their study habits include "timely review," the more their underlined text segments gain or lose importance for review purposes. (pp. 201–202)

It has been suggested that teachers model the use of underlining/highlighting (Blanchard, 1985; Poostay, 1984). It also seems important for teachers of youngsters who are deaf to provide guided practice in underlining/highlighting the most important concepts in a passage.

Focusing and Organizing Strategies

A few of the study strategies described in the literature are designed to help students accomplish two goals—focus on important text information and organize the information in a way that makes sense.

One of these strategies is *notetaking* while reading. According to Smith and Tompkins (1988), notetaking from text has four benefits:

❑ First, students actively attend to the written message, selecting important ideas to retain in notes.

❑ Second, students who paraphrase and add their own comments or examples are relating their prior knowledge to new information.

❑ Third, as learners elaborate on content by paraphrasing, indicating relationships among ideas, and developing their own examples, they are processing the content more deeply.

❑ Finally, in creating their own notes, students generate a transportable and permanent storage of important information that is available for review. (pp. 46–47)

The research has shown that students who profit from notetaking are those who are able to identify the central ideas in text material. Connected to this finding is the observation that notetaking is more productive for material that is relatively easy for the youngster to read and comprehend (Caverly & Orlando, 1991). It has also been found that the act of taking notes is less important than the actual studying of the notes (Smith & Tompkins, 1988), a finding that may be self-evident to teachers but not at all obvious to students.

Notetaking is one focusing and organizing study strategy. *Study guides* are another. Study guides are typically viewed as a set of questions the student must answer either during or after reading text material (Horton & Lovitt, 1989). It has been suggested that questions requiring different levels of comprehension be included in study guides. For example, Bean and Ericson (1989) recommended the use of Pearson and Johnson's taxonomy of textually explicit, textually implicit, and scriptally implicit questions.

Reading road maps were developed by Wood (1988) as elaborated versions of study guides. In a reading road map, a winding road is drawn down the left side of a page and questions are written down the right side of the page. Road signs are drawn alongside the winding road. The signs on the left of the road present the topics and page numbers, and the signs on the right side of the road provide the directions.

Study guides can be valuable as a study strategy with students who are deaf for three reasons. First, the questions focus the youngster's attention on key text information. Second, the questions can be designed to encourage higher-order thinking. And third, they provide a set of notes the youngsters can use for reviewing major concepts.

Focusing, Organizing, and Integrating Strategies

Several study strategies are designed to enable students to accomplish three goals—focus their attention on important text information, organize the information into a conceptual framework, and integrate it with previously known information so that it can be retained. Strategies in this category include outlining, semantic mapping, and graphic organizers.

The major difference between these study strategies and the ones discussed previously is that these particular strategies require the student to elucidate the relationships between concepts. The strategies are different from each other in the ways that connections between relationships are drawn.

Outlining requires that the student identify superordinate concepts and relate subordinate concepts to superordinate ones. *Semantic mapping* also requires the student to relate subordinate concepts to superordinate ones but semantic mapping goes a step further by providing a way for the student to relate subordinate concepts to one another.

Outlining and semantic mapping have been found to be effective with material that is at or above the student's reading level and with relatively lengthy material. It has also been found that students need explicit instruction in outlining and semantic mapping to be able to use these strategies competently (Caverly & Orlando, 1991; Laframboise, 1986–1987).

When used as a study strategy, *graphic organizers* were described by Smith and Tompkins (1988) as "a summary that contains verbal and perhaps pictorial information; in it the layout and presentation on the page indicate the relationships among ideas" (p. 48). Smith and Tompkins found that graphic organizers could be used by students, particularly low ability students, to summarize, understand, and retain information from text when the organizers reflected expository text structures.

Figure 5–2 illustrates the kinds of graphic organizers that can be used for each of the five basic expository text structures of collection, description, causation, problem/solution, and comparison. These graphic organizers are based on ones developed by Smith and Tompkins.

Focusing, Organizing, Integrating, and Retrieving Strategies

A few strategies are designed to enable youngsters to achieve all of the goals involved in studying. These study strategies incorporate activities to help the youngster select the most important information in the text material, organize this information in a way that makes sense, integrate it with previously known information, and retrieve it when needed.

It would seem that the comprehensiveness of these strategies would make them highly useful. After all, instead of learning a menu of strategies such as the ones I described previously, the youngster could learn one comprehensive strategy and use it all the time. This comprehensiveness, however, can be a drawback when specific components of the strategy do not feel comfortable to the youngster or are not appropriate for every study situation. Comprehensive study strategies are somewhat like all-symptom cold tablets; they may contain ingredients you don't need and the side-effects can leave you immobile.

SQ3R is one of these comprehensive strategies. Originally developed in 1946 by Robinson, it continues to be one of the most widely taught strategies today. SQ3R contains five steps. *S* is for survey, the step in which the student skims the material to get a general overview of the organization and content. *Q* is for question, and in this step, the student converts chapter headings and subheadings into questions. These first two steps take place before reading. The *3R* is for read, recite, and review. During reading, the student finds answers to the questions. After reading, the student recites the answers or writes them down. Lastly, the student reviews the answers until the information is fully remembered.

For the advantages of SQ3R to be realized, it has been found that teachers need to spend a substantial amount of time teaching the strategy and providing students with guided practice in applying it (Caverly & Orlando, 1991; Gustafson & Pederson, 1986).

FIGURE 5–2

Graphic Organizers for Expository Text Structures

Collection   _____

(time sequence or list)   1.   _____

                             2.   _____

                             3.   _____

Description

Causation   _____ Cause

                           _____

                           _____

                           _____

                  _____ Effect

                           _____

                           _____

                           _____

Problem/Solution   Problem   Solution

           _____   _____

              _____   _____

              _____   _____

              _____   _____

Comparison   _____   _____

                             Likenesses

          _____   _____   _____

          _____   _____   _____

          _____   _____   _____

                             Differences

          _____   _____   _____

          _____   _____   _____

          _____   _____   _____

Source: Smith & Tompkins (1988). Reprinted with permission of Patricia L. Smith and the International Reading Association.

PORPE is another study strategy that is designed to be comprehensive. It was developed by Simpson, Stahl, and Hayes (1989) and is unique from many other strategies in that it begins after the youngster has read the text material. PORPE consists of five steps: predict, organize, rehearse, practice and evaluate.

In the predict step, the student poses several essay questions the teacher might ask about the material. The student is encouraged to develop questions requiring synthesis, discussion, comparison-and-contrast, or evaluation of major concepts presented in the text. In the organize step, the student gathers information from the text to answer the questions and organizes the information into a map, chart, or outline. In the rehearse step, the student recites the answers aloud or in sign. In the practice step, the student writes the answers. In the evaluate step, the student evaluates his or her own answers. The authors recommended that in this final step, the student should be given a checklist to help determine how complete, accurate, and appropriate the answers are.

Implications for Instruction

All of these study strategies have been shown to benefit some students, with particular kinds of materials, under certain conditions. In other words, no one strategy has been found to be superior to the others. The ability to use all or most of them would likely enable students who are deaf to study a variety of text material effectively and efficiently. We can help our students to use study strategies skillfully by doing three things:

1. We need to explicitly teach youngsters who are deaf how to use each strategy.
2. We need to encourage them to be flexible in their choice of strategies.
3. We need to provide them with enough guided practice so that they are likely to use the strategies independently.

WRITING ACROSS THE CURRICULUM

In recent years, the literature on writing instruction has focused intently on the writing process. The consequence has been a trend toward a deemphasis of expository writing and writing in the content areas, particularly when this kind of writing involved direct instruction in form and content. The literature seems to reflect the obvious enthusiasm that teachers and researchers are feeling about process writing approaches. The literature may also be reflecting the concern of teachers and researchers that direct teaching models undermine the sense of ownership, relevance, and meaningfulness that youngsters should feel about their own writing. Yet the ten-sion between different paradigms of writing instruction may be more apparent than real to classroom teachers. It is my experience that classroom teachers continue to seek new approaches for teaching the many kinds of writing that deaf youngsters need to learn.

This section will focus on some of the ideas being presented in the literature on writing across the curriculum which are particularly valuable for youngsters who are deaf. However, I would like to note that the body of current literature on this topic is relatively small and many of the ideas are time-honored ones.

Summary Writing

Summary writing traditionally has been valued as a writing activity in all subject areas because it combines reading and writing, it has been found to improve comprehension and recall, and it requires the student to use higher-order thinking processes (Bromley, 1985; Brown, Day, & Jones, 1983; Noyce & Christie, 1989; Rinehart, Stahl, & Erickson, 1986). It has been observed that the ability to summarize improves with age, able readers write better summaries than less able readers, and even good readers may need explicit instruction in the rules of summary writing (Brown, Day, & Jones, 1982; Garner, Belcher, Winfield, & Smith, 1985).

Three models can be found in the literature for teaching summary writing. All of these models can be used with students who are deaf. The major drawback is that the models assume that the youngster can read the text material independently with relatively good comprehension. However, as discussed previously in this chapter, expository text material is often very challenging for deaf students. Teachers who incorporate summary writing into their instruction usually combine it with one of the reading strategies designed to give the students support in initially reading the material.

The first model, developed by Noyce and Christie (1989), consists of four steps:

1. Select a topic sentence. If you do not see a sentence by the author that summarizes the paragraph, write your own.

2. Delete unnecessary information. Text information may be repeated in a passage, or it may be trivial. Delete both redundant and unimportant ideas.

3. Collapse list of items. Substitute a collective term for a number of things that fall into the same category, e.g., instead of bracelets, pendants, pins, and watches, you might use jewelry. Also, substitute one encompassing action for a list of subcomponents of the action.

4. Collapse paragraphs. Some paragraphs expand on others and can be combined with them. Others are unnecessary and can be deleted. (pp. 234–235)

Noyce and Christie suggested that these rules be taught explicitly, that the teacher model the steps, and that the students be given practice in applying the rules.

The second model, developed by Guido and Colwell (1987), consists of four principles, several of which overlap with the Noyce and Christie model:

1. Don't include unnecessary detail (even if it's interesting to you).
2. Don't repeat anything you have already said.
3. Use a general term for a list of specific items.
4. Use one word to describe a list of actions that were included in one or several sentences. (pp. 94–95)

Guido and Colwell also suggested that teachers use direct instruction in teaching this model. The steps they recommended include presenting the principles, giving examples, providing practice, sharing applications, and offering feedback.

Taylor (1982) developed a model she called the hierarchical summary procedure, which includes study skills as well as summary writing. The summary writing part of the procedure involves the following three steps:

1. Previewing. The students skim three to five pages of text and create a skeleton outline. A skeleton outline includes major headings with five to six lines left open for each heading.
2. Reading. The students read the text.
3. Summarizing. The students complete their outline, using main idea statements and supporting details. In the margin, the students write key phrases that relate to more than one section of the outline and use lines to connect them. For each major section, the students write a topic sentence.

In the last two steps, the students study their summaries and retell the information to a classroom partner. Taylor noted that it is important for the students to generate their own topic sentences, main idea statements, and supporting details and not copy headings, subheadings, or phrases from the actual text.

Content Area Writing Activities

Writing in the content areas can accomplish three goals for students who are deaf: (a) increasing knowledge of expository text structure, (b) using writing to learn, and (c) gaining mastery of an assortment of discourse forms. The following writing activities can be used throughout the curriculum. Many of them were recommended by Noyce and Christie (1989) and Tompkins (1990).

❏ Research Reports
❏ Biography and Autobiography
    Actual
    Imaginary
❏ Letter Writing
    Personal
    To the Editor or Public Official
    Complaint
    Request for Information, Services, or Goods
    Invitation or Thank-You
❏ Essays
❏ Advertisements
    Print Advertisement
    Video Commercial
❏ Learning Logs
    Notes
    Vocabulary
    Observations
    Procedures
    Questions
    Lab Reports
❏ Story Problems
❏ Journals and Diaries
❏ News Reports
    Newspaper Articles
    Television Reports
    Book or Film Reviews
❏ Interviews
❏ Directions and Recipes
❏ Scripts

These writing activities can be used throughout the school year and within all subject area classes to provide children who are deaf with abundant experiences in writing across the curriculum. When combined with the process writing activities described in Chapter 4, the teacher can create a classroom environment that supports the learning of writing, learning about writing, and the using of writing to learn.

FINAL COMMENTS

It is not uncommon for teachers of the content areas to be more interested in their subject matter curriculum goals and objectives than in the children's reading, writing, and language goals. After all, at each grade level children are expected to master specific content area material. It is extremely difficult for teachers of deaf children to pay close attention to language and literacy while they are presenting complex concepts and ideas in science, social studies, math, health, and other subject areas. The purpose of this chapter was to provide teachers of content area subjects with teaching strategies designed to help them deal with the competing demands involved in encouraging the development of literacy while teaching content area information.

In the next chapter, I will present approaches that teachers can use to assess the deaf child's growth in reading and writing.

SUGGESTED READINGS

Duffy, G.G. (1990). *Reading in the Middle School (2nd ed.)*. Newark, DE: International Reading Association.

Gilles, C., Bixby, M., Crowley, P., Crenshaw, S.R., Henrichs, M., Reynolds, F. E., & Pyle, D. (1988). *Whole Language Strategies for Secondary Students*. New York: Richard C. Owen.

Moore, D.W., Moore, S.A., Cunningham, P.M., & Cunningham, J.W. (1986). *Developing Readers and Writers in the Content Areas*. New York: Longman.

Moore, D.W., Readence, J.E., & Rickelman, R.J. (1988). *Prereading Activities for Content Area Reading and Learning (2nd ed.)*. Newark, DE: International Reading Association.

Tompkins, G.E. *Teaching Writing: Balancing Process and Product*. New York: Merrill/Macmillan.

6

Monitoring the Learning Process in Reading and Writing

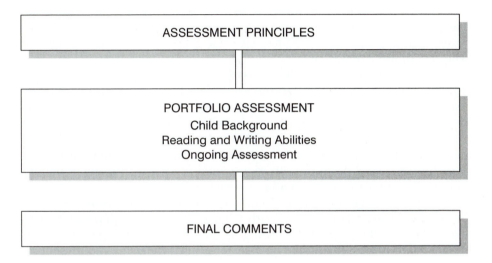

ASSESSMENT PRINCIPLES

PORTFOLIO ASSESSMENT
Child Background
Reading and Writing Abilities
Ongoing Assessment

FINAL COMMENTS

A ssessment, diagnosis, measurement, and evaluation are terms that are used to describe the process of gathering information about each child's strengths and weaknesses in learning and then making judgments about instruction. Purposes for literacy assessment tend to fall into three categories: administrative decisions, parental decisions, and instructional decisions. As Finn (1990) indicated, the assessment instruments and techniques the teacher uses depend on the purpose of assessment, and the way to determine purpose is to figure out what questions are being asked and who is asking the questions.

Administrators and public policymakers ask questions like, "How well are the students in my charge (or the students among my constituents) learning to read?" and "What do these children know compared to others the same age or in the same grade in other schools or school districts?" (Finn, 1990, p. 277). According to Baumann (1988b), the answers lead to decisions regarding evaluation of programs and materials, identification of students for special programs, promotion and retention, assessment of minimum competencies, and evaluation of teachers.

Parents ask questions like, "What does the child know or how does he or she perform in comparison with what the teacher expects of him or her?" (Finn, 1990, p. 277). According to Baumann (1988b), parental questions lead to decisions regarding when to enroll a child in school, whether to seek placement in a special program, and whether to request a specific teacher.

Teachers ask questions such as, "What does this child know and what can he or she do?" "What does the child need to learn next?" and "What can I learn by observing the child that will help determine my teaching strategy?" (Finn, 1990, p. 277). Baumann (1988b) noted that teachers' questions lead to instructional decisions regarding grouping, choice of teaching strategies and materials, and screening for further evaluations.

A further purpose of assessment is to provide feedback to the children. Students have questions about their own learning, questions that are at least as important as the ones administrators, parents, and teachers ask, and the answers help them decide what, how, when, and why they will learn. In this section, I will discuss the kinds of assessment that help answer student, parent, and teacher questions. With this focus in mind, I will concentrate on the informal approaches to assessment which I believe best answer these questions.

ASSESSMENT PRINCIPLES

The following set of principles should guide teachers in monitoring the literacy development of children who are deaf. Several of these guiding principles were based on ones developed by Valencia (1990) and Teale, Hiebert, and Chittenden (1987).

1. *Assessment and teaching are bound together.* Assessment should be grounded in what children are learning, assessment should be linked with authentic reading and writing activities, assessment should enhance the teacher's ability to observe and understand learning. Teaching goals should be focused enough to be assessed.

2. *Assessment is a continuous, systematic, and evolving process.* This principle means that some types of assessment take place moment-by-moment and some on a regularly scheduled basis. It also means that assessment changes over time as children demonstrate the ability to engage in new kinds of literacy tasks.

3. *Assessment is multidimensional.* Assessment techniques and instruments must be varied, and diverse contexts should be used to gather information on the full spectrum of knowledge and skills possessed by the youngsters.

4. *Assessment is a shared endeavor between teacher and student.* According to this principle, the goal of assessment is to inform the teacher and the student mutually so that they can make joint decisions about what to do next.

PORTFOLIO ASSESSMENT

Portfolios constitute a relatively recent addition to the topic of literacy assessment. Portfolios, which have been used for many years by artists and investment brokers, provide a means for matching assessment with whole language philosophy. A *portfolio* is a collection of items that "reflect the student's strengths, growth, and goals" (Reading/Language in Secondary Schools Subcommittee of the International Reading Association, 1990, p. 646).

In this section, I will describe the information that teachers of deaf children might want to include in a portfolio. In reading this discussion, two points should be kept in mind. The first is that these are suggestions only. There are no hard-and-fast rules for portfolios at this time. It is up to the teacher to choose the types of information and categories of items that have the best potential to reveal the kinds of literacy learning occurring in the classroom. The second point is that I will not advocate any specific test, procedure, or technique but rather will discuss examples that teachers might consider. Although this discussion of reading and writing assessment is separate from the assessment of language development presented in Chapter 1, the two discussions should be seen as complementary.

Child Background

When we look into the child's background for the purposes of a language assessment, we are interested in information such as developmental milestones, degree of hearing loss, presence of disabilities that might affect learning, relevant medical history, language(s) used at home, profile of the family structure, age at which the hearing loss was diagnosed, age at which the child began receiving educational services, and school progress reports.

We are equally interested in this kind of information when we are conducting an assessment of the child's literacy development. However, we also want to know the nature of the child's previous reading and writing instruction. For example, it is extremely important to know the kinds of reading materials the child used in the past, the types of writing the child did, and how the previous teacher evaluated the child's progress.

Reading and Writing Abilities

Regardless of the richness of background data available to the teacher, when the child is new to the classroom, there is a need to obtain information about the child's current reading and writing abilities. The teacher can gather this information informally and through standardized tests.

Informal Approaches

The advantages and disadvantages of informal approaches in literacy assessment are similar to the advantages and disadvantages of informal approaches in language assessment discussed in Chapter 1. Informal approaches offer the best potential for providing a link between literacy assessment and instruction because the assessment tasks closely resemble actual instruction and they engage the child in authentic reading and writing. The disadvantage of informal approaches is that the accuracy and completeness of the information depends heavily on the skill of the teacher.

Informal Reading Inventory   An informal reading inventory is one type of informal approach to reading assessment. In an informal reading inventory, the teacher begins by choosing reading passages at easy to progressively more difficult levels. Two equivalent passages are chosen at each level. Passage length is typically 25–50 words for the preprimer and primer levels, 50 words for first- and second-grade levels, and 100–200 words for third-grade level and above. The teacher then develops 6 to 10 factual and inferential questions for each passage.

It is usually recommended that teachers begin the procedure with passages the child would find easy to read. Child background information can be very helpful at this time for indicating a starting point. The teacher should mark the location of the passage in the actual book for the child to use and make a photocopy of the passage for his or her own use.

The child is asked to read the first passage aloud or in sign. During this reading, the teacher records any inaccuracies the child makes such as substituting, adding, or omitting words. It is important for teachers of children who are deaf to record the places in which the child uses a sign that is not conceptual or fingerspells a word because these responses sometimes indicate that the child does not recognize the word concept. During this reading, the teacher also makes note of the child's reading behaviors. Some of the observations the teacher might make are whether the child reads fluently or word-by-word, effortlessly or with intense concentration, with or without expression, and uses effective strategies for figuring out unknown words. After the passage is read, the teacher asks the comprehension questions and records the child's answers.

The child is asked to read the second passage silently. During this reading, the teacher can make note of reading behaviors such as signing to oneself or subvocalizing, rereading words and phrases, and finger pointing. When the child finishes reading the passage, the teacher asks the comprehension questions and records the child's answers.

This procedure is repeated with increasingly more difficult passages until the passage the child is reading is clearly at his or her frustration level. At that point, the teacher reads the passage aloud or in sign to the child and then asks the comprehension questions.

After completing the procedure, the teacher examines the child's reading inaccuracies, behaviors, and answers to the comprehension questions to determine the child's independent, instructional, frustration, and capacity reading levels. The *independent reading level* is considered to be the level at which the child recognizes 98% of the words, answers 90% of the comprehension questions correctly, and reads in a relaxed and fluent manner. The *instructional level* is considered to be the level at which the child recognizes 95% of the words, answers 75% of the comprehension questions correctly, and demonstrates a few behaviors that indicate the child is having some difficulty reading the material. At the *frustration level,* the child is only able to recognize 90% of the words and if forced to complete reading the passage, answers no more than 50% of the comprehension questions correctly. Furthermore, the child demonstrates the desire to avoid reading the material by exhibiting behaviors such as fidgeting and looking up constantly. The *capacity level* is the level at which the child can answer 75% of the comprehension questions correctly when the material is read to him or her.

Creating informal reading inventories is obviously time-consuming for the teacher. It is tempting for teachers to use one of the commercially available informal reading inventories, a couple of which are described in the Appendix. However, a published informal reading inventory no longer embodies the advantages of an informal approach. As Finn (1990) commented, "The passages on which the child is tested are not in the materials that will be used for instruction. Therefore, the direct linkage between the test and the placement of the child at his or her instructional level in the materials used in instruction is lost, as is direct linkage between the difficulties discovered during testing and the difficulties he or she will encounter in the materials used for instruction" (p. 304).

Diagnostic Reading Lesson   In a diagnostic reading lesson, the teacher develops a lesson implementing a reading strategy thought to be appropriate for the child, with reading material likely to be at the child's independent or instructional reading level. If a parent or administrator happened to be watching the teacher and child, it would probably be assumed that this was an ordinary teaching lesson and not an assessment procedure. The teacher conducts the lesson as a typical reading lesson but the purpose is to gather information about the child's reading abilities.

Any of the strategies discussed in Chapter 4 could be used to develop a diagnostic teaching lesson. One example is a Directed Reading Thinking Activity. A teacher who wants to use a DRTA as a diagnostic teaching lesson would choose a story or chapter at a level believed to be at the child's independent to instructional reading level. The teacher would develop and teach a lesson incorporating the steps in a DRTA—concept development, sight vocabulary, guided reading (prediction, silent reading, questions, purposeful oral or sign rereading), and discussion.

If the child demonstrated prior knowledge of most or all of the sight vocabulary, showed few difficulties with recognizing words in the selection, answered comprehension questions fully with little help from the teacher, and seemed relaxed during the reading, the teacher could assume that the text material could be read independently by the child. If the child did not previously know most of the sight vocabulary but was able to learn the words relatively quickly, could recognize most words in the selection but needed assistance with a few words or figurative expressions, and demonstrated good comprehension with help from the teacher, the teacher could assume that the text material would be appropriate for instruction with a strategy such as the DRTA that offers the child considerable teacher support. The teacher would have also learned the kinds of word identification strategies and comprehension strategies that the child used and whether these strategies were being used effectively or not.

Analytical Writing Scoring   Assessing the writing abilities of a child who is deaf can be extremely frustrating because it can be difficult to sort out the child's abilities to manipulate English sentence structures from other aspects of the child's writing. One of the techniques used to gather information about the child's writing that can avoid the problem of focusing too intensely on one aspect of writing is analytical writing scoring. In this technique, separate writing traits are assessed individually and each trait is given equal weight.

In Figure 6–1, criteria for analytical writing scoring are presented. Six writing traits are included—ideas and content, organization, voice, word choice, sentence structures, and mechanics. For each trait, the teacher evaluates the child's writing on a scale from 1 to 5.

The usefulness of this technique as a measure of the deaf child's writing abilities depends on how representative the child's composition is of the child's writing in general. For example, a child who writes prolifically and creatively about sports may write with no enthusiasm when asked to write a mystery. If the teacher chooses to evaluate the mystery using analytical writing scoring, the results might indicate false problems with the child's writing.

Analytical writing scoring provides more reliable assessment information if the teacher applies it to several different pieces of writing and with at least some pieces that are based on self-selected topics. This guideline should be followed not only at the beginning of the school year but at intervals during the year when the teacher wants to assess the child's writing.

Standardized Assessment Instruments

In Chapter 1, the advantages and disadvantages of standardized tests of language were discussed. Standardized tests of reading offer similar advantages and disadvantages. On the plus side, they are relatively easy to administer and results are not influenced by the skill or bias of the examiner. Also on the plus side, these tests offer data regarding reliability, validity, representativeness, and standard error of measurement. On the minus side, standardized reading tests tend to focus heavily on isolated reading skills such as phonic analysis and structural analysis, comprehension is measured with relatively short passages unrelated to one another, and knowledge of vocabulary is often assessed with words that are out of context.

It is an understatement to say that there is a fair amount of discussion regarding the usefulness of standardized tests to measure reading ability and reading growth. Diagnostic reading tests can give the teacher valuable information about the deaf child's current reading abilities when used in conjunction with informal approaches, although standardized reading tests should not be used as a sole measure of the child's current abilities. Furthermore, many school administrators require standardized tests to be given at periodic intervals and if the teacher must administer these tests, the information should be interpreted and used.

One way to elicit information from standardized tests beyond the grade equivalent score is to use a procedure referred to as probing. *Probing* takes place after the teacher has administered and scored the test. In probing, the teacher chooses a few items from the test that were answered correctly and a few that were answered incorrectly by the child. The teacher gives the child a clean copy of the test and asks the child to read and answer the marked items aloud or in sign. For each item, the teacher asks why the child chose that particular answer.

I have described several diagnostic reading tests and academic achievement tests in the Appendix. With the exception of the Stanford Achievement Test, none have been normed on students who are deaf. It is common knowledge that youngsters who are deaf tend to obtain depressed scores on standardized tests of reading, probably because these tests focus largely on the surface structure features of the reading process.

FIGURE 6-1
Analytical Writing Scoring

I. Ideas and Content

> 5   *Paper*: The topic is clear, there is a good balance between central ideas and details, and the paper is interesting.

> 3   *Paper*: Some ideas are clear and others are unclear or not appropriate; and there is too much emphasis on the central idea and not enough supporting details, or vice versa.

> 1   *Paper*: The topic is unclear and ideas seem unrelated to one another or very few ideas are presented.

II. Organization

> 5   *Paper*: Presentation of ideas is logical, relationships between ideas are clearly drawn, and details and examples fit in well to central ideas.

> 3   *Paper*: The presentation of ideas is unclear or not logical, connections between ideas are not made, and details and examples are sometimes not appropriate.

> 1   *Paper*: There is no obvious order to the presentation of ideas, and it is difficult to figure out how ideas relate to one another.

III. Voice

> 5   *Paper*: The writer demonstrates genuine interest in the topic, a desire to express ideas in an original way, and a concern that the reader respond to the writing.

> 3   *Paper*: The writer demonstrates knowledge but no deep interest in the topic, expresses him or herself in routinized ways, and seems aware of his or her audience but does not engage them in the writing.

Ongoing Assessment

Throughout the school year, the teacher can add to the child's portfolio any information that illustrates the child's growth in all areas related to literacy development. The following categories represent the assortment of items that teachers of children who are deaf might consider including in their portfolios.

Literacy Development Checklists

Literacy development checklists are often recommended as one element of a portfolio. For any reading development checklist, Mathews (1990) advised that four major components be included: concepts about print, attitudes toward reading, strategies for word identification, and comprehension strategies. She recommended that observations be recorded on the checklist

FIGURE 6-1
continued

---

      1 *Paper*: The writer demonstrates no sincere interest in the topic and seems unaware of an audience.

IV. Word Choice

      5 *Paper*: The writer chooses words carefully and with creativity.

      3 *Paper*: The writer chooses words that are clear but ordinary, and may use inappropriate or overused words or phrases.

      1 *Paper*: The writer uses a limited variety of words, the words used are not always clear, and some words are inappropriately used.

V. Sentence Structures

      5 *Paper*: Sentences are easy to read and understand, structures are grammatically correct, and a variety of structures are used.

      3 *Paper*: Most sentences are understandable but some structures are incorrect and similar structures are often used.

      1 *Paper*: Sentence structure errors are frequent and it is a difficult paper to read and understand.

VI. Mechanics (Grammar, Capitalization, Punctuation, Spelling, and Paragraphing)

      5 *Paper*: Errors in mechanics are few, and they don't interfere with the reading flow.

      3 *Paper*: Errors in mechanics sometimes draw the reader's attention away from the ideas being presented.

      1 *Paper*: Errors in mechanics are so glaring that it is extremely tedious to read the paper.

---

each term of the school year. Harp (1988) suggested that reading development checklists incorporate a Likert-type scale. For example, for the reading strategy "demonstrates predicting and confirming," the teacher could check "most of the time, sometimes, not noticed yet, or does not apply" (p. 161).

In their investigation of assessment in whole language classrooms, Cambourne and Turbill (1990) found that the teachers who participated in the study developed their own literacy development checklists based on the following categories: "(a) the strategies learners use as they read and write, (b) the level of explicit understanding learners have of the processes they can and should use when reading and writing (i.e., metatextual awareness), (c) learners' attitudes toward reading and writing, (d) learners' interests and backgrounds, and (e) the degree of control that learners display over language in all its forms" (pp. 342–343).

Reading and writing development checklists can be constructed from two possible sources of information. One source is the yearly goals and objectives developed by the teacher in the areas of reading and writing. These goals and objectives are typically based on the teacher's evaluation of the child's current abilities along with the teacher's own perspective regarding the important milestones and attributes of literacy development. Literacy development checklists can also be curriculum-based. The teacher who is expected to conduct curriculum-based assessment can transfer the learning objectives from the school district, statewide, or basal curriculum into a literacy development checklist.

Teachers usually record their observations on literacy development checklists at regularly scheduled intervals such as monthly or quarterly.

Reading Records

Another item usually suggested for a portfolio is a reading record. In a reading record, the student records the title and author of each book he or she has read and the date it was completed. Au, Scheu, Kawakami, and Herman (1990) commented that teachers can use the reading record for periodic conferences with the child regarding how much he or she is reading, the appropriateness of the material, the child's preferences, the child's reading habits, and books the child might be interested in reading next. The teacher's notes on these conferences can also become a part of the child's portfolio.

Writing Samples

Writing samples constitute a third element typically recommended for a portfolio. It is suggested that the choice of writing samples from the body of work the youngster is producing should be a collaborative decision between the student and teacher. Simmons (1990) proposed a Theirs/Mine/Ours system in which students choose a piece, teachers choose a piece, and they collaborate on a piece for every three pieces that are selected.

Writing samples should be collected periodically, with the frequency dependent on the amount and diversity of writing produced by the child.

Progress Notes, Observation Notes, and Anecdotes

Progress notes, observation notes, and anecdotes can be a fourth item in a portfolio. They can provide an important dimension to assessment but also can be the most difficult to manage. Cambourne and Turbill (1990) observed that conference time, both formal teacher-student conferences and informal conferences carried out as the teacher moved around the classroom, provided pivotal time for taking notes on individual student learning.

Atwell (1987) used a conference journal in which she wrote the names of each student in alphabetical order, allocated six to eight pages for each student for the year, and recorded the skills she taught in individual conferences as well as other anecdotal information she believed to be of interest to parents as well as to herself.

Valencia (1990) suggested that progress notes in a portfolio be submitted by both students and teachers.

Teacher-Made Tests

Portfolios often include teacher-made tests, particularly when those tests provide information regarding important milestones in the child's literacy development. For some tests, the teacher can announce in advance that the completed and graded test will become a part of each youngster's portfolio. For other tests, the decision to include it in the portfolio can be made in a conference between the youngster and the teacher. Also, some pieces of writing that children do are graded by the teacher. The actual writing, criteria used, and grade would also be a valuable part of a portfolio.

❏   A Case Study   ❏

John is an 11-year-old boy who is currently in the sixth grade. He has a profound hearing loss. He is mainstreamed for many content area subjects and is in Ms. Dickman's resource room for 1 hour and 15 minutes daily along with three other youngsters who are deaf. Ms. Dickman also has other groups of youngsters with hearing impairments who come to her resource room for scheduled periods of time daily.

At the beginning of the school year, Ms. Dickman had looked through John's cumulative file and learned that the etiology of his hearing loss was unknown, his parents and siblings were hearing, his hearing loss had been identified at 19 months of age, and he and his parents had begun participating in an early intervention program when he was almost 2 years old. She also learned that John's previous school progress reports indicated that his former teacher felt he was progressing satisfactorily in reading, and his SAT-HI score from the spring indicated that he was reading at the second-grade level. Ms. Dickman wrote a note to herself that at the fall parent-teacher conferences, she would ask John's parents about the kinds of reading he does at home, the parents' own reading habits, and whether they read to him on a regular basis.

The first week of school, Ms. Dickman administered the Gates-MacGinitie Reading Test, Level 2, Form K, and John received a grade equivalent score of 2.5 on vocabulary, 1.8 on comprehension, and 2.2 overall. She probed the test with John and learned that in the vocabulary section, John made a couple of errors because he had spelled the key words incorrectly and one of his mistakes was a misinterpretation of the target concept. The picture was a boy looking at his reflection in the mirror. The correct answer was "reflection" but John chose "affection," which an 11-year-old boy with high self-esteem might feel when he looks at himself in the mirror.

Ms. Dickman learned several things about John's thinking when she probed the comprehension section also. For most of the questions he answered incorrectly, there were one or two words that were pivotal for determining the correct answer and these words were in the last part of the sentence or last sentence of the paragraph. For example, in one item, John chose a picture of twins dressed identically for the statement, "The girls looked exactly alike, but they wore different kinds of clothes." In another item, he chose a picture of two-holed, lined paper for the paragraph, "Inez bought a three-ring notebook and some paper for it. But the paper had only two holes. Which paper should she have bought?"

After probing the test, Ms. Dickman realized that his score probably underestimated John's reading ability, particularly in the area of comprehension. She considered it likely that when given meaningful reading material which was longer than a few sentences, and when asked questions that relied less heavily on the surface structure of individual sentences, that John would demonstrate much better comprehension than the test results indicated. Ms. Dickman put the test and her observation notes about the probing into John's portfolio.

Ms. Dickman decided to teach a diagnostic reading lesson. She had already planned that fables and folktales would be the reading topic for the first month of school. For the first diagnostic reading lesson, she chose "The Elves and the Shoemaker" because with a 2.0 readability, she felt it would be relatively easy for John to read. She conducted a Directed Reading Thinking Activity and found that John read the story with good literal and inferential comprehension, and when he retold it, he included all the major story structure components.

For a second diagnostic reading lesson, she chose "The Cat and the Fiddler," which had a readability of 2.8. She conducted a Directed Reading Thinking Activity and found that John learned the sight vocabulary presented prior to reading fairly quickly, although he was initially unfamiliar with several of the words. She also noticed that he struggled with a few of the words and phrases in the story that she had not presented prior to the reading. She made note of the strategies that he used to figure out unknown words so that she could decide which strategies to teach in her reading strategy lessons. For example, she observed that John did not use context clues effectively. She also paid close attention to the answers John gave to the comprehension questions she asked. She found that even brief discussions helped him to more fully understand major concepts in the story.

Ms. Dickman briefly recorded her observations regarding the diagnostic reading lessons and put this paper into John's portfolio, along with her conclusion that she would choose folktales and fables written at the late second- and early third- grade levels to use with John as instructional reading materials for the first month of school. She also chose several fables and folktales written at the fourth- and fifth-grade levels to read to John for daily read-aloud during the month. She decided to use a Directed Reading Thinking Activity for her method of instruction but also planned to shift to a more student-directed approach, such as reading workshop, by the second half of the school year.

Ms. Dickman gathered books containing fables and folktales to include in her small classroom library so that John and the other youngsters in her resource room could choose to read some additional stories independently. She put a sheet in each child's portfolio with "Reading Record" written at the top. She explained to the students that each time they completed reading a story or book, they should arrange to have a conference with her and at that conference, the child could record the title, author, and date on the Reading Record. She told them that they could read books, stories, magazine articles, and newspaper articles on any topic of their choosing unless there were particular topics, books, or authors their parents did not want them to read.

Ms. Dickman then developed a literacy development checklist for John. This list is shown in Figure 6–2. She decided to record her observations on the checklist once each month by writing the date in the appropriate column next to each characteristic.

Ms. Dickman planned to teach reading five days each week for approximately 30 minutes of the 1 ½ hour period John spends in the resource room. She also planned to include sustained silent reading for approximately 15 minutes three days each week and read-aloud for 15 minutes daily. For writing instruction, she decided to incorporate writing workshop for 30

FIGURE 6–2

Literacy Development Checklist

	Most of the time	Sometimes	Not noticed yet	NA
Comprehension Strategies				
Uses prior knowledge of content (content schema)				
Uses knowledge of text structure (textual schema)				
—story schema				
—schema for expository text				
Predicts				
Uses metacognitive abilities to monitor comprehension				
Summarizes				
Generates self-questions				
Strategies for Understanding Words and Sentences				
Uses word recognition strategies				
—uses lexical cues				
—uses graphophonic cues				
—uses structural cues				
—uses context cues				
Uses text cohesion devices				
Understands sentence transformations				
Understands figurative language				
Demonstrates flexibility in using strategies				
Types of Reading				
Short stories				
Comic books				
Poetry				
Magazine articles				

FIGURE 6–2
continued

	Most of the time	Sometimes	Not noticed yet	NA
Newspaper articles				
Scripts				
Books				
—nonfiction:				
biography				
_____				
_____				
—fiction:				
fables and folktales				
mystery				
adventure				
_____				
_____				
Attitudes Toward Reading				
Approaches reading with enthusiasm				
Demonstrates confidence about reading abilities				
Reads text material thoroughly				
Takes risks in choice of reading material				
Is relaxed when reading				
Reads independently				
Writing Process				
Engages in planning				
Engages in writing/drafting				
Engages in revising				
Publishes				

FIGURE 6–2
continued

	Most of the time	Sometimes	Not noticed yet	NA
Writing Traits				
Ideas and content are clear				
Organization is logical				
Voice demonstrates sincerity				
Words are chosen carefully				
Sentence structures are correct and clear				
Mechanics do not interfere with content				
—grammar				
—capitalization				
—punctuation				
—spelling				
—paragraphing				
Writing Topics				
Dialogue journals				
Real-life stories				
Fables and folk tales				
Reports				
Summaries				
_____				
_____				
Attitudes Toward Writing				
Approaches writing with enthusiasm				
Demonstrates confidence in writing abilities				
Writes extensively				
Takes risks in types of writing				
Writes independently				

minutes at least three days each week, dialogue journal writing for 10 to 15 minutes two days each week, and writing across the curriculum for 30 minutes two days each week. During the writing across the curriculum period, Ms. Dickman planned to include writing projects from John's mainstream teacher; if there were no current projects, she would use the time to teach summary writing during the first month of school.

Ms. Dickman recognized that the writing John accomplished the first week or two of school might not be representative of his writing abilities. So she decided to postpone evaluating his writing but planned to keep several early pieces to place in his portfolio. She felt that by the beginning of the second month of school, she could use the analytical writing scoring procedure on one or two pieces of his writing, share her observations with John, and include her evaluation in John's portfolio. In the meantime, she included her goals for John's writing development on the literacy development checklist, recognizing that these goals might need to be modified once she was able to gather more information about John's current writing abilities.

Ms. Dickman decided to keep informal notes on John's progress and the progress of her other students in a notebook. She purchased a three-ring binder, put dividers in it, wrote each student's name on one of the dividers, and put notebook paper into each section. She planned to leave the notebook on her desk during the day so that she could jot down her observations easily. She also decided that once each week, she would regularly schedule time to write about any student on whom she had not entered notes in the past week.

Ms. Dickman then discussed the portfolio with John. She explained that the responsibility for maintaining the portfolio was with both of them. She suggested to him that he could include work he completed in the resource room, at home, and in his mainstream classroom as long as he felt that the item he put into the portfolio showed how much he was learning.   ❏

FINAL COMMENTS

This chapter began with a discussion of the purposes for literacy assessment. For administrators and public policymakers, the purpose for literacy assessment is to be able to compare how the students in the school, district, or state compare to students in other schools, districts, states, and countries. The administrator and public policymaker is clearly more interested in standardized test results than any other type of information. These test results can easily be part of portfolio assessment, though certainly not the whole of assessment.

For parents, the purpose of literacy assessment is to be able to compare their child's performance to the teacher's expectations. The literacy development checklist, informal notes, writing samples, reading record, and test results that are included in a portfolio can provide parents with a thorough answer to questions regarding how well their child is meeting teacher expectations.

For youngsters, the purpose for literacy assessment is to help them figure out how to become better readers and writers. The multifaceted data contained in portfolios can provide youngsters with meaningful information that can enable them to make choices regarding their own learning.

For teachers, the purpose for literacy assessment is to be able to determine an appropriate learning environment for each child. Portfolio assessment offers in-depth analysis of the many aspects involved in literacy development. Therefore, it provides teachers with precise, frequent, differential, and immediate feedback about each student's progress.

SUGGESTED READINGS

Baumann, J.F. (1988). *Reading Assessment: An Instructional Decision-Making Perspective*. New York: Merrill/Macmillan.

Daly, E. (1989). *Monitoring Children's Language Development: Holistic Assessment in the Classroom*. Portsmouth, NH: Heinemann.

Farr, R., & Carey, R.F. (1986). *Reading: What Can Be Measured? (2nd ed.)*. Newark, DE: International Reading Association.

Tierney, R.J., Carter, M.A., & Desai, L.E. (1991). *Portfolio Assessment in the Reading-Writing Classroom*. Norwood, MA: Christopher-Gordon.

7

Language and Literacy Development Through Parent-Child-Teacher Partnerships

PERSPECTIVES ON FAMILY-SCHOOL PARTNERSHIPS

LEGAL IMPETUS FOR PARENT INVOLVEMENT IN EDUCATIONAL DECISIONS

POTENTIAL SOURCES OF CONFLICT BETWEEN HOME AND SCHOOL

FINAL COMMENTS

Throughout this book I have discussed current theories and suggested practices regarding the language and literacy development in children who are deaf. The discussion has been directed to classroom teachers because this text is designed to be used by teachers of deaf students from preschool through high school. Yet, while the classroom is certainly an important place for language learning to happen, this final chapter will acknowledge the place and the individuals that are much more important to the child's language and literacy development than the classroom is. I am, of course, referring to the home and to the child's parents.

I begin with a set of statements that reflect assumptions about the roles and responsibilities of teachers and parents in the language and literacy development of children who are deaf:

1. To develop language, children need to be immersed within an environment in which language is used consistently by individuals who are fluent users of the language. Whether children are learning English or ASL, it is the responsibility of teachers to help their students develop that language in face-to-face communication. Whether children are learning English or ASL, it is the responsibility of teachers to help their students develop their ability to read and write English.

2. Parents are the first and most salient models of language acquisition for their children. Their influence and importance to their children's language development should not be overlooked or diminished.

3. Regardless of which language system any particular educational program decides to use in the classroom, the program must include parents in all educational decisions about their children. As Dunst, Trivette, and Deal (1988) wrote, "Parents have the rightful role in deciding what is important for themselves and their family, and the family and the family alone bears the responsibility for deciding its course of development—to the extent that the well-being and rights of all family members are protected. The role of a professional must be to support and strengthen the family's ability to nurture and promote the development of its members in a way that is both enabling and empowering" (p. x).

PERSPECTIVES ON FAMILY-SCHOOL PARTNERSHIPS

Partnerships do not always work smoothly. The mutual respect, good will, and shared interests that bring partners together are difficult to sustain when there is disagreement about goals, priorities, and specific actions. It is an understatement to say that parents and professionals do not necessarily work in harmony with one another. Trout and Foley (1989) captured a major source of the conflict in the following questions:

> Why, indeed, do families keep "distracting" us from our roles as language specialists or special educators with their endless questions, complaints, and stories about recently born healthy children of neighbors or siblings; with unsettling descriptions of marital strife; and with expressions of hopelessness or helplessness? Why are these parents unable to "accept" the illness or handicapping condition? Why do they claim to want help and then fail to "cooperate" with us, or even appear to sabotage our plans by failing to show up for appointments or to carry out homework assignments? And why must there be so much guilt (in spite of our protestations that there is nothing to feel guilty about), not to mention the rage, defensiveness, and sorrow? (p. 58)

I would like to add a set of questions that parents might ask:

> Why, indeed, do teachers keep "distracting" us from our roles as parents with their endless questions, complaints, and stories about the other children in class; with unsettling descriptions of classroom problems; and with expressions of frustration and disappointment? Why are these teachers unable to "accept" the school system's condition? Why do they overestimate or underestimate our children's condition? Why do they claim to want to help and then fail to "cooperate" with us, or even appear to sabotage our plans by saying things at meetings that make no sense to the average person and sending homework that requires our undivided attention when we have a million things to do and no energy left by the end of the day? And why must there be so much blame, not to mention the anger, defensiveness, and sorrow?

For partnership to be more than a catchword, parents and professionals must be able to find a common set of principles guiding their interactions. The following principles represent a point for beginning a partnership and avoiding the kind of blaming that all too often has characterized the relationship between home and school.

1. The child is part of a family system. When we intervene with the child, we impact on every other member of the child's family. In family systems theory, the family is viewed as a whole and each member understood by looking at the interactions and relationships among all the family members (Bailey & Simeonsson, 1988; Dunst, Trivette, & Deal, 1988; Turnbull, Summers, & Brotherson, 1983).

Viewing the child as an interdependent member of a family system is important for two reasons. The first is that it helps us realize that anything we do educationally for the child will influence the interactions and relationships between the child and his or her family members and among the mother, father, siblings, as well as perhaps the grandparents and others in the extended family.

The second reason is that viewing the child within the family context forces us to recognize and be sensitive to the many demands on families. It has been observed that when the family unit is supported, each member is strengthened. When the family unit is ignored, the result is often a weakening of every member and a lack of cooperation with the educational system that is purporting to help the child (Winton, 1986).

As we seek to understand each child's unique family structure, it is crucial to remember that traditional definitions of family structures and notions regarding the roles of family members no longer apply as families have changed in response to social, political, and economic pressures. Teachers must recognize that they will work with children from families with one parent, foster families, families with two adults of the same gender, homeless families, families that migrate frequently for work, blended families, extended families, and families with two biological parents. Teachers need to demonstrate awareness and sensitivity to the values, attitudes, beliefs, and customs of each child's family.

2. Parents need to be encouraged to develop the skills and knowledge that will enable them to become competent and capable. The traditional relationship between parents of deaf children and professionals has been paternalistic. Professionals have taken responsibility for the educational needs of the child, and often social and emotional needs as well, without expecting much more than cooperation from the parents. This principle suggests that the child benefits when parents are confident of their knowledge and skills and respected for their contributions to educational decision making.

The implication is that educators need to help parents to identify and build on their strengths and capabilities. It also means that educators need to spend less time helping parents to identify and correct family weaknesses and deficiencies (Dunst, Trivette, & Deal, 1988).

3. Families experience a life cycle in much the same way that individuals do and the changes inherent in major family events need to be understood by individuals working with any family member. The shifts experienced by families during transition times disrupt the interactions and relationships among family members. When individuals pass from one stage to another, they experience anxiety and stress. When families pass from one stage to another, the whole family experiences anxiety and stress (Winton, 1986).

Complicating this picture is that while the family undergoes passages through developmental phases, family members undergo their own individual life passages. Furthermore, mothers and fathers undergo change as they develop in their parental abilities. As Trout and Foley (1989) noted, "The capacity to parent competently does not, unfortunately, occur as suddenly as does the capacity to reproduce. It develops over time and requires experience, empathy, and practice. In families with a handicapped child, parental development is further complicated by the unexpected, the unknown, and the tragic" (p. 63).

4.   Educational decisions should be made collaboratively between parents and professionals. There is a great difference between soliciting parent input for the purposes of making educational decisions and jointly making educational decisions. Collaboration is crucial to any partnership. It recognizes that both partners have essential insights to contribute. When decisions are made collaboratively, both partners are vested in the implementation and results.

Ultimately, there are two arguments in favor of family-school partnerships. One is that it is the rightful role of parents to decide what is best for their child. The second is that decisions made as a result of an equal sharing of ideas will be fully supported by the parents and therefore are more likely to result in positive outcomes for the child.

LEGAL IMPETUS FOR PARENT INVOLVEMENT IN EDUCATIONAL DECISIONS

The legal impetus for parent involvement in educational decisions was a result of parent activism. The beginning of this impetus can be found in the civil rights movement of the 1950s and 60s. As Heward and Orlansky (1992) noted, the 1954 *Brown v. Board of Education of Topeka* decision in which the U.S. Supreme Court established the right of all children to equal opportunity to an education "began a period of intense concern and questioning among parents and handicapped children, who asked why the same principles of equal access to education did not apply to their children" (p. 36).

Parents initiated a number of court cases which resulted in decisions and publicity that directly led to legislation aimed at guaranteeing the rights of exceptional children. Public Law 94-142, the Education for All Handicapped Children Act, passed by the U.S. Congress in 1975, not only mandated a free, appropriate public education for all children with disabilities between the ages of 3 and 21 regardless of the type or degree of severity of their disability, but it also protected the rights of parents. One of the provisions of this law was a mandatory inclusion of parents in educational decisions regarding evaluation, placement, and delivery of instruction.

In 1986, Public Law 99-457, The Education of the Handicapped Act Amendments, was passed by the U.S. Congress. This law included two important sections. In one section, all the rights and protections of P.L. 94-142 were extended to children with disabilities who are 3 to 5 years of age. Another section of this law established a new state grant program to assist states in developing comprehensive, coordinated, multidisciplinary services for infants and toddlers (birth to age 3) with disabilities. Included among the components of a state system mandated by this law are a multidisciplinary evaluation of infant and toddler and family needs and a written

Individualized Family Service Plan (IFSP) developed collaboratively by the multidisciplinary team and the parents.

The Individualized Family Service Plan component of P.L. 99-457 has led to many interesting discussions in the literature concerning models for working with parents of infants and toddlers (e.g., Garwood, Fewell, & Neisworth, 1988; Krauss, 1990; Lowenthal, 1988; McGonigel & Garland, 1988; Robinson, Rosenberg, & Beckman, 1988). These discussions are actually a continuation within the field of early intervention to years of explorations into ideas, strategies, and techniques for creating partnerships with parents. Yet while there is an abundance of information, empirical and anecdotal, on working with families whose child is birth to age 3, there is very little to be found on models for building family school relationships when the child is school-age, unless one counts the many published suggestions for having successful parent-teacher conferences (as a parent myself, I have received many such lists from school principals prior to report cards being sent home).

The Individualized Education Plan component of P.L. 94-142 and the Individualized Family Service Plan component of P.L. 99-457 seem to have been the result, at least in part, of parents demanding their rightful voice in educational planning. But it is only the Individualized Family Service Plan that has led, so far at least, to the kind of dialogue and research that is likely to result in improved partnerships between parents and professionals.

POTENTIAL SOURCES OF CONFLICT BETWEEN HOME AND SCHOOL

Earlier in this chapter several principles for creating family/professional partnerships were presented. If these principles are followed, many sources of conflict between home and school can be avoided. This point is highlighted in a research study conducted by Bernstein and Barta (1988).

Bernstein and Barta surveyed 47 families with hearing impaired children and 37 professionals working with hearing impaired youngsters (teachers, speech/language pathologists, audiologists, psychologists, otolaryngologists, and pediatricians) regarding how these parents and professionals ranked the relative importance of topics of information typically included in parent education programs. While the researchers found overall congruence in parents' and professionals' perceptions of what constitutes important topics in a parent education program, they also found that parents expressed strong interest in programs that met their individual needs and in which the professionals listened to them:

> Numerous respondents wrote short comments on their questionnaires indicating their enthusiasm to be able to share their frustrations with professionals; they welcomed the opportunity to offer their views concerning their own needs as parents of deaf children. . .Parents in the survey seemed to want the most detail on topics that relate to practical matters which they perceive to relate to their own action vis a vis their child. (p. 245)

It seems clear that parents want professionals to help them develop their skills and knowledge, but they also want their own concerns and insights to be respected by professionals.

Potential sources of conflict between home and school can be illustrated by examining the relatively recent bilingual/bicultural education movement. In Chapter 2, the rationales underlying bilingual/bicultural programs were discussed and the various models currently being examined and implemented were presented. This section will look at some of the issues that bilingual/bicultural programs raise for parents, particularly the parents who are hearing (and we know that approximately 85–90% of children who are deaf have parents who are hearing).

One issue for parents is how the decision is made to move from a traditional program to a bilingual/bicultural program. Educators in these programs need to ask themselves, how much input is solicited from parents and how sincerely are parents' concerns received? Ultimately, much of the success of these programs will rest on parent cooperation and support.

Another issue involves how the parents will react to bringing a second culture into their homes. Educators need to ask themselves, how comfortable will parents feel about deaf culture and what conflicts will parents see between their home culture and deaf culture?

A third issue involves communication between parents and their children. Educators need to ask themselves how important is it for children who are deaf to be immersed in language for more than 6 hours each day, 140 days each year (the average length of a school year), who in the child's life has the greatest influence on language learning, what language should parents use to communicate with their children, how frustrated will parents feel trying to learn ASL, how likely is it that they will learn ASL, and how guilty will they feel if they don't learn ASL?

There are no single correct answers to any of these questions. However, the process of asking them will strengthen the family-school partnership within any bilingual/bicultural program.

FINAL COMMENTS

Years ago I was a teacher at a school for the deaf in the northeast region of the United States. One of my students was a 12-year-old boy who exhibited what I thought were emotional problems that were interfering with his ability to benefit from instruction in my language class. I talked to my supervisor about him, and after observing him in my class and talking with the other teachers in our department, she brought her concerns about this boy to the school psychologist. After observing him in several of his classes, the school psychologist concluded that this boy would benefit from professional counseling. She arranged for a conference with his parents and the suggestion for professional counseling was presented and discussed. Nothing happened. Several months later, this boy's father came to school for an evening open house. I chatted with him for quite a while and during our conversation, I broached the topic of counseling for his son. To my surprise, the father was quite receptive and I went home feeling pleased with myself. The boy did not come back to our school. After several days, my supervisor received a request that his school records be forwarded to a school in a different part of the city.

For a long time afterwards I believed that the boy's parents, and particularly his mother, were in denial about their son's problems. It took me many years to realize the extent of my own denial. I had been unable to recognize that my student was their son; that while I knew things about him they didn't know, they knew many things about him that I didn't know. They knew about their family, and I knew only about their son.

Actually, I didn't learn this lesson until I was a parent myself and I became the recipient of unsolicited advice from my children's teachers. Then I learned that parent-child-teacher partnerships can work only when we express sensitivity and respect toward one another.

I want to stress that I have only touched on some of the important issues involved in family-school partnerships. These and other issues are dealt with extensively in other sources, and it is my hope that the reader will use some of these sources for developing skills in working with families.

It is important to emphasize that teachers of children who are deaf need to be knowledgeable about many areas. This text has focused on language and literacy development specifically. The information in this text should help enable teachers to create classroom environments that foster the development of face-to-face language, reading, and writing in children who are deaf.

SUGGESTED READINGS

Bailey, D.B., Jr., Simeonsson, R.J. (1988). *Family Assessment in Early Intervention*. New York: Merrill/Macmillan.

Dunst, C.B., Trivette, C.M., & Deal, A.G. (1988). *Enabling and Empowering Families: Principles and Guidelines for Practice*. Cambridge, MA: Brookline.

Harding, E., & Riley, P. (1986). *The Bilingual Family*. Cambridge, England: Cambridge University.

Luterman, D. (1987). *Deafness in the Family*. San Diego, CA: Singular.

Appendix:
Standardized Tests

Standardized tests can serve as one part of a language and literacy assessment program. While naturalistic assessment strategies such as language sampling and diagnostic reading lessons can provide teachers with a wealth of information for making educational decisions, standardized tests can also provide valuable supplementary information. Much has been written regarding the limitations of standardized tests and the misuse of standardized test scores. Some educators even advocate the elimination of standardized testing. This stance ignores two realities. The first is that standardized tests can be used in ways that are productive to educational decision making. The second is that standardized tests will not disappear in the near future. I agree with Pikulski's (1990) point that "it seems imperative as responsible professionals we reduce the amount of time that we spend railing against standardized tests in an unproductive way and that we concentrate our efforts on three things: curtailing specific misuses and misinterpretations of standardized tests, improving existing tests, and proposing alternative assessment procedures that place standardized test scores in a broader context or begin to substitute for them" (p. 686).

Listed in this Appendix are the basic characteristics of a selected group of published tests in the areas of language, literacy, and academic achievement. All of these tests meet three criteria, (a) they were published for the first time or substantially revised within the last 12 years, (b) they received relatively positive reviews in the literature, and (c) they are reportedly used with regularity by teachers throughout the United States. In choosing and describing these tests, I relied on the following sources: Abraham and Stoker (1988), Bartlett, Slade, and Bellerose (1987), Baumann (1988b), Canney (1989), Conoley and Kramer (1989), Cooter (1988, 1989, 1990), Cooter and Curry (1989), Dale and Henderson (1987), Gearheart and Gearheart (1990), Irvin and Lynch-Brown (1988),

Jongsma (1982), Martin-Rehrmann (1990), Mathewson (1988), Mitchell (1985), Novoa and Lazarus (1988), Radencich (1986), Salvia and Ysseldyke (1991), Thompson, Biro, Vethivelu, Pious, and Hatfield (1987), Tibbits (1988), Westby (1988), Williams (1988), and Ziezula (1982). This list of tests is not exhaustive nor does it provide enough information for teachers to decide specifically which tests are appropriate for their students who are deaf. These descriptions are intended to narrow the choices from among the hundreds of standardized tests on the market today.

Language Screening Tests

Bankson Language Screening Test—2

Author: Nicolas W. Bankson
Copyright Date: 1990
Publisher: Pro-Ed (8700 Shoal Creek Dr., Austin, TX 78758)
Age Range: 3 to 7 years
Administration Time: 20–30 minutes
Purpose: To measure children's psycholinguistic skills
Description: The test is organized into three general categories: semantic knowledge (body parts, nouns, verbs, categories, functions, prepositions, opposites), morphological rules (pronouns, plurals, comparatives, superlatives, negation, questions, verb usage/verb tense, verb usage—auxiliary, modal, copula), and pragmatics (ritualizing, informing, controlling, imagining).

The normative sample is reported as 1,200 youngsters representative of the U.S. population on a number of variables. No norms for students who are deaf are provided. Reliability is reported as adequate, and evidence for validity is provided.

Sequenced Inventory of Communication Development (Revised)

Authors: Dona Lea Hedrick, Elizabeth M. Prather, and Annette R. Tobin
Copyright Date: 1984
Publisher: University of Washington Press (P.O. Box 50096, Seattle, WA 98145)
Age Range: 4 months to 4 years
Administration Time: 30–60 minutes
Purpose: To screen the communication behavior of children in order to identify areas requiring in-depth assessment
Description: The test includes a receptive section that includes items on sound and speech awareness, discrimination, and understanding. It also consists of an expressive section that includes eliciting imitating, initiating, and responding as well as analysis of a spontaneous language sample.

The normative sample is reported as several hundred. All subjects were hearing though the authors report that it has been used successfully with hearing impaired children. However, items involving sound discrimination and auditory response may not be appropriate for many students who are deaf. Reliability is reported as adequate though the sample size was quite small. Very limited evidence for validity is provided.

Test of Early Language Development

Authors: Wayne P. Hresko, D. Kim Reid, and Donald D. Hammill
Copyright Date: 1981
Publisher: Pro-Ed (8700 Shoal Creek Blvd., Austin, TX 78758)
Age Range: 3-0 to 7-11 years
Administration Time: approximately 15 minutes
Purpose: To evaluate the child's ability to comprehend and use language syntactically and semantically
Description: The test consists of 38 items designed to measure form, content, and interpretation of meaning. Form includes syntax, phonology, and morphology. Content includes word and concept knowledge.

The normative sample is reported as 1,184 youngsters representative, where possible, of the U.S. population on a number of variables. No norms for deaf students are provided. Reliability is reported as adequate, and evidence for validity is provided.

Vocabulary Tests

Carolina Picture Vocabulary Test

Authors: Thomas L. Layton and David W. Holmes
Copyright Date: 1985
Publisher: Pro-Ed (8700 Shoal Creek Blvd., Austin, TX 78758)
Age Range: 4-0 to 11-6 years
Administration Time: 10–15 minutes
Purpose: To assess the receptive sign vocabulary of hearing impaired children
Description: The test consists of 130 plates, each of which contains four line drawings. The child's task is to identify the correct picture from the examiner's sign.

The normative sample is reported as 767 hearing impaired youngsters from a nationwide population of children using manual communication as their primary means of communicating. Reliability is reported as adequate, and evidence for validity is provided. The examiner needs to be familiar with the sign system used by the child in order to use the appropriate signs (for example, an ASL sign may be quite different from a SEE sign for the same word). When signs are iconic, vocabulary knowledge may not be assessed accurately.

Peabody Picture Vocabulary Test—Revised

Authors: Lloyd M. Dunn and Leota M. Dunn
Copyright Date: 1981
Publisher: American Guidance Service (Publishers' Building, P.O. Box 99, Circle Pines, MN 55014)
Age Range: 2 to 6 years to adult
Administration Time: 10–20 minutes
Purpose: To assess the youngster's receptive vocabulary in face-to-face communication. It is intended to provide a quick estimate of verbal ability and scholastic aptitude.
Description: The test consists of a list of vocabulary words and a series of plates with four pictures per plate. The examiner reads each word aloud and the child points to the most appropriate picture.

The normative sample is reported as 4,200 youngsters between 2 1/2 and 18 years of age and 828 adults who were representative of the U.S. population on a number of variables. No norms for students who are deaf are provided. Reliability is reported as adequate and evidence for validity is provided.

The Word Test-Elementary (Revised)
and The Word Test-Adolescent

Authors: Rosemary Huisingh, Mark Barrett, Linda Zachman, Carolyn Blagden, and Jane Orman
Copyright Date: 1990
Publisher: LinguiSystems, Inc. (3100 4th Ave., P.O. Box 747, East Moline, IL 61244)
Age Range: 7 to 11 years for the Elementary level and 12 to 17 years for the Adolescent level
Administration Time: approximately 30 minutes
Purpose: To assess student knowledge about the critical features of words and about the relationships between words for the Elementary level. To assess semantic and vocabulary tasks reflective of school assignments as well as language usage in everyday life for the Adolescent level.
Description: The Elementary level tests six essential vocabulary and semantic areas: associations, multiple definitions, semantic absurdities, antonyms, definitions, and synonyms. The Adolescent level includes four tasks: brand names (explaining why a semantically descriptive name of a product or company is appropriate), synonyms, signs of the times (telling what a sign or message means and why it is important), and definitions.

The normative sample is reported as more than 2,000 youngsters for the Elementary level and more than 1,500 youngsters for the Adolescent level gathered nationwide. No norms for deaf students are provided. Reliability is reported as adequate and evidence for validity is provided for both levels.

Tests of Syntax and Semantics

Clinical Evaluation of Language Fundamentals (Revised)

Authors: Eleanor Semel, Elisabeth Wiig, and Wayne Secord
Copyright Date: 1987
Publisher: Psychological Corp. (555 Academic Ct., P.O. Box 839954, San Antonio, TX 78293)
Age Range: 5 to 16 years
Administration Time: 1 to 1 ½ hours
Purpose: To assess the language processing and production of children
Description: The diagnostic battery includes subtests designed to measure the child's phonology, syntax, semantics, memory and word finding, and retrieval.

The normative sample is reported as 2,400 youngsters. No norms for students who are deaf are provided. Reliability is reported as adequate and evidence for validity is provided.

Test for Auditory Comprehension of Language—Revised

Author: Elizabeth Carrow-Woolfolk
Copyright Date: 1985
Publisher: DLM Teaching Resources (P.O. Box 4000, One DLM Park, Allen, TX 75002)
Age Range: 3-0 to 9-11 years
Administration Time: 10–20 minutes
Purpose: To measure auditory comprehension of word classes and relations, grammatical morphemes, and elaborated sentence constructions
Description: The test consists of 120 items verbally presented by the examiner. Each item is accompanied by three pictures. The child is required to point to the correct picture.

The normative sample is reported as 1,003 youngsters who were representative of the U.S. population on a number of variables. No norms for students who are deaf are provided. Reliability is reported as adequate and evidence for validity is provided.

Test of Language Development—2, Primary and
Test of Language Development—2, Intermediate

Authors: Phyllis L. Newcomer and Donald D. Hammill
Copyright Date: 1988
Publisher: Pro-Ed (8700 Shoal Creek Blvd., Austin, TX 78758)
Age Range: 4-0 to 8-11 for the Primary level and 8-6 to 12-11 for the Intermediate level
Administration Time: 40–60 minutes
Purpose: To identify specific receptive and expressive language skills of primary age and intermediate level youngsters.

Description: Subtests for the Primary level are picture vocabulary, oral vocabulary, grammatic understanding, grammatic completion, sentence imitation, word articulation, and word discrimination. Subtests for the Intermediate level are sentence combining, vocabulary, word ordering, generals, grammatic comprehension, and malapropisms.

The normative sample for the Primary level is reported as more than 2,000 youngsters and for the Intermediate level as 1,000 youngsters who were representative of the U.S. population on a number of variables. No norms for students who are deaf are provided. Reliability is reported as adequate and evidence for validity is reported.

Test of Adolescent Language—2

Authors: Donald D. Hammill, Virginia L. Brown, Stephen C. Larsen, and J. Lee Wiederholt
Copyright Date: 1987
Publisher: Pro-Ed (8700 Shoal Creek Blvd., Austin, TX 78758)
Age Range: 12-0 to 18 years or students in grades 6 to 12
Administration Time: approximately 1 hour 45 minutes
Purpose: To assess the spoken and written vocabulary and grammar of adolescents
Description: The test includes eight subtests: listening/vocabulary, listening/grammar, speaking/vocabulary, writing/vocabulary, speaking/grammar, reading/vocabulary, reading/grammar, and writing/grammar.

The normative sample is reported as 2,628 adolescents who were representative of the U.S. population on a number of variables. No norms for deaf students are provided. Reliability is reported as adequate and evidence for validity is provided.

Tests of Syntax

Rhode Island Test of Language Structure

Author: Elizabeth E. Engen and Trygg Engen
Copyright Date: 1983
Publisher: Pro-Ed (8700 Shoal Creek Blvd., Austin, TX 78758)
Age Range: 3 to 20 years
Administration Time: approximately 30 minutes
Purpose: To assess the hearing impaired child's syntactic processing of sentences.
Description: The test consists of 50 simple and 50 complex sentences designed to represent 20 sentence types. Each sentence is accompanied by three pictures. The child is expected to match the sentence to the appropriate picture.

The normative sample is reported as 513 hearing impaired youngsters from several east coast states and 304 hearing youngsters from Rhode

Island. Reliability is reported as adequate, though the sample size was quite small, and evidence for validity is provided.

Tests of Language Use

Evaluating Communicative Competence (Revised)

Author: Charlann S. Simon
Copyright Date: 1986
Publisher: Communication Skill Builders (3830 E. Bellevue, P.O. Box 42050-E91, Tucson, AZ 85733)
Age Range: 9 to 17 years
Administration Time: approximately 60 minutes
Purpose: To assess the youngster's abilities in language processing, metalinguistic skills, and functional uses of language for various communicative purposes
Description: The test consists of 21 informal evaluation tasks. Some examples are giving directions, creative storytelling, justification of an opinion, identification of absurdities in sentences, integration of facts to solve a riddle, memory for facts, and twenty questions.

The normative sample is reported as 25 youngsters in kindergarten through eighth grade in Tempe, Arizona. No norms for students who are deaf are provided. The author describes the test as a criterion-referenced test. No reliability or validity data are provided.

Diagnostic Reading Tests

Gates-MacGinitie Reading Tests (3rd Edition)

Authors: Walter H. MacGinitie and Ruth K. MacGinitie
Copyright Date: 1989
Publisher: The Riverside Publishing Co. (8420 Bryn Mawr Ave., Chicago, IL 60631)
Age Range: emergent literacy to grade 12
Administration Time: approximately 55 minutes for all levels except the Pre-Reading and Readiness levels
Purpose: To measure reading readiness skills and language concepts, beginning reading skills at grade 1, and vocabulary and comprehension at grades 1.5 to 12.
Description: The Pre-Reading test assesses language skills, letter knowledge, and auditory discrimination of letter sounds. The grade 1 test assesses phonic skills and use of context clues. The grade 1.5 through 12 tests assess vocabulary and comprehension.

The normative sample is reported as 65,000 youngsters who were representative of the U.S. population on a number of variables. No norms for deaf students are provided. Reliability is reported as adequate and limited evidence for validity is provided.

Gray Oral Reading Test (Revised)

Authors: J. Lee Wiederholt and Brian R. Bryant
Copyright Date: 1986
Publisher: Pro-Ed (8700 Shoal Creek Blvd., Austin, TX 78758)
Age Range: grades 1 to 12
Administration Time: 15–30 minutes
Purpose: To assess reading skill development through oral reading
Description: Each form of the test contains 13 progressively more difficult oral reading passages. Oral miscues are noted by the examiner. The youngster is also asked a set of comprehension questions after reading each paragraph.

The normative sample is reported as 1,401 youngsters from 15 states who were representative of the U.S. population on a number of variables. No norms for students who are deaf are provided. Reliability is reported as adequate and evidence for validity is provided.

Metropolitan Achievement Tests—6, Reading Diagnostic Tests

Authors: Roger C. Farr, George A. Prescott, Irving H. Balow, and Thomas P. Hogan
Copyright Date: 1986
Publisher: The Psychological Corp. (555 Academic Ct., P.O. Box 9954, San Antonio, TX 78204)
Age Range: grades K-5 to 9-9
Administration Time: 1 1/2–2 1/2 hours
Purpose: To assess the child's reading strengths and weaknesses
Description: The test includes subtests in 11 skill areas, though not all areas are tested for each grade level. The areas include: visual discrimination, letter recognition, auditory discrimination, sight vocabulary, phoneme/grapheme: consonants, phoneme/grapheme: vowels, vocabulary in context, word part clues, rate of comprehension, skimming and scanning, and reading comprehension.

For the MAT-6, the normative sample is reported as 75,000 youngsters who were representative of the U.S. population on a number of variables. No norms are provided for deaf students. Reliability is reported as adequate and limited evidence for validity is provided.

Woodcock Reading Mastery Tests (Revised)

Author: Richard W. Woodcock
Copyright Date: 1987
Publisher: American Guidance Service (Publishers' Building, Circle Pines, MN 55014)

Age Range: 5 to 75+ years
Administration Time: 40–45 minutes
Purpose: To measure readiness skills, word recognition skills, and reading comprehension skills
Description: The test consists of a battery of six subtests: visual-auditory learning, letter identification, word identification, word attack, word comprehension, and passage comprehension.

The normative sample is reported as 6,089 youngsters from 60 different communities and who were representative of the U.S. population on a number of variables. No norms are provided for students who are deaf. Reliability is reported as adequate though data is limited, and limited evidence for validity is provided.

Informal Reading Inventories

Analytical Reading Inventory (Fourth Ed.)

Authors: Mary Lynn Woods and Alden J. Moe
Copyright Date: 1989
Publisher: Merrill/Macmillan (866 Third Ave., New York, NY 10022)
Age Range: primer to grade 9 reading level
Administration Time: approximately 30 minutes
Purpose: To identify the youngster's independent, instructional, frustration, and capacity (listening level) reading levels and to assess strengths and weaknesses in word recognition and comprehension.
Description: The test contains three forms for each grade level that are equivalent in terms of content, format, and readability. Each form consists of graded word lists and graded passages.

The test is not normed. No reliability or validity data are provided.

Standardized Reading Inventory

Author: Phyllis L. Newcomer
Copyright Date: 1986
Publisher: Pro-Ed (8700 Shoal Creek Blvd., Austin, TX 78758)
Age Range: grades 1 to 8 reading level
Administration Time: 15–60 minutes
Purpose: To assess word recognition and comprehension, diagnose reading strengths and weaknesses, and determine the youngster's independent, instructional, and frustration reading levels.
Description: The test consists of a set of graded word lists and graded passages for each of two forms.

The test is not normed. It is a criterion-referenced test that the author argues is standardized because the content was selected and checked empirically, administration procedures are defined, scoring is objective and consistent, and guidelines are provided for interpreting results. Reliability is reported as adequate; however, it is based on a limited sample of students. Limited evidence for validity is provided.

Academic Achievement Tests

California Achievement Tests

Author: California Test Bureau
Copyright Date: 1985
Publisher: CTB/McGraw-Hill (Del Monte Research Park, Monterey, CA 93940)
Age Range: kindergarten to grade 12
Administration Time: 2 1/2 to 3 hours for K-3.2, 5 hours for 2.6–4.2, 6 $\frac{3}{4}$ hours for 4.6–12.9
Purpose: To assess skill development in content areas
Description: The test is a battery of seven tests: reading, spelling, language, mathematics, study skills, science, and social studies. The Reading test includes subtests in visual recognition, sound recognition, word analysis, vocabulary, and comprehension. The Language test includes subtests in language mechanics and language expression.

The normative sample is reported as 300,000 youngsters in 1984 and 230,000 in 1985 who were representative of the U.S. population on a number of variables. No norms are provided for students who are deaf. Reliability is reported as adequate and evidence for validity is provided.

Iowa Tests of Basic Skills

Authors: A. N. Hieronymus, H. D. Hoover, E. F. Lindquist, and associates
Copyright Date: 1990
Publisher: The Riverside Publishing Co. (8420 Bryn Mawr Ave., Chicago, IL 60631)
Age Range: kindergarten to grade 9
Administration Time: 3–6 hours
Purpose: To assess general functioning and growth in the skills essential to academic success
Description: The test includes subtests in listening, writing, word analysis, vocabulary, reading comprehension, language skills (spelling, capitalization, punctuation), usage and expression, visual materials, reference materials, and mathematics skills (math concepts, math problem solving, math computation).

The normative sample is reported as several hundred thousand youngsters who were representative of the U.S. population on a number of variables. No norms are provided for students who are deaf. Reliability is reported as adequate and evidence for validity is provided.

Stanford Achievement Test

Authors: Eric F. Gardner, Herbert C. Rudman, Bjorn Karlsen, and Jack C. Merwin
Copyright Date: 1982
Publisher: The Psychological Corp. (555 Academic Court, P.O. Box 9954, San Antonio, TX 78204)
Age Range: grades 1 through 9
Administration Time: 4 1/2 to 6 1/2 hours
Purpose: To assess skill development in major content areas
Description: The test is divided by grade levels and includes 5 to 11 subtests at each level. Subtests include sounds and letters, word study skills, word reading, sentence reading, reading comprehension, vocabulary, listening to words and stories, listening comprehension, spelling, language/English, mathematics, concepts of number, mathematics computation, mathematics applications, science, social studies, and environment.

The normative sample is reported as more than 450,000 youngsters who were representative of the U.S. population on a number of variables. The SAT-HI was normed on hearing impaired students enrolled in special education programs through the U.S. Reliability is reported as adequate and evidence for validity is provided.

Woodcock-Johnson Psychoeducational Battery (Revised)

Authors: Richard W. Woodcock and M. Bonner Johnson
Copyright Date: 1989
Publisher: DLM Teaching Resources (P.O. Box 4000, One DLM Park, Allen, TX 75002)
Age Range: 2 to 90 years
Administration Time: 2 hours +
Purpose: To assess cognitive ability, scholastic aptitude, academic achievement, and interests
Description: The test consists of two parts. Part one, the Tests of Cognitive Ability, includes 21 subtests measuring 7 cognitive factors: long-term retrieval, short-term memory, visual processing, comprehension-knowledge, processing speed, auditory processing, and fluid reasoning. Part two, the Tests of Achievement, includes 18 subtests in 5 achievement clusters: reading, mathematics, written language, knowledge, and early development/skills.

The normative sample is reported as 6,300 youngsters. No norms are provided for students who are deaf. Reliability is reported as adequate and evidence for validity is provided.

References

Abraham, S., & Stoker, R. (1988). Language assessment of hearing-impaired children and youth: Patterns of test use. *Language, Speech, and Hearing Services in Schools*, *19*, 160–174.

Acredolo, L., & Goodwyn, S. (1988). Symbolic gesturing in normal infants. *Child Development*, *59*, 450–466.

Aguirre, A. (1982). *In search of a paradigm for bilingual education*. Los Angeles: Evaluation, Dissemination, and Assessment Center, California State University, Los Angeles.

Ainsworth, D. (1987). What century is this anyway? A critical look at technology in education and training. *Educational Technology*, *27*(9), 26–28.

Altwerger, B., Diehl-Faxon, J., & Dockstader-Anderson, K. (1985). Read-aloud events as meaning construction. *Language Arts*, *62*, 476–484.

Altwerger, B., Edelsky, C., & Flores, B. M. (1987). Whole language: What's new? *The Reading Teacher*, *41*, 144–154.

Alvarez, M. C. (1983). Using a thematic pre-organizer and guided instruction as aids to concept learning. *Reading Horizons*, *24*, 51–58.

Alvermann, D. E., & Boothby, P. R. (1986). Children's transfer of graphic organizer instruction. *Reading Psychology*, *7*, 87–100.

Alvermann, D. E., Dillon, D. R., & O'Brien, D. G. (1987). *Using discussion to promote reading comprehension*. Newark, DE: International Reading Association.

Alvermann, D. E., & Swafford, J. (1989). Do content area strategies have a research base? *Journal of Reading*, *32*, 388–394.

Anders, P. L., & Bos, C. S. (1986). Semantic feature analysis: An interactive strategy for vocabulary development and text comprehension. *Journal of Reading*, *29*, 610–616.

Anderson, J. (1983). Lix and Rix: Variations on a little-known readability index. *Journal of Reading*, *26*, 490–496.

Anderson, R. C., Spiro, R. J., & Anderson, M. C. (1978). Schemata as scaffolding for the representation of information in connected discourse. *American Educational Research Journal, 15*, 433–440.

Andrews, J. F. (1988). Deaf children's acquisition of prereading skills using the reciprocal teaching procedure. *Exceptional Children, 54*, 349–355.

Andrews, J. F., & Mason, J. M. (1986). How do deaf children learn about prereading? *American Annals of the Deaf, 131*, 210–217.

Ankney, P., & McClurg, P. (1981). Testing Manzo's guided reading procedure. *The Reading Teacher, 34*, 681–685.

Applebee, A. N. (1978). *The child's concept of story: Ages two to seventeen.* Chicago: University of Chicago.

Applebee, A. N. (1980). Children's narratives: New directions. *The Reading Teacher, 34*, 137–142.

Armbruster, B. B., Anderson, T. H., & Ostertag, J. (1987). Does text structure/summarization instruction facilitate learning from expository text? *Reading Research Quarterly, 22*, 331–346.

Arwood, E. L. (1983). *Pragmaticism: Theory and application.* Rockville, MD: Aspen.

Atwell, N. (1987). *In the middle: Writing, reading, and learning with adolescents.* Portsmouth, NH: Heinemann.

Au, K. H., & Scheu, J. A. (1989). Guiding students to interpret a novel. *The Reading Teacher, 43*, 104–110.

Au, K. H., Scheu, J. A., Kawakami, A. J., & Herman, P. A. (1990). Assessment and accountability in a whole literacy curriculum. *The Reading Teacher, 43*, 574–578.

Ausubel, D. P. (1960). The use of advance organizers in the learning and retention of meaningful material. *Journal of Educational Psychology, 51*, 267–272.

Babbs, P. J., & Moe, A. J. (1983). Metacognition: A key for independent learning from text. *The Reading Teacher, 36*, 422–426.

Bailey, D. B., & Simeonsson, R. J. (1988). *Family assessment in early intervention.* New York: Merrill/Macmillan.

Baker, C. (1988). *Key issues in bilingualism and bilingual education.* Clevedon, England: Multilingual Matters.

Baker, K. A., & deKanter, A. A. (1983). Federal policy and the effectiveness of bilingual education. In K. A. Baker & A.A. deKanter (Eds.) *Bilingual education* (pp. 33–86). Lexington, MA: Lexington Books.

Barrett, T. C. (1976). Taxonomy of reading comprehension. In R. Smith & T. C. Barrett, *Teaching reading in the middle grades* (pp. 51–58). Reading, MA: Addison-Wesley.

Barron, R. F. (1969). The use of vocabulary as an advance organizer. In H. L. Herber & P. L. Sanders (Eds.), *Research in reading in the content areas: First year report* (pp. 29–39). Syracuse, NY: Syracuse University, Reading and Language Arts Center.

Bartlett, A., Slade, D., & Bellerose, P. C. (1987). Test review: The Test of Early Language Development (TELD). *The Reading Teacher, 40,* 546–548.

Bates, E., Bretherton, I., Snyder, L., Shore, C., & Volterra, V. (1980). Vocal and gestural symbols at 13 months. *Merrill-Palmer Quarterly, 26,* 407–423.

Bates, E., Thal, D., Whitesell, K., Fenson, L., & Oakes, L. (1989). Integrating language and gesture in infancy. *Developmental Psychology, 25,* 1004–1019.

Baumann, J. F. (1988a). Direct instruction reconsidered. *Journal of Reading, 31,* 716–718.

Baumann, J. F. (1988b). *Reading assessment: An instructional decision-making perspective.* New York: Merrill/Macmillan.

Bean, T. W., & Ericson, B. O. (1989). Test previews and three level study guides for content area critical reading. *Journal of Reading, 32,* 337–341.

Bear, D. R., & Invernizzi, M. (1984). Student directed reading groups. *Journal of Reading, 28,* 248–252.

Beck, I. L. (1989). Improving practice through understanding reading. In L. B. Resnick & L. E. Klopfer (Eds.), *Toward the thinking curriculum: Current cognitive research* (pp. 40–58). Alexandria, VA: Association for Supervision and Curriculum Development.

Beers, T. (1987). Schema-theoretic models of reading: Humanizing the machine. *Reading Research Quarterly, 22,* 369–377.

Bensinger, J., Santomen, L., & Volpe, M. (1987). From fear to fluency: The writing process. In D. S. Copeland & D. C. Fletcher (Eds.), *Proceedings of the 1987 National Conference on Innovative Writing Programs and Research for Deaf and Hearing Impaired Students, Removing the writing barrier: A dream?* (pp. 18–29). New York: Lehman College, The City University of New York.

Berk, L. E., & Garvin, R. A. (1984). Development of private speech among low-income Appalachian children. *Developmental Psychology, 20,* 271–286.

Bernstein, M. E., & Barta, L. (1988). What do parents want in parent education? *American Annals of the Deaf, 133,* 235–246.

Betts, E. A. (1946). *Foundations of reading instruction.* New York: American Book.

Bidwell, S. M. (1990). Using drama to increase motivation, comprehension, and fluency. *Journal of Reading, 34,* 38–41.

Billingsley, B. S., & Wildman, T. M. (1988). The effects of prereading activities on the comprehension monitoring of learning disabled adolescents. *Learning Disabilities Research, 4,* 36–44.

Birnbaum, J. C. (1982). The reading and composing behaviors of selected fourth- and seventh-grade students. *Research in the Teaching of English, 16,* 241–260.

Blachowicz, C. L. Z. (1984). Reading and remembering: A constructivist perspective on reading comprehension and its disorders. *Visible Language, 18,* 391–403.

Blanchard, J. (1988). Plausible stories: A creative writing and story prediction activity. *Reading Research and Instruction, 28,* 60–65.

Blanchard. J. S. (1985). What to tell students about underlining. . .and why. *Journal of Reading, 29,* 199–203.

Blanchard, J. S., & Rottenberg, C. J. (1990). Hypertext and hypermedia: Discovering and creating meaningful learning environments. *The Reading Teacher, 43,* 656–661.

Blank, M. (1988). Classroom text: The next stage of intervention. In R. L. Schiefelbusch & L. L. Lloyd (Eds.), *Language perspectives: Acquisition, retardation, and intervention* (pp. 367–392). Austin, TX: Pro-Ed.

Blank, M., & Marquis, A. (1987). *Directing discourse.* Tucson, AZ: Communication Skill Builders.

Blanton, W. E., Wood, K. D., & Moorman, G. B. (1990). The role of purpose in reading instruction. *The Reading Teacher, 43,* 486–493.

Bloom, B. S., Engelhart, M. D., Furst, E. J., Hill, W. H., & Krathwohl, D. R. (1956). *Taxonomy of educational objectives. The classification of educational goals. Handbook I: Cognitive domain.* New York: David McKay.

Bloom, K., Russell, A., & Wassenberg, K. (1987). Turn taking affects the quality of infant vocalizations. *Journal of Child Language, 14,* 211–227.

Bloom, L., & Lahey, M. (1978). *Language development and language disorders.* New York: Wiley.

Bock, J. K., & Brewer, W. F. (1985). Discourse structure and mental models. In T. H. Carr (Ed.), *The development of reading skills* (pp. 55–75). San Francisco: Jossey-Bass.

Bode, B. A. (1989). Dialogue journal writing. *The Reading Teacher, 42,* 568–571.

Bohannon, J. N., & Stanowicz, L. (1988). The issue of negative evidence: Adult responses to children's language errors. *Developmental Psychology, 24,* 684–689.

Bouffler, C. (1984). Predictability: A redefinition of readability. *Australian Journal of Reading, 7,* 125–134.

Brennan, A. D., Bridge, C. A., & Winograd, P. N. (1986). The effects of structural variation on children's recall of basal reader stories. *Reading Research Quarterly, 21,* 91–103.

Bretherton, I., Bates, E., McNew, S., Shore, C., Williamson, C., & Beeghly-Smith, M. (1981). Comprehension and production of symbols in infancy: An experimental study. *Developmental Psychology, 17,* 728–736.

Brinton, B., & Fujiki, M. (1984). Development of topic manipulation skills in discourse. *Journal of Speech and Hearing Research, 27,* 350–358.

Britton, J., Burgess, T., Martin, N., McLeod, A., & Rosen, H. (1975). *The development of writing abilities (11–18).* London, England: Macmillan Education.

Brodesky, R. L., & Cohen, H. (1988). The American Sign Language/English studies project: A progress report. *American Annals of the Deaf, 133,* 330–335.

Bromley, K. D. (1985). Precis writing and outlining enhance content learning. *The Reading Teacher, 38,* 406–411.

Brountas, M. (1987). Whole language really works. *Teaching PreK–8, 18,* 57–60.

Brown, A. L. (1980). Metacognitive development and reading. In R. J. Spiro, B. C. Bruce, & W. F. Brewer (Eds.), *Theoretical issues in reading comprehension* (pp. 453–481). Hillsdale, NJ: Lawrence Erlbaum.

Brown, A. L., Day, J. D., & Jones, R. S. (1983). The development of plans for summarizing texts. *Child Development, 54,* 968–979.

Brown, M. H., Cromer, P. S., & Weinberg, S. H. (1986). Shared book experiences in kindergarten: Helping children come to literacy. *Early Childhood Research Quarterly, 1,* 397–405.

Brown, M. J. M. (1981). What does the author say, what does the author mean? Reading in the social studies. *Theory Into Practice, 20,* 199–205.

Brown, R. (1973). *A first language: The early stages.* Cambridge, MA: Harvard University.

Brown, R., & Hanlon, C. (1970). Derivational complexity and order of acquisition in child speech. In J. R. Hayes (Ed.), *Cognition and the development of language* (pp. 11–53). New York: Wiley.

Bruner, J. (1983). *Child's talk: Learning to use language.* New York: Wiley.

Bullard, C. S., & Schirmer, B. R. (1991). Understanding questions: Hearing impaired children with learning problems. *The Volta Review, 93,* 235–245.

Burmeister, L. E. (1976). A chart for the new Spache formula. *The Reading Teacher, 29,* 384–385.

Buss, R. R., Yussen, S. R., Mathews, S. R., Miller, G. E., & Rembold, K. L. (1983). Development of children's use of a story schema to retrieve information. *Developmental Psychology, 19,* 22–28.

Butler, C. (1980). When the pleasurable is measurable: Teachers reading aloud. *Language Arts, 57,* 882–885.

Buttery, T. J., & Parks, D. (1988). Instructive innovation: Interactive videodisc system. *Reading Improvement, 25,* 56–59.

Cairney, T. H. (1987). Story frames—story cloze. *The Reading Teacher, 41,* 239–241.

Calkins, L. M. (1986). *The art of teaching writing.* Portsmouth, NH: Heinemann.

Callahan, D., & Drum, P. A. (1984). Reading ability and prior knowledge as predictors of eleven and twelve year olds' text comprehension. *Reading Psychology, 5,* 145–154.

Cambourne, B., & Turbill, J. (1990). Assessment in whole-language classrooms: Theory into practice. *The Elementary School Journal, 90,* 337–349.

Caniglia, J., Cole, N. J., Howard, W., Krohn, E., & Rice, M. (1975). *Apple tree*. Beaverton, OR: Dormac.

Canney, G. (1989). Test review: Metropolitan Achievement Tests (MAT6) Reading Diagnostic Tests. *Journal of Reading, 33,* 148–150.

Carnine, D., & Kinder, D. (1985). Teaching low-performing students to apply generative and schema strategies to narrative and expository material. *Remedial and Special Education, 6,* 20–30.

Carroll, J. J., & Gibson, E. J. (1986). Infant perception of gestural contrasts: Prerequisites for the acquisition of a visually specified language. *Journal of Child Language, 13,* 31–49.

Caselli, M. C. (1983). Communication to language: Deaf children's and hearing children's development compared. *Sign Language Studies, 39,* 113–144.

Caverly, D. C., & Orlando, V. P. (1991). Textbook study strategies. In R. F. Flippo & D. C. Caverly (Eds.), *Teaching reading & study strategies at the college level* (pp. 86–165). Newark, DE: International Reading Association.

Cazden, C. B. (1988). *Classroom discourse: The language of teaching and learning*. Portsmouth, NH: Heinemann.

Chaplin, M. T. (1982). Rosenblatt revisited: The transaction between reader and text. *Journal of Reading, 26,* 150–154.

Chapman, J. (1979). Confirming children's use of cohesive ties in text: Pronouns. *The Reading Teacher, 33,* 317–322.

Christensen, K. M. (1988). I see what you mean: Nonverbal communication strategies of young deaf children. *American Annals of the Deaf, 133,* 270–275.

Christie, J. F. (1990). Dramatic play: A context for meaningful engagements. *The Reading Teacher, 43,* 542–5 5.

Ciocci, S. R., & Morrell-Schumann, M. (1987). The writing process: Applications in a program for deaf and hearing-impaired students. In D. S. Copeland & D. C. Fletcher (Eds.), *Proceedings of the 1987 National Conference on Innovative Writing Programs and Research for Deaf and Hearing Impaired Students, Removing the writing barrier: A dream?* (pp. 120–150). New York: Lehman College, The City University of New York.

Clarke, B. R. (1983). Competence in communication for hearing impaired children: A conversation, activity, experience approach. *B. C. Journal of Special Education, 7,* 15–27.

Clarke, B. R., & Stewart, D. A. (1986). Reflections on language programs for the hearing impaired. *The Journal of Special Education, 20,* 153–165.

Clarke, L. K. (1988). Invented versus traditional spelling in first graders' writings: Effects on learning to spell and read. *Research in the Teaching of English, 22,* 281–309.

Cline, R. K. J., & Kretke, G. L. (1980). An evaluation of long-term SSR in the junior high school. *Journal of Reading, 23,* 503–506.

Collins, C. (1980). Sustained silent reading period: Effect on teachers' behaviors and students' achievement. *The Elementary School Journal, 81,* 109–114.

Collins, C. (1988). Using context to develop meaning. In C. Gilles, M. Bixby, P. Crowley, S. R. Crenshaw, M. Henrichs, F.E. Reynolds, & D. Pyle (Eds.), *Whole language strategies for secondary students* (pp. 48–49). New York: Richard C. Owen.

Colman, P. (1989). Utilizing interactive instructional systems. *Media & Methods, 25*(4), 18, 48–50.

Combs, M. (1987). Modeling the reading process with enlarged texts. *The Reading Teacher, 40,* 422–426.

The Commission on Reading, National Council of Teachers of English. (1989). Basal readers and the state of American reading instruction: A call for action. *Language Arts, 66,* 896–898.

Conoley, J. C., & Kramer, J. J. (Eds.). (1989). *The tenth mental measurements yearbook.* Lincoln, NE: The Buros Institute of Mental Measurements, The University of Nebraska-Lincoln.

Conway, D. (1985). Children (re)creating writing: A preliminary look at the purposes of free-choice writing of hearing-impaired kindergartners. *The Volta Review, 87,* 91–126.

Conway, D. F., Mettler, R., Downs, K., Loverin, J., Bush, R., Hurrell, M., Robertson, D., & Truax, R. (1988, July). *Literature, language, and learning Part I: Dialogue journals.* Paper presented at the International Convention of the Alexander Graham Bell Association for the Deaf, Orlando, FL.

Cooke, N. L., Heron, T. E., & Heward, W. L. (1983). *Peer tutoring: Implementing classwide programs in the primary grades.* Columbus, OH: Special Press.

Cooper, D. C., & Anderson-Inman, L. (1988). Language and socialization. In M. A. Nippold (Ed.), *Later language development: Ages nine through nineteen* (pp. 225–245). San Diego: Singular.

Cooter, R. B. (1988). Test review: Woodcock Reading Mastery Tests-Revised (Forms G and H) (WRMT-R). *The Reading Teacher, 42,* 154–155.

Cooter, R. B. (1989). Test review: Gates-MacGinitie Reading Tests, Third Edition, Levels 5/6, 7/9, and 10/12. *Journal of Reading, 32,* 656–658.

Cooter, R. B. (Ed.) (1990). *The teacher's guide to reading tests.* Scottsdale, AZ: Gorsuch Scarisbrick.

Cooter, R. B., & Curry, S., (1989). Test Review: Gates-MacGinitie Reading Tests, Third Edition. *The Reading Teacher, 43,* 256–258.

Copra, E. R. (1990). Using interactive video discs for bilingual education. *Perspectives in Education and Deafness, 8*(5), 9–11.

Cox, B., & Sulzby, E. (1982). Evidence of planning in dialogue and monologue by five-year-old emergent readers. In J. A. Niles & L. A. Harris (Eds.), *New inquiries in reading research and instruction* (pp. 124–130). Rochester, NY: The National Reading Conference.

Crafton, L. K. (1983). Learning from reading: What happens when students generate their own background information? *Journal of Reading, 26,* 587–592.

Crowell, D. C., Kawakami, A. J., & Wong, J. L. (1986). Emerging literacy: Reading-writing experiences in a kindergarten classroom. *The Reading Teacher, 40,* 144–149.

Cudd, E. T., & Roberts, L. L. (1987). Using story frames to develop reading comprehension in a 1st grade classroom. *The Reading Teacher, 41,* 74–79.

Cullinan, B. E. (1987). Inviting readers to literature. In B. E. Cullinan (Ed.), *Children's literature in the reading program* (pp.2–14). Newark, DE: International Reading Association.

Cummins, J. (1979). *Linguistic interdependence and the educational development of bilingual children.* Los Angeles: National Dissemination and Assessment Center, California State University, Los Angeles.

Cummins, J. (1984). *Bilingualism and special education: Issues in assessment and pedagogy.* Clevedon, England: Multilingual Matters.

Cummins, J. (1987). Bilingualism, language proficiency, and metalinguistic development. In P. Homel, M. Palij, & D. Aaronson (Eds.), *Childhood bilingualism: Aspects of linguistic, cognitive, and social development* (pp. 57–73). Hillsdale, NJ: Lawrence Erlbaum.

Cummins, J., Harley, B., Swain, M., & Allen, P. (1990). Social and individual factors in the development of bilingual proficiency. In B. Harley, P. Allen, J. Cummins, & M. Swain (Eds.), *The development of second language proficiency* (pp. 119–133). Cambridge, England: Cambridge University.

Curtiss, S., Prutting, C. A., & Lowell, E. L. (1979). Pragmatic and semantic development in young children with impaired hearing. *Journal of Speech and Hearing Research, 22,* 534–552.

Daines, D. (1986). Are teachers asking higher level questions? *Education, 106,* 368–374.

Dale, P. S., & Henderson, V. L. (1987). An evaluation of the Test of Early Language Development as a measure of receptive and expressive language. *Language, Speech, and Hearing Services in Schools, 18,* 179–187.

Darch, C. B., Carnine, D. W., & Kameenui, E. J. (1986). The role of graphic organizers and social structure in content area instruction. *Journal of Reading Behavior, 18,* 275–295.

Davis, Z. T., & McPherson, M. D. (1989). Story map instruction: A road map for reading comprehension. *The Reading Teacher, 43,* 232–240.

Davison, A., & Kantor, R. N. (1982). On the failure of readability formulas to define readable texts: A case study for adaptations. *Reading Research Quarterly, 17,* 187–209.

Delquadri, J., Greenwood, C. R., Whorton, D., Carta, J. J., & Hall, R. V. (1986). Classwide peer tutoring. *Exceptional Children, 52,* 535–542.

Demetrus, M. J., Post, K. N., & Snow, C. E. (1986). Feedback to first language learners: The role of repetitions and clarification questions. *Journal of Child Language, 13*, 275–292.

Denner, P. R., McGinley, W. J., & Brown, E. (1989). Effects of story impressions as a prereading/writing activity on story comprehension. *The Journal of Educational Research, 82*, 320–326.

DePaulo, B. M., & Bonvillian, J. D. (1978). The effect on language development of the special characteristics of speech addressed to children. *Journal of Psycholinguistic Research, 7*, 189–211.

deVilliers, P. A., & deVilliers, J. G. (1979). *Early language*. Cambridge, MA: Harvard University.

Dewitz, P., Carr, E. M., & Patberg, J. P. (1987). Effects of inference training on comprehension and comprehension monitoring. *Reading Research Quarterly, 22*, 99–121.

Diaz, R. M. (1986). Issues in the empirical study of private speech: A response to Frawley and Lantolf's commentary. *Developmental Psychology, 22*, 709–711.

Dillon, D. (1990). Dear readers. *Language Arts, 67*, 7–9.

Dobson, L. (1989). Connections in learning to write and read: A study of children's development through kindergarten and first grade. In J. M. Mason (Ed.), *Reading and writing connections* (pp. 83–103). Boston: Allyn and Bacon.

Donaldson, J. (1984). Bookwebbing across the curriculum. *The Reading Teacher, 37*, 435–437.

Dore, J. (1975). Holophrases, speech acts and language universals. *Journal of Child Language, 2*, 21–40.

Dreher, M. J., & Singer, H. (1980). Story grammar instruction unnecessary for intermediate grade students. *The Reading Teacher, 34*, 261–268.

Dreher, M. J., & Singer, H. (1989). The teacher's role in students' success. *The Reading Teacher, 42*, 612–617.

Dreyer, L. G. (1984). Readability and responsibility. *Journal of Reading, 27*, 334–338.

Dry, E., & Earle, P. T. (1988). Can Johnny have time to read? *American Annals of the Deaf, 133*, 219–222.

Dudley-Marling, C. C., & Rhodes, L. K. (1987). Pragmatics and literacy. *Language, Speech, and Hearing Services in Schools, 18*, 41–52.

Duffelmeyer, F. A. (1985). Teaching word meaning from an experience base. *The Reading Teacher, 39*, 6–9.

Dunst, C. J., Trivette, C. M., & Deal, A. G. (1988). *Enabling and empowering families: Principles and guidelines for practice*. Cambridge, MA: Brookline.

Dyson, A. H. (1983). The role of oral language in early writing processes. *Research in the Teaching of English, 17*, 1–30.

Dyson, A. H. (1984). "N spell my Grandmama": Fostering early thinking about print. *The Reading Teacher, 38*, 262–271.

Dyson, A. H. (1986). Transitions and tensions: Interrelationships between the drawing, talking, and dictating of young children. *Research in the Teaching of English, 20,* 379–409.

Earle, R. A. (1969). Use of the structured overview in mathematics classes. In H. L. Herber & P. L. Sanders (Eds.), *Research in reading in the content areas: First year report* (pp. 49–58). Syracuse, NY: Syracuse University, Reading and Language Arts Center.

Earle, R. A., & Barron, R. F. (1973). An approach for teaching vocabulary in content subjects. In H. L. Herber & P. L. Sanders (Eds.), *Research in reading in the content areas: Second year report* (pp. 84–100). Syracuse, NY: Syracuse University, Reading and Language Arts Center.

Eeds, M., & Cockrum, W. A. (1985). Teaching word meanings by expanding schemata vs. dictionary work vs. reading in context. *Journal of Reading, 28,* 492–497.

Emig, J. (1971). *The composing process of twelfth graders.* Urbana, IL: National Council of Teachers of English.

Erickson, J. G. (1985). How many languages do you speak? An overview of bilingual education. *Topics in Language Disorders, 5*(4), 1–14.

Erickson, M. E. (1987). Deaf readers reading beyond the literal. *American Annals of the Deaf, 132,* 291–294.

Ewoldt, C. (1978). Reading for the hearing or hearing impaired: A single process. *American Annals of the Deaf, 123,* 945–948.

Ewoldt, C. (1984). Problems with rewritten materials, as exemplified by "To Build a Fire." *American Annals of the Deaf, 129,* 23–28.

Ewoldt, C. (1985). A descriptive study of the developing literacy of young hearing-impaired children. *The Volta Review, 87,* 109–126.

Ewoldt, C. (1987). Emerging literacy in three- to seven-year-old deaf children. In D. S. Copeland & D. C. Fletcher (Eds.), *Proceedings of the 1987 National Conference on Innovative Writing Programs and Research for Deaf and Hearing Impaired Students, Removing the writing barrier: A dream?* (pp. 5–17). New York: Lehman College, City University of New York.

Ewoldt, C., & Hammermeister, F. (1986). The language-experience approach to facilitating reading and writing for hearing-impaired students. *American Annals of the Deaf, 131,* 271–274.

Fagan, W. T. (1989). Empowered students; empowered teachers. *The Reading Teacher, 42,* 572–578.

Farnsworth, K. (1981). Storytelling in the classroom—not an impossible dream. *Language Arts, 58,* 162–167.

Feldman, M. J. (1985). Evaluating pre-primer basal readers using story grammar. *American Educational Research Journal, 22,* 527–547.

Finn, P. J. (1990). *Helping children learn to read* (rev. ed.). New York: Longman.

Fitzgerald, E. (1949). *Straight language for the deaf.* Washington, DC: The Volta Bureau.

Fitzgerald, J. (1984). The relationship between reading ability and expectations for story structures. *Discourse Processes*, 7, 21–41.

Fitzgerald, J. (1987). Research on revision in writing. *Review of Educational Research*, 57, 481–506.

Fitzgerald, J. (1988). Helping young writers to revise: A brief review for teachers. *The Reading Teacher*, 42, 124–129.

Fitzgerald, J. (1989). Enhancing two related thought processes: Revision in writing. *The Reading Teacher*, 43, 42–48.

Fitzgerald, J., Spiegel, D. L., & Webb, T. B. (1985). Development of children's knowledge of story structure and content. *Journal of Educational Research*, 79, 101–108.

Fivush, R., & Fromhoff, F. A. (1988). Style and structure in mother-child conversations about the past. *Discourse Processes*, 11, 337–355.

Flatley, J. K., & Gittinger, D. J. (1990). Teaching abstract concepts: Keys to the world of ideas. *Perspectives in Education and Deafness*, 8(3), 7–9.

Flower, L., & Hayes, J. R. (1980). The dynamics of composing: Making plans and juggling constraints. In L. W. Gregg & E. R. Steinberg (Eds.), *Cognitive processes in writing* (pp. 31–50). Hillsdale, NJ: Lawrence Erlbaum.

Foster, S. (1983). Topic and the development of discourse structure. *The Volta Review*, 85, 44–54.

Fountas, I. C., & Hannigan, I. L. (1989). Making sense of whole language: The pursuit of informed teaching. *Childhood Education*, 65, 133–137.

Franklin, M. B., & Barten, S. S. (Eds.). (1988). *Child language: A reader*. New York: Oxford University.

Frauenglass, M. H., & Diaz, R. M. (1985). Self-regulatory functions of children's private speech: A critical analysis of recent challenges to Vygotsky's theory. *Developmental Psychology*, 21, 357–364.

Frawley, W., & Lantolf, J. P. (1986). Private speech and self-regulation: A commentary on Frauenglass and Diaz. *Developmental Psychology*, 22, 706–708.

Fredericks, A. D. (1986). Mental imagery activities to improve comprehension. *The Reading Teacher*, 40, 78–81.

Freedman, G., & Reynolds, E. G. (1980). Enriching basal reader lessons with semantic webbing. *The Reading Teacher*, 33, 677–684.

French, M. M. (1988). Story retelling for assessment and instruction. *Perspectives for Teachers of the Hearing Impaired*, 7(2), 20–22.

Fry, E. B. (1989). Reading formulas—maligned but valid. *Journal of Reading*, 32, 292–297.

Fuhler, C. J. (1990). Let's move toward literature-based reading instruction. *The Reading Teacher*, 43, 312–315.

Furman, L. N., & Walden, T. A. (1990). Effect of script knowledge on preschool children's communicative interactions. *Developmental Psychology*, 26, 227–233.

Furrow, D., & Nelson, K. (1986). A further look at the motherese hypothesis: A reply to Gleitman, Newport, & Gleitman. *Journal of Child Language, 13*, 163–176.

Fusaro, J. A., & Slike, S. B. (1979). The effect of imagery on the ability of hearing-impaired children to identify words. *American Annals of the Deaf, 124*, 829–832.

Gaines, R., Mandler, J. M., & Bryant, P. (1981). Immediate and delayed story recall by hearing and deaf children. *Journal of Speech and Hearing Research, 24*, 463–469.

Galda, L. (1982). Playing about a story: Its impact on comprehension. *The Reading Teacher, 36*, 52–55.

Galda, L. (1984). Narrative competence: Play, storytelling, and story comprehension. In A. D. Pellegrini & T. D. Yawkey (Eds.), *The development of oral and written language in social contexts* (pp. 105–117). Norwood, NJ: Ablex.

Gambrell, L. B. (1980). Think-time: Implications for reading instruction. *The Reading Teacher, 34*, 143–146.

Gambrell, L. B. (1982). Induced mental imagery and the text prediction performance of first and third graders. In J. A. Niles & L. A. Harris (Eds.), *New inquiries in reading research and instruction* (pp. 131–135). Rochester, NY: The National Reading Conference.

Gambrell, L. B. (1983). The occurrence of think-time during reading comprehension instruction. *The Journal of Educational Research, 77*, 77–80.

Gambrell, L. B. (1985). Dialogue journals: Reading-writing interaction. *The Reading Teacher, 38*, 512–515.

Gambrell, L. B. (1987). Children's oral language during teacher-directed reading instruction. In J. E. Readence & R. S. Baldwin (Eds.), *Research in literacy: Merging perspectives* (pp. 195–199). Rochester, NY: The National Reading Conference.

Gambrell, L. B., & Bales, R. J. (1986). Mental imagery and the comprehension-monitoring performance of fourth- and fifth-grade poor readers. *Reading Research Quarterly, 21*, 454–464.

Gambrell, L. B., & Bales, R. (1987). Visual imagery: A strategy for enhancing listening, reading and writing. *Australian Journal of Reading, 10*, 147–153.

Gambrell, L. B., Pfeiffer, W. R., & Wilson, R. M. (1985). The effects of retelling upon reading comprehension and recall of text information. *The Journal of Educational Research, 78*, 216–220.

Gardner, R. C. (1979). Attitudes and motivation: Their role in second-language acquisition. In H. T. Trueba & C. Barnett-Mizrahi (Eds.), *Bilingual multicultural education and the professional: From theory to practice* (pp. 319–327). Rowley, MA: Newbury House.

Garner, R., Belcher, V., Winfield, E., & Smith, T. (1985). Multiple measures of text summarization proficiency: What can fifth-grade students do? *Research in the Teaching of English, 19*, 140–153.

Garrison, J. W., & Hoskisson, K. (1989). Confirmation bias in predictive reading. *The Reading Teacher, 42,* 482–486.

Garton, A., & Pratt, C. (1989). *Learning to be literate: The development of spoken and written language.* Oxford, England: Basil Blackwell.

Garwood, S. G., Fewell, R. R., & Neisworth, J. T. (1988). Public Law 94–142: You can get there from here! *Topics in Early Childhood Special Education, 8,* 1–11.

Gearheart, C., & Gearheart, B. (1990). *Introduction to special education assessment: Principles and practices.* Denver: Love.

Geers, A., & Moog, J. (1989). Factors predictive of the development of literacy in profoundly hearing-impaired adolescents. *The Volta Review, 91,* 69–86.

Genesee, F. (1989). Early bilingual development: One language or two? *Journal of Child Language, 16,* 161–179.

Gentry, J. R. (1982). An analysis of developmental spelling in GNYS AT WRK. *The Reading Teacher, 36,* 192–200.

Geoffrion, L. D. (1982). An analysis of teletype conversation. *American Annals of the Deaf, 127,* 747–752.

Gersten, R., Woodward, J., & Darch, C. (1986). Direct instruction: A research-based approach to curriculum design and teaching. *Exceptional Children, 53,* 17–31.

Gillet, J. W., & Gentry, J. R. (1983). Bridges between Nonstandard and Standard English with extensions of dictated stories. *The Reading Teacher, 36,* 360–364.

Gipe, J. P. (1980). Use of a relevant context helps kids learn new word meanings. *The Reading Teacher, 33,* 398–402.

Gipe, J. P., & Arnold, R. D. (1979). Teaching vocabulary through familiar associations and contexts. *Journal of Reading Behavior, 11,* 281–284.

Gleason, J. B. (Ed.). (1989). *The development of language* (2nd ed.). New York: Merrill/Macmillan.

Gleitman, L. R., Newport, E. L., & Gleitman, H. (1984). The current status of the motherese hypothesis. *Journal of Child Language, 11,* 43–79.

Glenn, C. G. (1978). The role of episodic structure and of story length in children's recall of simple stories. *Journal of Verbal Learning and Verbal Behavior, 17,* 229–247.

Golden, J. M. (1984). Children's concept of story in reading and writing. *The Reading Teacher, 37,* 578–584.

Goldin-Meadow, S., & Morford, M. (1985). Gesture in early child language: Studies of deaf and hearing children. *Merrill-Palmer Quarterly, 31,* 145–176.

Goodman, K. (1986). *What's whole in whole language?* Portsmouth, NH: Heinemann.

Goodman, K. S. (1989). Whole-language research: Foundations and development. *The Elementary School Journal, 90,* 207–221.

Goodman, K. S., Smith, E. B., Meredith, R., & Goodman, Y. M. (1987). *Language and thinking in school: A whole-language curriculum*. New York: Richard C. Owen.

Goodman, Y. M. (1989). Roots of the whole-language movement. *The Elementary School Journal, 90*, 113–127.

Goodman, Y. M. (1982). Retellings of literature and the comprehension process. *Theory Into Practice, 21*, 301–307.

Gormley, K. A. (1981). On the influence of familiarity on deaf students' text recall. *American Annals of the Deaf, 126*, 1024–1030.

Gormley, K. A., & Franzen, A. M. (1978). Why can't the deaf read? Comments on asking the wrong question. *American Annals of the Deaf, 123*, 542–547.

Gourley, J. W. (1978). The basal is easy to read—or is it? *The Reading Teacher, 32*, 174–182.

Graves, D. H. (1975). An examination of the writing process of seven-year-old children. *Research in the Teaching of English, 9*, 227–241.

Graves, D. H. (1983). *Writing: Teachers and children at work*. Portsmouth, NH: Heinemann.

Graves, M. F. (1986). Vocabulary learning and instruction. In E. Z. Rothkopf (Ed.), *Review of research in education* (pp. 49–89). Washington, DC: American Educational Research Association.

Graves, M. F., Cooke, C. L., & Laberge, M. J. (1983). Effects of previewing difficult short stories on low ability junior high school students' comprehension, recall, and attitudes. *Reading Research Quarterly, 17*, 262–276.

Graves, M. F., & Prenn, M . C. (1986). Costs and benefits of various methods of teaching vocabulary. *Journal of Reading, 29*, 596–602.

Gray, M. A. (1986). Let them play! *Reading Instruction Journal, 30*, 19–22.

Grieser, D. L., & Kuhl, P. K. (1988). Maternal speech to infants in a tonal language: Support for universal prosodic features in motherese. *Developmental Psychology, 24*, 14–20.

Griffith, P. L., Johnson, H. A., & Dastoli, S. L. (1985). If teaching is conversation, can conversation be taught? Discourse abilities in hearing impaired children. In D. N. Ripich & F. M. Spinelli (Eds.), *School discourse problems* (pp. 149–177). San Diego: College-Hill.

Griffith, P. L., & Ripich, D. N. (1988). Story structure recall in hearing-impaired learning-disabled and nondisabled children. *American Annals of the Deaf, 133*, 43–50.

Guido, B., & Colwell, C. G. (1987). A rationale for direct instruction to teach summary writing following expository text reading. *Reading Research and Instruction, 26*, 89–98.

Gustafson, D. J., & Pederson, J. (1986). SQ3R and the strategic reader. *Wisconsin State Research Association Journal, 31*(1), 25–28.

Guthrie, J. T. (1982). Metacognition: Up from flexibility. *The Reading Teacher, 35*, 510–512.

Hacker, C. J. (1980). From schema theory to classroom practice. *Language Arts, 57,* 866–871.

Haggard, M. R. (1985). An interactive strategies approach to content reading. *Journal of Reading, 29,* 204–210.

Haggard, M. R. (1988). Developing critical thinking with the Directed Reading-Thinking Activity. *The Reading Teacher, 41,* 526–533.

Hakuta, K. (1987). The second-language learner in the context of the study of language acquisition. In P. Homel, M. Palij, & D. Aaronson (Eds.), *Childhood bilingualism: Aspects of linguistic, cognitive, and social development* (pp. 31–55). Hillsdale, NJ: Lawrence Erlbaum.

Hall, N. (1987). *The emergence of literacy.* Portsmouth, NH: Heinemann.

Haller, E. P., Child, D. A., & Walberg, H. J. (1988). Can comprehension be taught? A quantitative synthesis of "metacognitive" studies. *Educational Researcher, 17*(9), 5–8.

Halliday, M. A. K. (1975). *Learning how to mean: Explorations in the development of language.* New York: Elsevier North-Holland.

Halliday, M. A. K. (1984). Three aspects of children's language development: Learning language, learning through language, and learning about language. In Y. M. Goodman, M. Haussler, & D. Strickland (Eds.), *Oral and written language development research: Impact on the schools* (pp. 165–192). Urbana, IL: National Council of Teachers of English.

Hammermeister, F. K., & Israelite, N. K. (1983). Reading instruction for the hearing impaired: An integrated language arts approach. *The Volta Review, 85,* 136–148.

Hansen, E. J. (1989). Interactive video for reflection: Learning theory and a new use of the medium. *Educational Technology, 29*(7), 7–15.

Hansen, J. (1981). The effects of inference training and practice on young children's reading comprehension. *Reading Research Quarterly, 16,* 391–417.

Hansen, J. (1987). *When writers read.* Portsmouth, NH: Heinemann.

Hansen, J., & Pearson, P. D. (1983). An instructional study: Improving the inferential comprehension of good and poor fourth-grade readers. *Journal of Educational Psychology, 75,* 821–829.

Hanson, V. L., & Padden, C. (1989, May). *Computers and videodisc for bilingual ASL/English instruction.* Paper presented at the annual meeting of the International Reading Association, New Orleans, LA.

Harding, E., & Riley, P. (1986). *The bilingual family: A handbook for parents.* Cambridge, England: Cambridge University.

Hare, V. C., Rabinowitz, M., & Schieble, K. M. (1989). Text effects on main idea comprehension. *Reading Research Quarterly, 24,* 72–88.

Harp, B. (1988). When the Principal asks "How are you helping your kids understand the reading process instead of just recalling information?" *The Reading Teacher, 42,* 74–75.

Harris, T. L., & Hodges, R. E. (Eds.). (1981). *A dictionary of reading and related terms*. Newark, DE: International Reading Association.

Harrison, M. F., Layton, T. L., & Taylor, T. D. (1987). Antecedent and consequent stimuli in teacher-child dyads. *American Annals of the Deaf, 132*, 227–231.

Harste, J. C. (1989a). The basalization of American reading instruction: One researcher responds. *Theory Into Practice, 28*, 265–273.

Harste, J. C. (1989b). The future of whole language. *The Elementary School Journal, 90*, 243–249.

Harste, J. C. (1989c). *New policy guidelines for reading: Connecting research and practice*. Urbana, IL: National Council of Teachers of English.

Harste, J. (1990). Jerry Harste speaks on reading and writing. *The Reading Teacher, 43*, 316–318.

Harste, J. C., Short, K. G., & Burke, C. (1988). *Creating classrooms for authors: The reading-writing connection*. Portsmouth, NH: Heinemann.

Harste, J. C., Woodward, V. A., & Burke, C. L. (1984). *Language stories and literacy lessons*. Portsmouth, NH: Heinemann.

Hartson, E. K. (1984). The effects of story structure in texts on the reading comprehension of 1st and 2nd grade students. *The California Reader, 17*(3), 6–10.

Hasenstab, M. S. (1983). Child language studies: Impact on habilitation of hearing-impaired infants and preschool children. *The Volta Review, 85*, 88–100.

Hawes, K. S., & Schell, L. M. (1987). Teacher-set pre-reading purposes and comprehension. *Reading Horizons, 27*, 164–169.

Heald-Taylor, B. G. (1984). Scribble in first grade writing. *The Reading Teacher, 38*, 4–8.

Heath, S. B. (1983). *Ways with words: Language, life, and work in communities and classrooms*. Cambridge, England: Cambridge University.

Heimlich, J. E., & Pittelman, S. D. (1986). *Semantic mapping: Classroom applications*. Newark, DE: International Reading Association.

Heller, M. F. (1986). How do you know what you know? Metacognitive modeling in the content areas. *Journal of Reading, 29*, 415–422.

Heller, M. F. (1988). Comprehending and composing through language experience. *The Reading Teacher, 42*, 130–135.

Herman, P. A., & Dole, J. (1988). Theory and practice in vocabulary learning and instruction. *The Elementary School Journal, 89*, 43–54.

Hertzog, M., Stinson, M. S., & Keiffer, R. (1989). Effects of caption modification and instructor intervention on comprehension of a technical film. *Educational Technology Research & Development, 37*(2), 59–68.

Heward, W. L., & Orlansky, M. D. (1992). *Exceptional children* (4th ed.). New York: Merrill/Macmillan.

Hickman, J., & Cullinan, B. E. (1989). A point of view on literature and learning. In J. Hickman & B. E. Cullinan (Eds.), *Children's literature in the classroom: Weaving Charlotte's Web* (pp. 3–12). Needham Heights, MA: Christopher Gordon.

Hicks, G. M. (1983). Sustained silent reading as an aid to reading achievement. *New England Reading Association Journal, 18,* 24–28.

Hiebert, E. H., & Colt, J. (1989). Patterns of literature-based reading instruction. *The Reading Teacher, 43,* 14–20.

Hirsh-Pasek, K., Treiman, R., & Schneiderman, M. (1984). Brown & Hanlon revisited: Mothers' sensitivity to ungrammatical forms. *Journal of Child Language, 11,* 81–88.

Hoff-Ginsberg, E. (1986). Function and structure in maternal speech: Their relation to the child's development of syntax. *Developmental Psychology, 22,* 155–163.

Hoff-Ginsberg, E. (1990). Maternal speech and the child's development of syntax: A further look. *Journal of Child Language, 17,* 85–99.

Hoffman, S., & McCully, B. (1984). Oral language functions in transaction with children's writing. *Language Arts, 61,* 41–50.

Holdaway, D. (1979). *The foundations of literacy.* Sydney, Australia: Ashton Scholastic.

Holdaway, D. (1982). Shared book experience: Teaching reading using favorite books. *Theory Into Practice, 21,* 293–300.

Holdgrafer, G. (1987). Getting children to talk: A model of natural adult teaching/child learning strategies for language. *Canadian Journal for Exceptional Children, 3*(3), 71–76.

Holland, K. W., & Hall, L. E. (1989). Reading achievement in the first grade classroom: A comparison of basal and whole language approaches. *Reading Improvement, 26,* 323–329.

Holmes, B. C. (1983). The effect of prior knowledge on the question answering of good and poor readers. *Journal of Reading Behavior, 15*(4), 1–18.

Holmes, B. C. (1985). The effect of four different modes of reading on comprehension. *Reading Research Quarterly, 20,* 575–585.

Holmes, K. M., & Holmes, D. W. (1981). Normal language acquisition: A model for language programming for the deaf. *American Annals of the Deaf, 126,* 23–31.

Holt, S. B., & O'Tuel, F. S. (1989). The effect of sustained silent reading and writing on achievement and attitudes of seventh and eighth grade students reading two years below grade level. *Reading Improvement, 26,* 290–297.

Homel, P., & Palij, M. (1987). Bilingualism and language policy: Four case studies. In P. Homel, M. Palij, & D. Aaronson (Eds.), *Childhood bilingualism: Aspects of linguistic, cognitive, and social development* (pp. 11–27). Hillsdale, NJ: Lawrence Erlbaum.

Horowitz, R. (1985a). Text patterns: Part I. *Journal of Reading, 28,* 448–454.

Horowitz, R. (1985b). Text patterns: Part II. *Journal of Reading, 28,* 534–541.

Horton, S. V., & Lovitt, T. C. (1989). Using study guides with three classifications of secondary students. *The Journal of Special Education, 22*, 447–462.

Hosie, P. (1987). Adopting interactive videodisc technology for education. *Educational Technology, 27*(7), 5–10.

Howe, C. (1981). *Acquiring language in a conversational context.* London, England: Academic.

Howe, S. F. (1985). Interactive video: Salt & pepper technology. *Media & Methods, 21*(5), 8–14.

Hubbard, R. (1985). Second graders answer the question "Why publish?" *The Reading Teacher, 38*, 658–662.

Huck, C. S. (1982). "I give you the end of a golden string." *Theory Into Practice, 21*, 315–321.

Huck, C. S. (1987). Literature as the content of reading. *Theory Into Practice, 26*, 374–382.

Hull, G. A. (1989). Research on writing: Building a cognitive and social understanding of composing. In L. B. Resnick & L. E. Klopfer (Eds.), *Toward the thinking curriculum: Current cognitive research* (pp. 104–128). Alexandria, VA: Association for Supervision and Curriculum Development.

Humes, A. (1983). Research on the composing process. *Review of Educational Research, 53*, 201–216.

Idol, L. (1987). Group story mapping: A comprehension strategy for both skilled and unskilled readers. *Journal of Learning Disabilities, 20*, 196–205.

Indrisano, R. (1979). Putting research to work. *Instructor, 88*(10), 98–100.

Ingram, D. (1989). *First language acquisition: Method, description, and explanation.* Cambridge, England: Cambridge University.

Irvin, J. L., & Lynch-Brown, C. (1988). A national survey of U.S. university reading clinics: Clientele, functions, and tests. *Journal of Reading, 31*, 436–442.

Irwin, J. W., & Davis, C. A. (1980). Assessing readability: The checklist approach. *Journal of Reading, 24*, 124–130.

Isenberg, J., & Jacob, E. (1983). Literacy and symbolic play: A review of the literature. *Childhood Education, 59*, 272–274, 276.

Isenhath, J. O. (1990). *The linguistics of American Sign Language.* Jefferson, NC: McFarland & Co.

Isom, B. A., & Casteel, C. P. (1986). Prereaders' understanding of function of print: Characteristic trends in the process. *Reading Psychology, 7*, 261–266.

Israelite, N. K. (1988). On readability formulas: A critical analysis for teachers of the deaf. *American Annals of the Deaf, 133*, 14–18.

Israelite, N. K., & Helfrich, M. A. (1988). Improving text coherence in basal readers: Effects of revisions on the comprehension of hearing-impaired and normal-hearing readers. *The Volta Review, 90*, 261–273.

Jacobs, H. H. (1989a) The growing need for interdisciplinary curriculum content. In H. H. Jacobs (Ed.), *Interdisciplinary curriculum: Design and implementation* (pp. 1–11). Alexandria, VA: Association for Supervision and Curriculum Development.

Jacobs, H. H. (1989b). Design options for an integrated curriculum. In H. H. Jacobs (Ed.), *Interdisciplinary curriculum: Design and implementation* (pp. 13–24). Alexandria, VA: Association for Supervision and Curriculum Development.

Jacobs, H. H. (1989c). The interdisciplinary concept model: A step-by-step approach for developing units of study. In H. H. Jacobs (Ed.), *Interdisciplinary curriculum: Design and implementation* (pp. 53–65). Alexandria, VA: Association for Supervision and Curriculum Development.

James, S. L. (1990). *Normal language acquisition*. Austin, TX: Pro-Ed.

James, S. L., & Seebach, M. A. (1982). The pragmatic function of children's questions. *Journal of Speech and Hearing Research, 25*, 2–11.

Jenkins, J. R., & Heliotis, J. G. (1981). Reading comprehension instruction: Findings from behavioral and cognitive psychology. *Topics in Language Disorders, 1*(2), 25–41.

Jenkins, J. R., Stein, M. L., & Wysocki, K. (1984). Learning vocabulary through reading. *American Educational Research Journal, 21*, 767–787.

Johnson, A. R., Johnston, E. B., & Weinrich, B. D. (1984). Assessing pragmatic skills in children's language. *Language, Speech, and Hearing Services in Schools, 15*, 2–9.

Johnson, D. D., & Pearson, P. D. (1984). *Teaching reading vocabulary* (2nd ed.). New York: Holt, Rinehart and Winston.

Johnson, D. D., Pittelman, S. D., & Heimlich, J. E. (1986). Semantic mapping. *The Reading Teacher, 39*, 778–783.

Johnson, D. W., & Johnson, R. T. (1986). Mainstreaming and cooperative learning strategies. *Exceptional Children, 52*, 553–561.

Johnson, D. W., Johnson, R. T., & Holubec, E. J. (1986). *Circles of learning: Cooperation in the classroom* (rev. ed.). Edina, MN: Interaction.

Johnson, G. S., & Bliesmer, E. P. (1983). Effects of narrative schema training and practice in generating questions on reading comprehension of seventh grade students. In G. H. McNinch (Ed.), *Reading research to reading practice* (pp. 91–94). Athens, GA: The American Reading Forum.

Johnson, H. A., & Barton, L. E. (1988). TDD conversations: A context for language sampling. *American Annals of the Deaf, 133*, 19–25.

Johnson, K. L. (1987). Improving reading comprehension through pre-reading and post-reading exercises. *Reading Improvement, 24*, 81–83.

Johnson, M. A., & Roberson, G. F. (1988). The language experience approach: Its use with young hearing-impaired students. *American Annals of the Deaf, 133*, 223–225.

Johnson, N. S., & Mandler, J. M. (1980). A tale of two structures: Underlying and surface forms in stories. *Poetics, 9,* 51–86.

Johnson, R. E., Liddell, S. K., & Erting, C. J. (1989). *Unlocking the curriculum: Principles for achieving access in deaf education.* Washington, DC: Gallaudet University.

Johnston, P. (1985). Teaching students to apply strategies that improve reading comprehension. *The Elementary School Journal, 85,* 635–645.

Jones, L. L. (1982). An interactive view of reading: Implications for the classroom. *The Reading Teacher, 35,* 772–777.

Jones, M. B., & Nessel, D. D. (1985). Enhancing the curriculum with experience stories. *The Reading Teacher, 39,* 18–22.

Jongsma, E. A. (1982). Test review: Peabody Picture Vocabulary Test— Revised (PPVT-R). *Journal of Reading, 25,* 360–364.

Joyce, B. R. (1987). Learning how to learn. *Theory Into Practice, 26,* 416–428.

Joyce, B., & Weil, M. (1986). *Models of teaching* (3rd ed.). Englewood Cliffs, NJ: Prentice-Hall.

Kaisen, J. (1987). SSR/Booktime: Kindergarten and 1st grade sustained silent reading. *The Reading Teacher, 40,* 532–536.

Kapinus, B. A., Gambrell, L. B., & Koskinen, P. S. (1987). Effects of practice in retelling upon the reading comprehension of proficient and less proficient readers. In J. E. Readence & R. S. Baldwin (Eds.), *Research in literacy: Merging perspectives* (pp. 135–141). Rochester, NY: The National Reading Conference.

Karnowski, L. (1989). Using LEA with process writing. *The Reading Teacher, 42,* 462–465.

Kauchak, D., & Eggen, P. D. (1989). *Learning and teaching: Research based methods.* Boston: Allyn and Bacon.

Kessler, C. (1984). *Language acquisition processes in bilingual children.* Los Angeles: Evaluation, Dissemination and Assessment Center, California State University, Los Angeles.

Kimmel, S., & MacGinitie, W. H. (1985). Helping students revise hypotheses while reading. *The Reading Teacher, 38,* 768–771.

Kinzer, C. K. (1986). A 5 part categorization for use of microcomputers in reading classrooms. *Journal of Reading, 30,* 226–232.

Klare, G. R. (1988). The formative years. In B. L. Zakaluk & S. J. Samuels (Eds.), *Readability: Its past, present, and future* (pp. 14–34). Newark, DE: International Reading Association.

Koenke, K. (1987). Readability formulas: Use and misuse. *The Reading Teacher, 40,* 672–674.

Kolich, E. M. (1988). Vocabulary learning—what works? Perspectives from the research literature. *Reading Improvement, 25,* 117–124.

Koskinen, P. S., Gambrell, L. B., Kapinus, B. A., & Heathington, B. S. (1988). Retelling: A strategy for enhancing students' reading comprehension. *The Reading Teacher, 41,* 892–896.

Koskinen, P. S., Wilson, R. M., & Jensema, C. J. (1986). Using closed-captioned television in the teaching of reading to deaf students. *American Annals of the Deaf, 131*, 43–46.

Krauss, M. W. (1990). New precedent in family policy: Individualized Family Service Plan. *Exceptional Children, 56*, 388–395.

Krein, E. L., & Zaharias, J. A. (1986). Analysis of able and disabled sixth-grade readers' knowledge of story structure: A comparison. *Reading Horizons, 27*, 45–53.

Kretschmer, J. C. (1984). Computerizing and comparing the Rix readability index. *Journal of Reading, 27*, 490–499.

Kretschmer, R. R., & Kretschmer, L. W. (1979). The acquisition of linguistic and communicative competence: Parent-child interactions. *The Volta Review, 81*, 306–322.

Kyle, J. G. (1980). Reading development of deaf children. *Journal of Research in Reading, 3*, 86–97.

Laframboise, K. L. (1986–1987). The use of study techniques with young and less-able students. *Journal of Reading Education, 12*(2), 23–31.

Laine, C., & Schultz, L. (1985). Composition theory and practice: The paradigm shift. *The Volta Review, 87*(5), 9–20.

Lambert, W. E. (1974). Culture and language as factors in learning and education. In F. E. Aboud & R. D. Meade (Eds.), *Cultural factors in learning and education* (pp. 91–122). Bellingham, WA: Western Washington State College.

Lambert, W. E. (1987). The effects of bilingual and bicultural experiences on children's attitudes and social perspectives. In P. Homel, M. Palij, & D. Aaronson (Eds.), *Childhood bilingualism: Aspects of linguistic, cognitive, and social development* (pp. 223–228). Hillsdale, NJ: Lawrence Erlbaum.

Lambert, W. E. (1990). Persistent issues in bilingualism. In B. Harley, P. Allen, J. Cummins, & M. Swain (Eds.), *The development of second language proficiency* (pp. 201–218). Cambridge, England: Cambridge University.

Lange, B. (1981). Making sense with schemata. *Journal of Reading, 24*, 442–445.

Lange, B. (1982). Readability formulas: Second looks, second thoughts. *The Reading Teacher, 35*, 858–861.

Langer, J. A. (1985). Children's sense of genre. *Written Communication, 2*, 157–187.

Langer, J. A., & Applebee, A. N. (1986). Reading and writing instruction: Toward a theory of teaching and learning. In E. Z. Rothkopf (Ed.), *Review of research in education* (pp. 171–194). Washington, DC: American Educational Research Association.

Lapp, D., Flood, J., & Gleckman, G. (1982). Classroom practices can make use of what researchers learn. *The Reading Teacher, 35*, 578–585.

Larking, L. (1984). ReQuest helps children comprehend: A study. *Australian Journal of Reading, 7,* 135–139.

LaSasso, C. (1983). Using the language experience approach with language-handicapped readers. *The Journal of Reading, 27,* 152–154.

LaSasso, C. (1987). Survey of reading instruction for hearing-impaired students in the United States. *The Volta Review, 89,* 85–98.

LaSasso, C., & Davey, B. (1987). The relationship between lexical knowledge and reading comprehension for prelingually, profoundly hearing-impaired students. *The Volta Review, 89,* 211–220.

Layton, J. R. (1980). A chart for computing the Dale-Chall Readability Formula above fourth grade level. *Journal of Reading, 24,* 239–244.

Lee, L. (1974). *Developmental sentence analysis.* Evanston, IL: Northwestern University.

Leechford, S., & Manarino, P. (1982). The effects of sustained silent reading on attitudes and interests of sixth-grade readers. *Tar Heel Reading Journal, 2*(1), 15–17, 21.

Lenz, B. K., Alley, G. R., & Schumaker, J. B. (1987). Activating the inactive learner: Advance organizers in the secondary content classroom. *Learning Disability Quarterly, 10,* 53–67.

Leu, D. J., & Kinzer, C. K. (1991). *Effective reading instruction, K–8* (2nd ed.). New York: Merrill/Macmillan.

Levine, S. G. (1984). USSR—a necessary component in teaching reading. *Journal of Reading, 27,* 394–400.

Levy, A. K., Schaefer, L., & Phelps, P. C. (1986). Increasing preschool effectiveness: Enhancing the language abilities of 3- and 4-year-old children through planned sociodramatic play. *Early Childhood Research Quarterly, 1,* 133–140.

Lewis, E. G. (1981). *Bilingualism and bilingual education.* Oxford, England: Pergamon.

Lindberg, B. (1988). Teaching literature: The process approach. *Journal of Reading, 31,* 732–735.

Lindholm, K. J., & Padilla, A. M. (1978). Language mixing in bilingual children. *Journal of Child Language, 5,* 327–335.

Lipson, M. Y. (1982). Learning new information from text: The role of prior knowledge and reading ability. *Journal of Reading Behavior, 14,* 243–261.

Lipson, M. Y. (1984). Some unexpected issues in prior knowledge and comprehension. *The Reading Teacher, 37,* 760–764.

Livingston, S. (1989). Revision strategies of deaf student writers. *American Annals of the Deaf, 134,* 21–26.

Lococo, J. (1985). *Pragmatics: Identification and intervention strategies.* Workshop presented for the Portland Public Schools, Portland, OR.

Long, S. A., Winograd, P. N., & Bridge, C. A. (1989). The effects of reader and text characteristics on imagery reported during and after reading. *Reading Research Quarterly, 24,* 353–372.

Loughlin, C. E., & Martin, M. D. (1987). *Supporting literacy: Developing effective learning environments*. New York: Teachers College, Columbia University.

Lowenthal, B. (1988). United States Public Law 99-457: An ounce of prevention. *The Exceptional Child, 35*, 57–60.

Lucariello, J., & Nelson, K. (1987). Remembering and planning talk between mothers and children. *Discourse Processes, 10*, 219–235.

Luetke-Stahlman, B. (1988). Assessing the semantic language development of hearing impaired students. *A.C.E.H.I. Journal, 14*(1), 5–12.

Luetke-Stahlman, B. (1989). Pragmatic communication for young children: Assessing abilities, building skills. *Perspectives in Education and Deafness, 8*(2), 16–19.

Luterman, D. (1987). *Deafness in the family*. San Diego: Singular.

MacGregor, S. K., & Thomas, L. B. (1988). A computer-mediated text system to develop communication skills for hearing-impaired students. *American Annals of the Deaf, 133*, 280–284.

Mallon, B., & Berglund, R. (1984). The language experience approach to reading: Recurring questions and their answers. *The Reading Teacher, 37*, 867–871.

Mandler, J. M. (1978). A code in the node: The use of story schema in retrieval. *Discourse Processes, 1*, 14–35.

Mandler, J. M. (1987). On the psychological reality of story structure. *Discourse Processes, 10*, 1–29.

Mandler, J. M., & Johnson, N. S. (1977). Remembrance of things parsed: Story structure and recall. *Cognitive Psychology, 9*, 111–151.

Mangano, N. G., Palmer, D., & Goetz, E. T. (1982). Improving reading comprehension through metacognitive training. *Reading Psychology, 3*, 365–374.

Manson, M. (1982). Explorations in language arts for preschoolers (who happen to be deaf). *Language Arts, 59*, 33–39, 45.

Manzo, A. V. (1969). The ReQuest procedure. *Journal of Reading, 13*, 123–126, 163.

Manzo, A. V. (1975). Guided reading procedure. *Journal of Reading, 18*, 287–291.

Manzo, A. V., & Casale, U. P. (1985). Listen-read-discuss: A content reading heuristic. *Journal of Reading, 28*, 732–734.

Marino, J. L., Gould, S. M., & Haas, L. W. (1985). The effects of writing as a prereading activity on delayed recall of narrative text. *The Elementary School Journal, 86*, 199–205.

Marr, M. B., & Gormley, K. (1982). Children's recall of familiar and unfamiliar text. *Reading Research Quarterly, 18*, 89–104.

Marshall, N. (1979). Readability and comprehensibility. *Journal of Reading, 22*, 542–544.

Marshall, N. (1984). The effects of differential instruction on story comprehension. *Florida Reading Quarterly, 20*(3), 3–7.

Martin-Rehrmann, J. (1990). Test review: Analytic Reading Inventory (ARI) (Fourth Edition). *Journal of Reading, 33*, 564–565.

Martinez, M., & Roser, N. (1985). Read it again: The value of repeated readings during storytime. *The Reading Teacher, 38*, 782–786.

Mason, J. M., & Allen, J. (1986). A review of emergent literacy with implications for research and practice in reading. In E. T. Rothkopf (Ed.), *Review of research in education* (pp. 3–47). Washington, DC: American Educational Research Association.

Mason, J. M., & Au, K. H. (1990). *Reading instruction for today* (2nd ed.). New York: HarperCollins.

Mason, J. M., Peterman, C. L., Powell, B. M., & Kerr, B. M. (1989). Reading and writing attempts by kindergartners after book reading by teachers. In J. M. Mason (Ed.), *Reading and writing connections* (pp. 105–120). Boston: Allyn and Bacon.

Mathews, J. K. (1990). From computer management to portfolio assessment. *The Reading Teacher, 43*, 420–421.

Mathewson, G. C. (1988). Test review: Standardized Reading Inventory (SRI). *The Reading Teacher, 41*, 462–465.

Mavrogenes, N. A. (1983). Teaching implications of the schemata theory of comprehension. *Reading World, 22*, 295–305.

Mavrogenes, N. A. (1986). What every reading teacher should know about emergent literacy. *The Reading Teacher, 40*, 174–178.

McAnally, P. L., Rose, S., & Quigley, S. P. (1987). *Language learning practices with deaf children*. San Diego: Singular.

McAndrew, D. A. (1983). Underlining and notetaking: Some suggestions from research. *Journal of Reading, 27*, 103–108.

McCallum, R. D. (1988). Don't throw the basals out with the bath water. *The Reading Teacher, 42*, 204–208.

McCaslin, M. M. (1989). Whole language: Theory, instruction, and future implementation. *The Elementary School Journal, 90*, 223–229.

McCauley, R. J., & Swisher, L. (1984). Psychometric review of language and articulation tests for preschool children. *Journal of Speech and Hearing Disorders, 49*, 34–42.

McClure, E., Mason, J., & Barnitz, J. (1979). An exploratory study of story structure and age effects on children's ability to sequence stories. *Discourse Processes, 2*, 213–249.

McCollum, P. A. (1981). Concepts in bilingualism and their relationship to language assessment. In J. G. Erickson & D. R. Omark (Eds.), *Communication assessment of the bilingual bicultural child: Issues and guidelines* (pp. 25–41). Baltimore: University Park.

McConaughy, S. H. (1980). Using story structure in the classroom. *Language Arts, 57*, 157–165.

McConaughy, S. H. (1982). Developmental changes in story comprehension and levels of questioning. *Language Arts, 59*, 580–589.

McCormick, L., & Schiefelbusch, R. L. (1990). *Early language intervention: An introduction*. New York: Merrill/Macmillan.

McGee, L. M. (1982). Awareness of text structure: Effects on children's recall of expository text. *Reading Research Quarterly, 17*, 581–590.

McGee, L. M., & Lomax, R. G. (1990). On combining apples and oranges: A response to Stahl and Miller. *Review of Educational Research, 60*, 133–140.

McGee, L. M., & Richgels, D. J. (1985). Teaching expository text structure to elementary students. *The Reading Teacher, 38*, 739–748.

McGonigel, M. J., & Garland, C. W. (1988). The Individualized Family Service Plan and the early intervention team: Team and family issues and recommended practices. *Infants and Young Children, 1*, 10–21.

McKeown, M. G., Beck, I. L., Omanson, R. C., & Pople, M. T. (1985). Some effects of the nature and frequency of vocabulary instruction on the knowledge and use of words. *Reading Research Quarterly, 20*, 522–535.

McLaughlin, B. (1990). The relationship between first and second languages: Language proficiency and language aptitude. In B. Harley, P. Allen, J. Cummins, & M. Swain (Eds.), *The development of second language proficiency* (pp. 158–174). Cambridge, England: Cambridge University.

McLaughlin, B., White, D., McDevitt, T., & Raskin, R. (1983). Mothers' and fathers' speech to their young children: Similar or different? *Journal of Child Language, 10*, 245–252.

McNeil, J. D. (1987). *Reading comprehension: New directions for classroom practice* (2nd ed.). Glenview, IL: Scott, Foresman.

McNergney, R., Lloyd, J., Mintz, S., & Moore, J. (1988). Training for pedagogical decision making. *Journal of Teacher Education, 39*(5), 37–43.

Menyuk, P. (1971). *The acquisition and development of language*. Englewood Cliffs, NJ: Prentice-Hall.

Menyuk, P. (1988). *Language development: Knowledge and use*. Glenview, IL: Scott, Foresman.

Meyer, B. J. F. (1975). *The organization of prose and its effects on memory*. Amsterdam, Holland: North-Holland.

Meyer, B. J. F., & Freedle, R. O. (1984). Effects of discourse type on recall. *American Educational Research Journal, 21*, 121–143.

Mezynski, K. (1983). Issues concerning the acquisition of knowledge: Effects of vocabulary training on reading comprehension. *Review of Educational Research, 53*, 253–279.

Miller, L. C., Lechner, R. E., & Rugs, D. (1985). Development of conversational responsiveness: Preschoolers' use of responsive listener cues and relevant comments. *Developmental Psychology, 21*, 473–480.

Minton, M. J. (1980). The effect of sustained silent reading upon comprehension and attitudes among ninth graders. *Journal of Reading, 23*, 498–502.

Mitchell, J. V. (Ed.). (1985). *The ninth mental measurements yearbook*. Lincoln, NE: The Buros Institute of Mental Measurements, The University of Nebraska-Lincoln.

Moeller, M. P., Osberger, M. J., & Eccarius, M. (1986). Cognitively based strategies for use with hearing-impaired students with comprehension deficits. *Topics in Language Disorders, 6*(4), 37–50.

Mohay, H. (1982). A preliminary description of the communication systems evolved by two deaf children in the absence of a sign language model. *Sign Language Studies, 34*, 73–90.

Moldofsky, P. B. (1983). Teaching students to determine the central story problem: A practical application of schema theory. *The Reading Teacher, 36*, 740–745.

Montague, M., & Tanner, M. L. (1987). Reading strategy groups for content area instruction. *Journal of Reading, 30*, 716–723.

Monteith, M. K. (1979). Schemata: An approach to understanding reading comprehension. *Journal of Reading, 22*, 368–371.

Moore, D. W., & Readence, J. E. (1984). A quantitative and qualitative review of graphic organizer research. *The Journal of Educational Research, 78*, 11–17.

Moore, J. C., Jones, C. J., & Miller, D. C. (1980). What we know after a decade of sustained silent reading. *The Reading Teacher, 33*, 445–450.

Moore, P. (1987). On the incidental learning of vocabulary. *Australian Journal of Reading, 10*, 12–19.

Moore, P. J. (1988). Reciprocal teaching and reading comprehension: A review. *Journal of Research in Reading, 11*, 3–14.

Morrow, L. M. (1985a). Reading and retelling stories: Strategies for emergent readers. *The Reading Teacher, 38*, 870–875.

Morrow, L. M. (1985b). Retelling stories: A strategy for improving young children's comprehension, concept of story structure, and oral language complexity. *The Elementary School Journal, 85*, 647–661.

Morrow, L. M. (1986). Effects of structural guidelines in story retelling on children's dictation of original stories. *Journal of Reading Behavior, 18*, 135–152.

Morrow, L. M. (1987). The effects of one-to-one story readings on children's questions and responses. In J. E. Readence & R. S. Baldwin (Eds.), *Research in literacy: Merging perspectives* (pp. 75–83). Rochester, NY: The National Reading Conference.

Morrow, L. M. (1988). Young children's responses to one-to-one story readings in school settings. *Reading Research Quarterly, 23*, 89–107.

Morrow, L. M. (1989). *Literacy development in the early years: Helping children read and write*. Englewood Cliffs, NJ: Prentice Hall.

Morrow, L. M., & Weinstein, C. S. (1982). Increasing children's use of literature through program and physical design changes. *The Elementary School Journal, 83*, 131–137.

Mulcahy, P. I., & Samuels, S. J. (1987). Problem-solving schemata for text types: A comparison of narrative and expository text structures. *Reading Psychology, 8*, 247–256.

Muth, K. D. (1987). Teachers' connection questions: Prompting students to organize text ideas. *Journal of Reading, 31*, 254–259.

Nagy, W. E. (1988). *Teaching vocabulary to improve reading comprehension.* Urbana, IL: National Council of Teachers of English.

Nagy, W. E., Herman, P. A., & Anderson, R. C. (1985). Learning words from context. *Reading Research Quarterly, 20*, 233–253.

Nelson, C. E., Prosser, T., & Tucker, D. (1987). The decline of traditional media and materials in the classroom. *Educational Technology, 27*(1), 48–49.

Nelson, O. (1989). Storytelling: Language experience for meaning making. *The Reading Teacher, 42*, 386–390.

Newkirk, T. (1987). The non-narrative writing of young children. *Research in the Teaching of English, 21*, 121–144.

Newton, L. (1985). Linguistic environment of the deaf child: A focus on teachers' use of nonliteral language. *Journal of Speech and Hearing Research, 28*, 336–344.

Nippold, M. A. (1988a). Figurative language. In M. A. Nippold (Ed.), *Later language development: Ages nine through nineteen* (pp. 179–210). San Diego: Singular.

Nippold, M. A. (1988b). The literate lexicon. In M. A. Nippold (Ed.), *Later language development: Ages nine through nineteen* (pp. 29–47). San Diego: Singular.

Nolte, R. Y., & Singer, H. (1985). Active comprehension: Teaching a process of reading comprehension and its effects on reading achievement. *The Reading Teacher, 39*, 24–31.

Norton, D. E. (1982). Using a webbing process to develop children's literature units. *Language Arts, 59*, 348–356.

Novoa, L. M., & Lazarus, P. J. (1988). Test review: Test of Language Development—Primary (TOLD-P). *The Reading Teacher, 41*, 592–595.

Nower, B. (1985). Scratching the itch: High school students and their topic choices for writing. *The Volta Review, 87*, 171–185.

Noyce, R. M., & Christie, J. F. (1989). *Integrating reading and writing instruction in grades K–8.* Boston: Allyn and Bacon.

Obler, L. K. (1989). Language beyond childhood. In J. B. Gleason (Ed.), *The development of language* (2nd ed.) (pp. 275–301). New York: Merrill/Macmillan.

Ogle, D. M. (1986). K-W-L: A teaching model that develops active reading of expository text. *The Reading Teacher, 39*, 564–570.

Ohlhausen, M. M., & Roller, C. M. (1988). The operation of text structure and content schemata in isolation and in interaction. *Reading Research Quarterly, 23*, 70–88.

Olson, M. W. (1984). A dash of story grammar and. . .Presto! A book report. *The Reading Teacher, 37,* 458–461.

Olson, R. C. (1987). Writing across the curriculum program at Gallaudet. In D. S. Copeland & D. C. Fletcher (Eds.), *Proceedings of the 1987 National Conference on Innovative Writing Programs and Research for Deaf and Hearing Impaired Students, Removing the writing barrier: A dream?* (pp. 151–179). New York: Lehman College, The City University of New York.

Orlich, D. C., Kauchak, D. P., Harder, R. J., Pendergrass, R. A., Callahan, R. C., & Keogh, A. J. (1990). *Teaching strategies: A guide to better instruction.* Lexington, MA: D. C. Heath.

Owens, R. E. (1992.) *Language development: An introduction* (3rd ed.). New York: Merrill/Macmillan.

Palij, M., & Homel, P. (1987). The relationship of bilingualism to cognitive development: Historical, methodological, and theoretical considerations. In P. Homel, M. Palij, & D. Aaronson (Eds.), *Childhood bilingualism: Aspects of linguistic, cognitive, and social development* (pp. 131–148). Hillsdale, NJ: Lawrence Erlbaum.

Palincsar, A. S. (1986). Metacognitive strategy instruction. *Exceptional Children, 53,* 118–124.

Palincsar, A. S., & Brown, A. L. (1986). Interactive teaching to promote independent learning from text. *The Reading Teacher, 39,* 771–777.

Palincsar, A. S., & Brown, A. L. (1988). Teaching and practicing thinking skills to promote comprehension in the context of group problem solving. *Remedial and Special Education, 9,* 53–59.

Palincsar, A. S., & Brown, A. L. (1989). Instruction for self-regulated reading. In L. B. Resnick & L. E. Klopfer (Eds.), *Toward the thinking curriculum: Current cognitive research* (pp. 19–39). Alexandria, VA: Association for Supervision and Curriculum Development.

Pappas, C. C., & Brown, E. (1987). Young children learning story discourse: Three case studies. *The Elementary School Journal, 87,* 455–466.

Pasch, M., Sparks-Langer, G., Gardner, T. G., Starko, A. J., & Moody, C. D. (1991). *Teaching as decision making.* New York: Longman.

Paul, P. V., & Quigley, S. P. (1990). *Education and deafness.* New York: Longman.

Paz, E. Y. (1980). *The development of bilingual education models.* Los Angeles: National Dissemination and Assessment Center, California State University, Los Angeles.

Pearson, P. D. (1989). Reading the whole-language movement. *The Elementary School Journal, 90,* 231–241.

Pearson, P. D., & Johnson, D. D. (1978). *Teaching reading comprehension.* New York: Holt, Rinehart and Winston.

Pearson, P. D., & Spiro, R. J. (1982). Toward a theory of reading comprehension instruction. In K. G. Butler & G. P. Wallach (Eds.), *Language disorders and learning disabilities* (pp. 71–88). Rockville, MD: Aspen.

Pease, D. M., Gleason, J. B., & Pan, B. A. (1989). Gaining meaning: Semantic development. In J. B. Gleason (Ed.), *The development of language* (2nd Ed.) (pp. 101–134). New York: Merrill/Macmillan.

Peck, J. (1989). Using storytelling to promote language and literacy development. *The Reading Teacher, 43*, 138–141.

Pehrsson, R. S., & Denner, P. R. (1988). Semantic organizers: Implications for reading and writing. *Topics in Language Disorders, 8*(3), 24–37.

Pellegrini, A. D. (1984). The development of the functions of private speech: A review of the Piaget-Vygotsky debate. In A. D. Pellegrini & T. D. Yawkey (Eds.), *The development of oral and written language in social contexts* (pp. 57–69). Norwood, NJ: Ablex.

Pellegrini, A. D., & Galda, L. (1982). The effects of thematic-fantasy play training on the development of children's story comprehension. *American Educational Research Journal, 19*, 443–452.

Peterson, L. N., & French, L. (1988). Summarization strategies of hearing-impaired and normally hearing college students. *Journal of Speech and Hearing Research, 31*, 327–337.

Petitto, L. A. (1987). On the autonomy of language and gesture: Evidence from the acquisition of personal pronouns in American Sign Language. *Cognition, 27*, 1–52.

Peyton, J. K., & Seyoum, M. (1989). The effect of teacher strategies on students' interactive writing: The case of dialogue journals. *Research in the Teaching of English, 23*, 310–334.

Piaget, J. (1926). *The language and thought of the child*. London, England: Kegan, Paul, Trench, & Trubner.

Pickering, C. T. (1989). Whole language: A new signal for expanding literacy. *Reading Improvement, 26*, 144–149.

Pieronek, F. T. (1979). Using basal guidebooks—the ideal integrated reading lesson plan. *The Reading Teacher, 33*, 167–172.

Pikulski, J. J. (1990). The role of tests in a literacy assessment program. *The Reading Teacher, 43*, 686–688.

Pillar, A. M. (1979). Using children's literature to foster moral development. *The Reading Teacher, 33*, 148–151.

Poostay, E. J. (1984). Show me your underlines: A strategy to teach comprehension. *The Reading Teacher, 37*, 828–830.

Prince, A. T., & Mancus, D. S. (1987). Enriching comprehension: A schema altered basal reading lesson. *Reading Research and Instruction, 27*, 45–54.

Prinz, P. M. (1991). Literacy and language development within microcomputer-videodisc-assisted interactive contexts. *Journal of Childhood Communication Disorders, 14*, 67–80.

Prinz, P. M., & Masin, L. (1985). Lending a helping hand: Linguistic input and sign language acquisition in deaf children. *Applied Psycholinguistics, 6*, 357–370.

Prinz, P. M., & Prinz, E. A. (1985). If only you could hear what I see: Discourse development in sign language. *Discourse Processes, 8*, 1–19.

Probst, R. E. (1988). Transactional theory in the teaching of literature. *Journal of Reading, 31,* 378–381.

Propp, G., Nugent, G., Stone, C., & Nugent, R. (1981). Videodisc for the hearing impaired. *The Volta Review, 83,* 321–327.

Prutting, C. A. (1982). Pragmatics as social competence. *Journal of Speech and Hearing Disorders, 47,* 123–134.

Prutting, C. A., & Kirchner, D. M. (1987). A clinical appraisal of the pragmatic aspects of language. *Journal of Speech and Hearing Disorders, 52,* 105–119.

Pugh, B. L. (1955). *Steps in language development for the deaf.* Washington, DC: The Volta Bureau.

Purcell-Gates, V. (1989). What oral/written language differences can tell us about beginning instruction. *The Reading Teacher, 42,* 290–294.

Radencich, M. C. (1986). Test review: Gray Oral Reading Test—Revised. *Journal of Reading, 30,* 137–139.

Rahman, T., & Bisanz, G. L. (1986). Reading ability and use of a story schema in recalling and reconstructing information. *Journal of Educational Psychology, 78,* 323–333.

Raphael, T. E. (1982). Question-answering strategies for children. *The Reading Teacher, 36,* 186–190.

Raphael, T. E. (1984). Teaching learners about sources of information for answering comprehension questions. *Journal of Reading, 27,* 303–311.

Raphael, T. E. (1986). Teaching question-answer relationships, revisited. *The Reading Teacher, 39,* 516–522.

Raphael, T. E., & McKinney, J. (1983). An examination of fifth- and eighth-grade children's question-answering behavior: An instructional study in metacognition. *Journal of Reading Behavior, 15*(3), 67–86.

Raphael, T. E., Myers, A. C., Tirre, W. C., Fritz, M., & Freebody, P. (1981). The effects of some known sources of reading difficulty on metacomprehension and comprehension. *Journal of Reading Behavior, 13,* 325–334.

Raphael, T. E., & Pearson, P. D. (1985). Increasing students' awareness of sources of information for answering questions. *American Educational Research Journal, 22,* 217–235.

Raphael, T. E., & Wonnacott, C. A. (1985). Heightening fourth-grade students' sensitivity to sources of information for answering comprehension questions. *Reading Research Quarterly, 20,* 282–296.

Rasinski, T. V., & Fredericks, A. D. (1990). The best reading advice for parents. *The Reading Teacher, 43,* 344–345.

Ray, S. (1989). Context and the psychoeducational assessment of hearing impaired children. *Topics in Language Disorders, 9*(4), 33–44.

Reading/Language in Secondary Schools Subcommittee of the International Reading Association. (1989). Developing strategic learners. *Journal of Reading, 33,* 61–63.

Reading/Language in Secondary Schools Subcommittee of the International Reading Association. (1990). Portfolios illuminate the path for dynamic, interactive readers. *Journal of Reading, 33,* 644–647.

Reading/Language Through The Years Subcommittee On Secondary Schools and the IRA Board of Directors. (1990). A position statement from the International Reading Association on secondary school reading. *Journal of Reading, 33,* 285–287.

Reagan, T. (1985). The deaf as a linguistic minority: Educational considerations. *Harvard Educational Review, 55,* 265–277.

Reagan, T. (1988). Multiculturalism and the deaf: An educational manifesto. *Journal of Research and Development in Education, 22,* 1–6.

Recht, D. R., & Leslie, L. (1988). Effect of prior knowledge on good and poor readers' memory of text. *Journal of Educational Psychology, 80,* 16–20.

Redlinger, W. E., & Park, T. (1980). Language mixing in young bilinguals. *Journal of Child Language, 7,* 337–352.

Reed, S. K., (1988). *Cognition: Theory and applications* (2nd ed.). Pacific Grove, CA: Brooks/Cole.

Reimer, B. L. (1983). Recipes for language experience stories. *The Reading Teacher, 36,* 396–401.

Reutzel, D. R. (1985a). Reconciling schema theory and the basal reading lesson. *The Reading Teacher, 39,* 194–197.

Reutzel, D. R. (1985b). Story maps improve comprehension. *The Reading Teacher, 38,* 400–404.

Rice, M. L., & Kemper, S. (1984). *Child language and cognition.* Baltimore: University Park.

Richgels, D. J. (1982). Schema theory, linguistic theory, and representations of reading comprehension. *Journal of Educational Research, 76,* 54–62.

Richgels, D. J., McGee, L. M., Lomax, R. G., & Sheard, C. (1987). Awareness of four text structures: Effects on recall of expository text. *Reading Research Quarterly, 22,* 177–196.

Richgels, D. J., McGee, L. M., & Slaton, E. A. (1989). Teaching expository text structure in reading and writing. In K. D. Muth (Ed.), *Children's comprehension of text* (pp. 167–184). Newark, DE: International Reading Association.

Rickards, J. P. (1980). Notetaking, underlining, inserted questions, and organizers in text: Research conclusions and educational implications. *Educational Technology, 20*(6), 5–11.

Rinehart, S. D., Stahl, S. A., & Erickson, L. G. (1986). Some effects of summarization training on reading and studying. *Reading Research Quarterly, 21,* 422–438.

Risko, V. J., & Alvarez, M. C. (1983). Thematic organizers: Application to remedial reading. In G. H. McNinch (Ed.), *Reading research to reading practice* (pp. 85–87). Athens, GA: The American Reading Forum.

Risko, V. J., & Alvarez, M. C. (1986). An investigation of poor readers' use of a thematic strategy to comprehend text. *Reading Research Quarterly, 21*, 298–316.

Rittenhouse, R. K., & Kenyon, P. L. (1987). Educational and social language in deaf adolescents: TDD and school-produced comparisons. *American Annals of the Deaf, 132*, 210–212.

Roberts, T. A. (1988). Development of pre-instruction versus previous experience: Effects on factual and inferential comprehension. *Reading Psychology, 9*, 141–157.

Robinson, C. C., Rosenberg, S. A., & Beckman, P. J. (1988). Parent involvement in early childhood special education. In J. B. Jordan, J. J. Gallagher, P. L. Hutinger, & M. B. Karnes (Eds.), *Early childhood special education: Birth to three* (pp. 109–127). Reston, VA: The Council for Exceptional Children.

Robinson, F. P. (1946). *Effective study* (2nd ed.). New York: Harper & Row.

Rockler, M. J. (1988). *Innovative teaching strategies*. Scotsdale, AZ: Gorsuch, Scarisbrick.

Rogers, D. (1989). "Show-me bedtime reading": An unusual study of the benefits of reading to deaf children. *Perspectives for Teachers of the Hearing Impaired, 8*(1), 2–5.

Rogers, D. L., Perrin, M. S., & Waller, C. B. (1987). Enhancing the development of language and thought through conversations with young children. *Journal of Research in Childhood Education, 2*, 17–29.

Roller, C. M., & Schreiner, R. (1985). The effects of narrative and expository organizational instruction on sixth-grade children's comprehension of expository and narrative prose. *Reading Psychology, 6*, 27–42.

Romaine, S. (1989). *Bilingualism*. Oxford, England: Basil Blackwell.

Roney, R. C. (1989). Back to the basics with storytelling. *The Reading Teacher, 42*, 520–523.

Rosenblatt, L. M. (1978). *The reader, the text, the poem*. Carbondale, IL: Southern Illinois University.

Rosenblatt, L. M. (1989). Writing and reading: The transactional theory. In J. M. Mason (Ed.), *Reading and writing connections* (pp. 153–176). Boston: Allyn and Bacon.

Rosenthal, M. K. (1982). Vocal dialogues in the neonatal period. *Developmental Psychology, 18*, 17–21.

Roser, N., & Juel, C. (1982). Effects of vocabulary instruction on reading comprehension. In J. A. Niles & L. A. Harris (Eds.), *New inquiries in reading research and instruction* (pp. 110–118). Rochester, NY: The National Reading Conference.

Roskos, K. (1988). Literacy at work in play. *The Reading Teacher, 41*, 562–566.

Roth, F. P., & Spekman, N. J. (1984a). Assessing the pragmatic abilities of children: Part 1. Organizational framework and assessment parameters. *Journal of Speech and Hearing Disorders, 49*, 2–11.

Roth, F. P., & Spekman, N. J. (1984b). Assessing the pragmatic abilities of children: Part 2. Guidelines, considerations, and specific evaluation procedures. *Journal of Speech and Hearing Disorders, 49*, 12–17.

Rowe, D. W., & Rayford, L. (1987). Activating background knowledge in reading comprehension assessment. *Reading Research Quarterly, 22*, 160–176.

Rowe, M. B. (1974). Wait-time and rewards as instructional variables, their influence on language, logic and fate control: Part one—wait-time. *Journal of Research in Science Teaching, 11*, 81–94.

Rowe, M. B. (1986). Wait time: Slowing down may be a way of speeding up. *Journal of Teacher Education, 37*(1), 43–50.

Ruddell, R. B. (1986). Vocabulary learning: A process model and criteria for evaluating instructional strategies. *Journal of Reading, 29*, 581–587.

Rumelhart, D. E. (1975). Notes on a schema for stories. In D. G. Bobrow & A. Collins (Eds.), *Representation and understanding: Studies in cognitive science* (pp. 211–236). New York: Academic.

Rumelhart, D. E. (1977). Understanding and summarizing brief stories. In D. LaBerge & S. J. Samuels (Eds.), *Basic processes in reading: Perception and comprehension* (pp. 265–303). Hillsdale, NJ: Lawrence Erlbaum.

Rumelhart, D. E. (1980). Schemata: The building blocks of cognition. In R. J. Spiro, B. C. Bruce, & W. F. Brewer (Eds.), *Theoretical issues in reading comprehension* (pp. 33–58). Hillsdale, NJ: Lawrence Erlbaum.

Rush, R. T. (1985). Assessing readability: Formulas and alternatives. *The Reading Teacher, 39*, 274–283.

Rutter, D. R., & Durkin, K. (1987). Turn-taking in mother-infant interaction: An examination of vocalizations and gaze. *Developmental Psychology, 23*, 54–61.

Ryder, R. J. (1986). Teaching vocabulary through external context clues. *Journal of Reading, 30*, 61–65.

Sachs, J., Goldman, J., & Chaille, C. (1984). Planning in pretend play: Using language to coordinate narrative development. In A. D. Pellegrini & T. D. Yawkey (Eds.), *The development of oral and written language in social contexts* (pp. 119–128). Norwood, NJ: Ablex.

Sadoski, M. C. (1980). Ten years of uninterrupted sustained silent reading. *Reading Improvement, 17*, 153–156.

Sadoski, M. (1983). An exploratory study of the relationship between reported imagery and the comprehension and recall of a story. *Reading Research Quarterly, 19*, 110–123.

Sadoski, M. (1985). The natural use of imagery in story comprehension and recall: Replication and extension. *Reading Research Quarterly, 20*, 658–667.

Sadow, M. W. (1982). The use of story grammar in the design of questions. *The Reading Teacher, 35*, 518–522.

Sage, H. (1987). *Incorporating literature in ESL instruction*. Englewood Cliffs, NJ: Prentice-Hall.

Salvia, J., & Ysseldyke, J. E. (1991). *Assessment in special and remedial education* (5th ed.). Boston: Houghton Mifflin.

Sarachan-Deily, A. B. (1985). Written narratives of deaf and hearing students: Story recall and inference. *Journal of Speech and Hearing Research, 28*, 151–159.

Saville-Troike, M. (1979a). First- and second-language acquisition. In H. T. Trueba & C. Barnett-Mizrahi (Eds.), *Bilingual multicultural education and the professional: From theory to practice* (pp. 104–119). Rowley, MA: Newbury House.

Saville-Troike, M. (1979b). Culture, language, and education. In H. T. Trueba & C. Barnett-Mizrahi (Eds.), *Bilingual multicultural education and the professional: From theory to practice* (pp. 139–156). Rowley, MA: Newbury House.

Sawyer, W. (1987). Literature and literacy: A review of research. *Language Arts, 64*, 33–39.

Schatz, E. K., & Baldwin, R. S. (1986). Context clues are unreliable predictors of word meanings. *Reading Research Quarterly, 21*, 439–453.

Schewe, A., & Froese, V. (1987). Relating reading and writing via comprehension, quality, and structure. In J. E. Readence & R. S. Baldwin (Eds.), *Research in literacy: Merging perspectives* (pp. 273–279). Rochester, NY: The National Reading Conference.

Schickedanz, J. A. (1990). The jury is still out on the effects of whole language and language experience approaches for beginning reading: A critique of Stahl and Miller's study. *Review of Educational Research, 60*, 127–131.

Schirmer, B. R. (1984). Dynamic model of oral and/or signed language diagnosis. *Language, Speech, and Hearing Services in Schools, 15*, 76–82.

Schirmer, B. R. (1985). An analysis of the language of young hearing-impaired children in terms of syntax, semantics, and use. *American Annals of the Deaf, 130*, 15–19.

Schirmer, B. R. (1989). Framework for using a language acquisition model in assessing semantic and syntactic development and planning instructional goals for hearing-impaired children. *The Volta Review, 91*, 87–94.

Schirmer, B. R., & Winter, C. R. (1991, April). *Cognitive schema used by hearing impaired youngsters to comprehend narrative text*. Paper presented at the annual conference of the American Educational Research Association, Chicago, IL.

Schmitt, M. C., & O'Brien, D. G. (1986). Story grammars: Some cautions about the translation of research into practice. *Reading Research and Instruction, 26*, 1–8.

Schuder, T., Clewell, S. F., & Jackson, N. (1989). Getting the gist of expository text. In K. D. Muth (Ed.), *Children's comprehension of text* (pp. 224–242). Newark, DE: International Reading Association.

Schwabe, A. M., Olswang, L. B., & Kriegsmann, E. (1986). Requests for information: Linguistic, cognitive, pragmatic, and environmental variables. *Language, Speech, and Hearing Services in Schools, 17,* 38–55.

Schwartz, R. M., & Raphael, T. E. (1985). Concept of definition: A key to improving students' vocabulary. *The Reading Teacher, 39,* 198–205.

Scott, C. M. (1988). Spoken and written syntax. In M. A. Nippold (Ed.), *Later language development: Ages nine through nineteen* (pp. 49–95). San Diego: Singular.

Sebesta, S. L., Calder, J. W., & Cleland, L. N. (1982). A story grammar for the classroom. *The Reading Teacher, 36,* 180–184.

Seels, B. (1989). The instructional design movement in educational technology. *Educational Technology, 29*(5), 11–15.

Seidman, S. A. (1986). A survey of schoolteachers' utilization of media. *Educational Technology, 26*(10), 19–23.

Shah, D. C. (1986). Composing processes and writing instruction at the middle/junior high school level. *Theory Into Practice, 25,* 109–116.

Shanahan, T. (1980). The impact of writing instruction on learning to read. *Reading World, 19,* 357–368.

Shanahan, T., & Lomax, R. G. (1986). An analysis and comparison of theoretical models of the reading-writing relationship. *Journal of Educational Psychology, 78,* 116–123.

Shanklin, N. L., & Rhodes, L. K. (1989). Comprehension instruction as sharing and extending. *The Reading Teacher, 42,* 496–500.

Shannon, P. (1982). Some subjective reasons for teacher's reliance on commercial reading materials. *The Reading Teacher, 35,* 884–889.

Shuy, R. W. (1981). A holistic view of language. *Research in the Teaching of English, 15,* 101–111.

Shuy, R. W. (1987). Dialogue as the heart of learning. *Language Arts, 64,* 890–897.

Simmons, D. C., Griffin, C. C., & Kameenui, E. J. (1988). Effects of teacher-constructed pre- and post-graphic organizer instruction on sixth-grade science students' comprehension and recall. *The Journal of Educational Research, 82,* 15–21.

Simmons, J. (1990). Portfolios as large-scale assessment. *Language Arts, 67,* 262–268.

Simpson, M. L., Stahl, N. A., & Hayes, C. G. (1989). PORPE: A research validation. *Journal of Reading, 33,* 22–28.

Sinatra, R. C., Stahl-Gemake, J., & Berg, D. N. (1984). Improving reading comprehension of disabled readers through semantic mapping. *The Reading Teacher, 38,* 22–29.

Sinatra, R., Stahl-Gemake, J., & Morgan, N. W. (1986). Using semantic mapping after reading to organize and write original discourse. *Journal of Reading, 30,* 4–13.

Singer, H. (1978). Active comprehension: From answering to asking questions. *The Reading Teacher, 31,* 901–908.

Slater, W. H. (1985). Teaching expository text structure with structural organizers. *Journal of Reading, 28,* 712–718.

Slaughter, H. B. (1988). Indirect and direct teaching in a whole language program. *The Reading Teacher, 42,* 30–34.

Slaughter, J. P. (1983). Big books for little kids: Another fad or a new approach for teaching beginning reading? *The Reading Teacher, 36,* 758–762.

Smith, D. (1987). Talking with young children about their reading. *Australian Journal of Reading, 10,* 120–122.

Smith, F. (1978). *Reading without nonsense.* New York: Teachers College, Columbia University.

Smith, F. (1983). Reading like a writer. *Language Arts, 60,* 558–567.

Smith, J. A., & Bowers, P. S. (1989). Approaches to using literature for teaching reading. *Reading Improvement, 26,* 345–348.

Smith, P. L., & Tompkins, G. E. (1988). Structured notetaking: A new strategy for content area readers. *Journal of Reading, 32,* 46–53.

Snow, C. E. (1979). Conversations with children. In P. Fletcher & M. Garman (Eds.), *Language acquisition: Studies in first language development* (pp. 69–89). Cambridge, England: Cambridge University.

Spiegel, D. L. (1981). Six alternatives to the Directed Reading Activity. *The Reading Teacher, 34,* 914–920.

Spiegel, D. L. (1989). Content validity of whole language materials. *The Reading Teacher, 43,* 168–169.

Squire, J. R. (1984). Composing and comprehending: Two sides of the same basic process. In J. M. Jensen (Ed.), *Composing and comprehending* (pp. 23–31). Urbana, IL: National Conference on Research in English.

Staab, C. F. (1983). Language functions elicited by meaningful activities: A new dimension in language programs. *Language, Speech, and Hearing Services in Schools, 14,* 164–170.

Stahl, S. A. (1985). To teach a word well: A framework for vocabulary instruction. *Reading World, 24*(3), 16–27.

Stahl, S. A. (1986). Three principles of effective vocabulary instruction. *Journal of Reading, 29,* 663–668.

Stahl, S. A., & Fairbanks, M. M. (1986). The effects of vocabulary instruction: A model-based meta-analysis. *Review of Educational Research, 56,* 72–110.

Stahl, S. A., & Miller, P. D. (1989). Whole language and language experience approaches for beginning reading: A quantitative research synthesis. *Review of Educational Research, 59,* 87–116.

Stahl, S. A., & Vancil, S. J. (1986). Discussion is what makes semantic maps work in vocabulary instruction. *The Reading Teacher, 40,* 62–67.

Staton, J. (1985). Using dialogue journals for developing thinking, reading, and writing with hearing-impaired students. *The Volta Review, 87,* 127–154.

Staton, J. (1988). Dialogue journals. *Language Arts, 65,* 198–201.

Stauffer, R. G. (1969). *Teaching reading as a thinking process.* New York: Harper & Row.

Stein, N. L., & Glenn, C. G. (1979). An analysis of story comprehension in elementary school children. In R. O. Freedle (Ed.), *New directions in discourse processing* (pp. 53–120). Norwood, NJ: Ablex.

Stein, N. L., & Nezworski, T. (1978). The effects of organization and instructional set on story memory. *Discourse Processes, 1,* 177–193.

Stephens, M. I. (1988). Pragmatics. In M. A. Nippold (Ed.), *Later language development: Ages nine through nineteen* (pp. 247–262). San Diego: Singular.

Stevens, K. C. (1980). The effect of background knowledge on the reading comprehension of ninth graders. *Journal of Reading Behavior, 12,* 151–154.

Stewart, D. A. (1985). Language dominance in deaf students. *Sign Language Studies, 49,* 375–386.

Stewart, D. A. (1987). Linguistic input for the American Sign Language/English bilingual. *A.C.E.H.I. Journal, 13*(2), 58–70.

Stone, P. (1988). *Blueprint for developing conversational competence: A planning/instruction model with detailed scenarios.* Washington, DC: Alexander Graham Bell Association for the Deaf.

Stotsky, S. (1983). Research on reading/writing relationships: A synthesis and suggested directions. *Language Arts, 60,* 627–642.

Strackbein, D., & Tillman, M. (1987). The joy of journals—with reservations. *Journal of Reading, 31,* 28–31.

Strickland, D. S. (1982). Comprehending what's new in comprehension. *Reading Instruction Journal, 25,* 9–12.

Strickland, D. S., Dillon, R. M., Funkhouser, L., Glick, M., & Rogers, C. (1989). Classroom dialogue during literature response groups. *Language Arts, 66,* 192–200.

Strickland, D. S., & Morrow, L. M. (1988). Creating a print-rich environment. *The Reading Teacher, 42,* 156–157.

Strickland, D. S., & Morrow, L. M. (1989). Environments rich in print promote literacy behavior during play. *The Reading Teacher, 43,* 178–179.

Strickland, D. S., & Morrow, L. M. (1990). Integrating the emergent literacy curriculum with themes. *The Reading Teacher, 43,* 604–605.

Sulzby, E. (1982). Oral and written language mode adaptations in stories by kindergarten children. *Journal of Reading Behavior, 14,* 51–59.

Summers, E. G., & McClelland, J. V. (1982). A field-based evaluation of sustained silent reading (SSR) in intermediate grades. *The Alberta Journal of Educational Research, 28,* 100–112.

Tager-Flusberg, H. (1989). Putting words together: Morphology and syntax in the preschool years. In J. B. Gleason (Ed.), *The development of language* (2nd ed.) (pp. 135–165). New York: Merrill/Macmillan.

Tatham, S. M. (1978). Comprehension taxonomies: Their uses and abuses. *The Reading Teacher, 32,* 190–194.

Taylor, B. M. (1982). A summarizing strategy to improve middle grade students' reading and writing skills. *The Reading Teacher, 36*, 202–205.

Taylor, B. M., & Beach, R. W. (1984). The effects of text structure instruction on middle-grade students' comprehension and production of expository text. *Reading Research Quarterly, 19*, 134–146.

Taylor, B. M., Frye, B. J., & Maruyama, G. M. (1990). Time spent reading and reading growth. *American Educational Research Journal, 27*, 351–362.

Taylor, B. M., & Samuels, S. J. (1983). Children's use of text structure in the recall of expository material. *American Educational Research Journal, 20*, 517–528.

Taylor, D. M. (1987). Social psychological barriers to effective childhood bilingualism. In P. Homel, M. Palij, & D. Aaronson (Eds.), *Childhood bilingualism: Aspects of linguistic, cognitive, and social development* (pp. 183–195). Hillsdale, NJ: Lawrence Erlbaum.

Taylor, N. E., & Connor, U. (1982). Silent vs. oral reading: The rational instructional use of both processes. *The Reading Teacher, 35*, 440–443.

Teale, W. H. (1987). Emergent literacy: Reading and writing development in early childhood. In J. E. Readence & R. S. Baldwin (Eds.), *Research in literacy: Merging perspectives* (pp. 44–74). Rochester, NY: The National Reading Conference.

Teale, W. H., Hiebert, E. H., & Chittenden, E. A. (1987). Assessing young children's literacy development. *The Reading Teacher, 40*, 772–777.

Terrell, B. Y. (1985). Learning the rules of the game: Discourse skills in early childhood. In D. N. Ripich & F. M. Spinelli (Eds.), *School discourse problems* (pp. 13–27). San Diego: College-Hill.

Thal, D., & Bates, E. (1988). Language and gesture in late talkers. *Journal of Speech and Hearing Research, 31*, 115–123.

Thelen, J. N. (1986). Vocabulary instruction and meaningful learning. *Journal of Reading, 29*, 603–609.

Thompson, M., Biro, P., Vethivelu, S., Pious, C., & Hatfield, N. (1987). *Language assessment of hearing-impaired school age children*. Seattle: University of Washington.

Thorndyke, P. W. (1977). Cognitive structures in comprehension and memory of narrative discourse. *Cognitive Psychology, 9*, 77–110.

Thorndyke, P. W., & Hayes-Roth, B. (1979). The use of schemata in the acquisition and transfer of knowledge. *Cognitive Psychology, 11*, 82–106.

Thorum, A. R. (1981). *Language assessment instruments: Infancy through adulthood*. Springfield, IL: Charles C. Thomas.

Thurlow, M., Graden, J., Ysseldyke, J. E., & Algozzine, R. (1984). Student reading during reading class: The lost activity in reading instruction. *The Journal of Educational Research, 77*, 267–272.

Tibbits, D. F. (1988). Test review: Test of Adolescent Language-2(TOAL-2). A multidimensional approach to assessment. *Journal of Reading, 32*, 178–181.

Tierney, R. J., & Leys, M. (1986). What is the value of connecting reading and writing? In B. T. Peterson (Ed.), *Convergences: Transactions in reading and writing* (pp. 15–29). Urbana, IL: National Council of Teachers of English.

Tierney, R. J., & Pearson, P. D. (1983). Toward a composing model of reading. *Language Arts, 60,* 568–580.

Tobin, K. (1986). Effects of teacher wait time on discourse characteristics in mathematics and language arts classes. *American Educational Research Journal, 23,* 191–200.

Tobin, K. (1987). The role of wait time in higher cognitive learning. *Review of Educational Research, 57,* 69–95.

Tomasello, M., & Mannle, S. (1985). Pragmatics of sibling speech to one-year-olds. *Child Development, 56,* 911–917.

Tomlinson-Keasey, C., Brawley, R., & Peterson, B. (1986). An analysis of an interactive videodisc system for teaching language skills to deaf students. *The Exceptional Child, 33,* 49–55.

Tompkins, G. E. (1990). *Teaching writing: Balancing process and product.* New York: Merrill/Macmillan.

Townsend, M. A. R., & Clarihew, A. (1989). Facilitating children's comprehension through the use of advance organizers. *Journal of Reading Behavior, 21,* 15–35.

Trachtenburg, P., & Ferruggia, A. (1989). Big books from little voices: Reaching high risk beginning readers. *The Reading Teacher, 42,* 284–289.

Trelease, J. (1989). *The new read-aloud handbook.* New York: Penguin.

Trout, M., & Foley, G. (1989). Working with families of handicapped infants and toddlers. *Topics in Language Disorders, 10*(1), 57–67.

Truax, R. (1985). Linking research to teaching to facilitate reading-writing-communication connections. *The Volta Review, 87,* 155–169.

Trueba, H. T. (1979). Bilingual-education models: Types and designs. In H. T. Trueba & C. Barnett-Mizrahi (Eds.), *Bilingual multicultural education and the professional: From theory to practice* (pp. 54–73). Rowley, MA: Newbury House.

Tunnell, M. O., & Jacobs, J. S. (1989). Using "real" books: Research findings on literature based reading instruction. *The Reading Teacher, 42,* 470–477.

Turnbull, A. P., Summers, J. A., & Brotherson, M. J. (1984). *Working with families with disabled members: A family systems approach.* Lawrence, KS: University of Kansas.

Vacca, J. L., Vacca, R. T., & Gove, M. K. (1991). *Reading and learning to read.* New York: HarperCollins.

Valencia, S. (1990). A portfolio approach to classroom reading assessment: The whys, whats, and hows. *The Reading Teacher, 43,* 338–340.

VanDongen, R., & Westby, C. E. (1986). Building the narrative mode of thought through children's literature. *Topics in Language Disorders, 7*(1), 70–83.

Vaughan, J. L., Castle, G., Gilbert, K., & Love, M. (1982). Varied approaches to preteaching vocabulary. In J. A. Niles & L. A. Harris (Eds.), *New inquiries in reading research and instruction* (pp. 94–98). Rochester, NY: The National Reading Conference.

Vernon, M. (1987). Controversy within sign language. *A.C.E.H.I. Journal, 12*(3), 155–164.

Vernon, M., & Andrews, J. F. (1990). *The psychology of deafness*. New York: Longman.

Vihman, M. M. (1982). The acquisition of morphology by a bilingual child: A whole-word approach. *Applied Psycholinguistics, 3,* 141–160.

Vihman, M. M. (1985). Language differentiation by the bilingual infant. *Journal of Child Language, 12*, 297–324.

Volterra, V. (1981). Gestures, signs, and words at two years: When does communication become language. *Sign Language Studies, 33*, 351–362.

Volterra, V., & Erting, C. J. (Eds.). (1990). *From gesture to language in hearing and deaf children*. Berlin, Germany: Springer-Verlag.

Vygotsky, L. S. (1962). *Thought and language*. Cambridge, MA: M.I.T. Press.

Wagner, B. J. (1985). Integrating the language arts. *Language Arts, 62,* 557–560.

Wagner, B. J. (1988). Does classroom drama effect the arts of language? *Language Arts, 65*, 46–55.

Wanska, S. K., & Bedrosian, J. L. (1985). Conversational structure and topic performance in mother-child interaction. *Journal of Speech and Hearing Research, 28*, 579–584.

Warren, S. F., & Kaiser, A. P. (1986). Incidental language teaching: A critical review. *Journal of Speech and Hearing Disorders, 51*, 291–299.

Warren-Leubecker, A., & Bohannon, J. N. (1984). Intonation patterns in child-directed speech: Mother father differences. *Child Development, 55*, 1379–1385.

Warren-Leubecker, A., & Bohannon, J. N. (1989). Pragmatics: Language in social contexts. In J. B. Gleason (Ed.), *The development of language* (2nd ed.) (pp. 327–368). New York: Merrill/Macmillan.

Weaver, C. (1988). *Reading process and practice: From socio-psycholinguistics to whole language*. Portsmouth, NH: Heinemann.

Weaver, P. A., & Dickinson, D. K. (1982). Scratching below the surface structure: Exploring the usefulness of story grammars. *Discourse Processes, 5*, 225–243.

Weiss, A. L. (1986). Classroom discourse and the hearing-impaired child. *Topics in Language Disorders, 6*(3), 60–70.

Wells, G. (1981). *Learning through interaction: The study of language development*. Cambridge, England: Cambridge University.

Wells, G. (1982). Story reading and the development of symbolic skills. *Australian Journal of Reading, 5*, 142–152.

Wells, G. (1986). *The meaning makers: Children learning language and using language to learn*. Portsmouth, NH: Heinemann.

Wells, G., & Wells, J. (1984). Learning to talk and talking to learn. *Theory Into Practice, 23*, 190–197.

Westby, C. (1988). Test review: Test of Language Development-2 Primary, Test of Language Development-2 Intermediate. *The Reading Teacher, 42*, 236–237.

Whaley, J. F. (1981). Readers' expectations for story structures. *Reading Research Quarterly, 17*, 90–114.

Widomski, C. L. (1983). Building foundations for reading comprehension. *Reading World, 22*, 306–313.

Wiesendanger, K. D., & Bader, L. (1989). SSR: Its effects on students' reading habits after they complete the program. *Reading Horizons, 29*, 162–166.

Wiesendanger, K. D., & Birlem, E. D. (1984). The effectiveness of SSR: An overview of the research. *Reading Horizons, 24*, 197–201.

Wilbur, R. B. (1987). *American Sign Language: Linguistic and applied dimensions* (2nd ed.). Austin, TX: Pro-Ed.

Wilcox, M. J., & Webster, E. J. (1980). Early discourse behavior: An analysis of children's responses to listener feedback. *Child Development, 51*, 1120–1125.

Wilen, W. W. (1990). Forms and phases of discussion. In W. W. Wilen (Ed.), *Teaching and learning through discussion* (pp. 3–24). Springfield, IL: Charles C. Thomas.

Wilkinson, I., & Bain, J. (1984). Story comprehension and recall in poor readers: Everyone a schemer? *Australian Journal of Reading, 7*, 147–156.

Wilkinson, L. C., Wilkinson, A. C., Spinelli, F., & Chiang, C. P. (1984). Metalinguistic knowledge of pragmatic rules in school-age children. *Child Development, 55*, 2130–2140.

Williams, J. P., Taylor, M. B., & deCani, J. S. (1984). Constructing macrostructure for expository text. *Journal of Educational Psychology, 76*, 1065–1075.

Williams, R. T. (1988). Test review: Test of Adolescent Language-2 (TOAL-2). *Journal of Childhood Communication Disorders, 11*, 308–311.

Wing, C. S. (1982). Language processes and linguistic levels: A matrix. *Language, Speech, and Hearing Services in Schools, 13*, 2–10.

Winser, B. (1988). Readers getting control of reading. *Australian Journal of Reading, 11*, 257–268.

Winton, P. (1986). Effective strategies for involving families in intervention efforts. *Focus on Exceptional Children, 19*(2), 1–10, 12.

Wittrock, M. C. (1982). Three studies of generative reading comprehension. In J. A. Niles & L. A. Harris (Eds.), *New inquiries in reading research and instruction* (pp. 85–88). Rochester, NY: The National Reading Conference.

Wixson, K. K. (1986). Vocabulary instruction and children's comprehension of basal stories. *Reading Research Quarterly, 21*, 317–329.

Wolk, S., & Allen, T. E. (1984). A 5-year follow-up of reading comprehension achievement of hearing-impaired students in special education programs. *The Journal of Special Education, 18,* 161–176.

Wong, B. Y. L. (1985). Self-questioning instructional research: A review. *Review of Educational Research, 55,* 227–268.

Wong, J. A. & Au, K. H. (1985). The concept-text-application approach: Helping elementary students comprehend expository text. *The Reading Teacher, 38,* 612–618.

Wood, D. J., Wood, H. A., Griffiths, A. J., Howarth, S. P., & Howarth, C. I. (1982). The structure of conversations with 6- to 10-year-old deaf children. *Journal of Child Psychology, Psychiatry, and Allied Disciplines, 23,* 295–308.

Wood, H. A., & Wood, D. J. (1984). An experimental evaluation of the effects of five styles of teacher conversation on the language of hearing-impaired children. *Journal of Child Psychology, Psychiatry, and Allied Disciplines, 25,* 45–62.

Wood, K. D. (1988). Guiding students through informational text. *The Reading Teacher, 41,* 912–919.

Wood, M. (1985). Linking schema theory and metacognition research to the word identification strategies of beginning readers. *The New England Reading Association Journal, 20,* 18–24, 34.

Wood, M. (1989). Invented spelling revisited. *Reading Today, 6*(6), 22.

Yaden, D. (1988). Understanding stories through repeated read-alouds: How many does it take? *The Reading Teacher, 41,* 556–560.

Yawkey, T. D., & Hrncir, E. J. (1983). Pretend play tools for oral language growth in the preschool. *The Journal of Creative Behavior, 16,* 265–271.

Ysseldyke, J. E., & Algozzine, B. (1983). Where to begin in diagnosing reading problems. *Topics in Learning and Learning Disabilities, 2*(4), 60–69.

Zakaluk, B. L., & Samuels, S. J. (1988). Toward a new approach to predicting text comprehensibility. In B. L. Zakaluk & S. J. Samuels (Eds.), *Readability: Its past, present, and future* (pp. 121–144). Newark, DE: International Reading Association.

Ziezula, F. R. (Ed.). (1982). *Assessment for hearing-impaired people: A guide for selecting psychological, educational, and vocational tests.* Washington, DC: Gallaudet College.

Zorfass, J. M. (1981). Metalinguistic awareness in young deaf children: A preliminary study. *Applied Psychololinguistics, 2,* 333–352.

Subject Index

Author Index

ISBN 0-675-21295-2

9 780675 212953

90000>